NIGHT CAME
TO THE FARMS
OF THE
GREAT PLAINS

Dedicated to all the wheat farmers
of the Great Plains

NIGHT CAME
TO THE FARMS
OF THE
GREAT PLAINS

by Raymond D. North

Acres U.S.A.
Kansas City, Missouri

NIGHT CAME TO THE FARMS OF THE GREAT PLAINS

Copyright © 1991 Raymond D. North

Published in cooperation with
The National Organization for Raw Materials

Acres U.S.A.
Box 9547, Kansas City, Missouri 64133

ISBN: 0-911311-29-7
Library of Congress Catalog card number: 91-071312

Table of Contents

A WORD FROM THE PUBLISHER

FOR REASONS THAT TROUBLED the international money lenders no end, American manufacturers remained sublimely indifferent to foreign markets between 1813 and 1914, a full century. At the end of that era, a market basket of goods cost approximately the same as it had 100 years earlier. Generally speaking, this era saw the act of production create the credits for the consumption of that production, the basic result—even with wars and depressions involved—being structural balance for the American economy, low unemployment and prices seldom ruptured by cheap import invasion.

Toward the end of the era in question, Henry Ford had taken the lead in raising the American industrial wage to fifty cents an hour so that—with other industrialists following suit—a common worker could buy a Model T car. Moreover, broad spectrum distribution of land meant broad spectrum distribution of basic farm income, agriculture then and now being the biggest sector in the economy. Later, in the 1930s, statistical workers selected 1910-1914 as base period "100" for parity computations. This meant that the "100" era had relatively full employment and a stable price structure. Using this platform of structural balance, the U.S. built the world's greatest steel industry, and pushed almost all manufactures to new heights. Indeed, the act of production created the money for consumption of that production under these equitable pricing conditions.

This situation stuck like a sharp bone in the throats of the international lenders. Free international trade required a price dislocation between nations, thus the policy of the international lenders to "so reduce the purchasing power of the American people that they can no longer even approximately consume their own products."

The quoted words are from *The Breakdown of Money*, by Christopher Hollis. Hollis was a British historian on loan to Notre Dame University during the 1930s. He wrote,

> As long as that purchasing power was adequate, the American manufacturer was indifferent to foreign markets. But with domestic purchasing power reduced, foreign markets become essential to him. And, the more that he could be persuaded to look abroad for this market, the easier it will be to change his whole attitude toward wages. At present he is in favor of high tariff and high wages, for he looks on the working man as his customer. But, if he can be induced to look abroad for his markets, then wages become merely an item of costs and it is to the manufacturer's interest to reduce them as low as possible. If they are reduced—and the odium for reducing them of course, allowed to fall on the manufacturer—then American industry becomes at once a much more profitable investment for the financier, while the foreign goods can flow into free trade America to pay the interest on the foreign loans.

The opening gun in the drive to break the purchasing power of the American dollar had been fired as early as 1873 via the mechanism of silver, then an international money. From that date up to 1896, the price of silver broke from $1.32 an ounce to sixty-five cents an ounce. This was accomplished on the commodity exchanges by manipulation, much as the grain traders broke soybean prices on the Chicago Board of Trade in 1989. For every cent that silver went down between 1873 and 1896, the price of wheat in the high plains went down a penny a bushel also.

These probes continued well into the Wilson administration, at which time the international lenders struck pay dirt. Almost overnight the American republic amended its past and recast its future in terms of the price dislocation requirements of free international trade.

The Federal Reserve came into being, as did the income tax and the foundation apparatus for preserving the mature fortunes and manufacturing an oligarchy. The Federal Reserve failed all of its objectives accidentally on purpose, the income tax did away with the requirement for tariffs to fund the government, and the foundations law became an insurance policy for the preservation of the wealthy. Even the Senate was affected by the Wilson assault on the Constitution, since its members—by Constitutional Amendment—were no longer under the control of the political apparatus of state lawmakers. Sentence by sentence, and paragraph by paragraph—with laws, bureau rules and judicial decrees—the Constitution was annihilated until now little more than the requirement of two Senators per state remains. The target of breaking the purchasing power of the American dollar via lowered commodity prices was achieved soon enough by import invasion, and the Great Depression followed.

There was that short interlude—the 1940s—when a stabilization measure and the Steagall Amendment returned raw material prices to parity, but this was all swept aside the minute Dwight D. Eisenhower took office. In homage to free international trade, the farmers of the Great Plains were cast into an economic abyss. The metes and bounds of that story have been covered in my book *Unforgiven* and in the papers of the National Organization for Raw Materials (NORM).

Harry S Truman called the 80th Congress a do-nothing Congress, the worst in history. It was this Congress that gave him an Aiken bill to sign, and then allowed the barest subsidies to keep American producers in business. Truman was sandbagged in this political game, threatened by a veto override, tired to death, and assured of his own defeat in the 1948 election by everyone who could write for print. Harry Truman had made his mistakes, but failing to understand the economics of the nation was not one of them. No one was ready to listen to statesmanship in 1948. The international flim-flam men won the day, and the plan the Council on Foreign Relations (CFR) types suckered USDA Secretary Charlie Brannan into accepting made the last years of the Truman administration look like a convention of free-trade fellow travelers, something Truman never was.

Suffice it to say that as long as American agriculture had parity, lenders of every stripe went hungry. At the end of the war parity years, the banks were chock full of money, but applicants for loans were few. In fact there was only a market for 16% of the available funds at one time. The minute USDA Secretary Ezra Taft Benson struck down parity, farm operators started the painful process of consuming their capital, and loan applications soared. Government lending agencies were created or expanded to take risky customers off the hands of the commercial banks.

Unforgiven provides a few details that are now of maximum interest:

As prices continued to sink, one wave of pundits after another hit farmers with the productivity routine. The Committee for Economic Development, with Goldsmith's *A Study of Saving in the United States* in tow much of the time, did its hatchet work on a continuing basis, starting immediately after WWII. Policy papers such as *Toward a Realistic Farm Program, Economic Policy for American Agriculture* and *An Adaptive Program for Agriculture* explained to farmers how they had to get bigger, more efficient, and finally depart the scene. The Bible-style texts of Don Paarlberg and Dale Hathaway also arrived to help style public policy so that the job of liquidating agriculture might proceed without bringing on open revolt from the farmers, and by the time those volumes had been thumbed to death in the learning halls, Johns Hopkins Press struck off another entry, this one titled *Policy Directions for U.S. Agriculture.* The last was issued under the auspices of Resources for the Future, Inc., a non-profit organization based in Washington for the altruistic purpose of serving the powers that be. The writer, one Marion Clawson, came to the Resources for the Future Foundation via the customary route—out of USDA and the Interior Department. His message came to the public from the mature fortunes of the nation by way of the tax-supported instrumentalities that no longer knew which hand did the long range feeding.

Instead of support programs, Clawson fell back on the Brannan idea, direct payments to certain farmers, or institutionalized poverty, so those who remained could double their production, enjoy prices held down by imports, and starve to death in the end.

Pensioning farmers and speeding the exodus from the countryside could not solve either the farm problem or the city problem because rural America required the gross dollar, and without the gross dollar rural towns would starve as well. The sore of low farm income thus became the cancer that consumed fully a third of the American population by the end of the 1960s.

The "too many resources in agriculture" pitch failed to express or prove a concept of economic growth, because too many resources in agriculture could become too many resources in widget-making, entertaining or professoring, for that matter. Unfortunately the "gut agriculture" seers dismissed this problem with a "we'll get to that later" gesture.

The mechanism for this debauchery of agriculture is not well understood by farmers even today, and because of this information shortfall, farm organizations talked nonsense and lost members from the beginning of the Eisenhower administration to the present, the process being exacerbated with the arrival of satellite technology.

Soon enough prices became governed by an invisible currency in the skies linked to the monetary systems of almost every nation on earth.

This electronic currency [wrote Harold Wills, a NORM associate] consists of a satellite rotating with Mother Earth so that it stays in place above Brussels, Belgium, and is linked to a banking network able to transfer the equivalent of cash between any two or more points on earth in a matter of seconds. An offer can be made, it can be accepted, and electronic entries can convert it into cash in currency of the selling nation as easily as when a farmer hauls a load of wheat to his local grain elevator and receives a check for his efforts.

The farmer, of course, receives the price offered by the elevator and which may or may not have any relationship to parity. In global electronic transactions, the relationship is the same but the volume is much larger, a million or so bushels instead of a truckload. Also, there are more middlemen who must receive a piece of the action. Here, in a very simplified form, is how this system operates.

A buyer in Malawi wants to purchase a million tons of American wheat (or any other commodity or product) and has a specific price he is willing to pay. His first stop is at the National Bank of Malawi, which has access to the satellite. In Iraq, it would be the Rafidian Bank of Iraq. In either case, this intent is the equivalent of cash.

Then, the satellite is used to make contact with an American seller, invariably one of the huge, global grain corporations. A price is offered and it is accepted. At this point, nothing but paper exists. The grain may be located on the farms or in country elevators. If an industrial product instead of wheat is involved, it may not even be manufactured yet. In fact, it may need to be acquired from an additional party not even aware of this heavenly linkage.

When an agreement is reached, the equivalent of a purchase order goes into orbit—but not until the seller's bank is notified so it can alert its upstream correspondent institutions. A FAX machine is used for this chore.

Today, almost every core center bank has a global correspondent linkage for the immediate transfer of debits and credits, needed because today's world does not recognize national or even continental boundaries. It is one huge package composed of buyers and sellers with this network as the transfer mechanism. Once a deal has been made on this imaginary tonnage of wheat, the seller's bank is notified and, immediately, the equivalent of an electronic letter of intent is bucked upstairs to the core center institution and from it, by satellite, to the National Bank of Malawi. It releases the equivalent of money back through the heavenly network to the U.S. core center bank and it, in turn, issues a credit chip to the local bank (a downstream correspondent) and the seller is notified that a deposit has been made in his account.

This entire sequence can be completed in a matter of minutes, with absolutely no "real" cash changing hands. All that is left to be done is to acquire the wheat and ship it to Malawi, or Iraq, or anywhere else on earth this satellite transfer procedure is used.

Naturally, as in all transactions, the balance of power lies with the buyer—or buyers if three or more nations are involved in the transaction. The buyer dictates price and delivery. And, with buyers, sellers and the global financial system all in global satellite linkage with each other, rigging prices to make quick deals is not only very possible but also a part of the game. With no sales made, there is no profit. And, this theoretical load of wheat (or any other product) may change hands as many as three or more times in a single day, accompanied by three or more satellite exchanges of financial instruments!

Where does the U.S. federal government fit into this operation? It doesn't! It has no jurisdiction over the skies and any threat to them would trigger an immediate capital exodus that could be completed in a matter of minutes, triggering a crisis in this country. Washington's hands are tied even tighter because the entire electronic network is linked to the International Monetary Exchange (IME) operations in Brussels, Belgium, the coordinating agency for the world's monetary systems.

Where does the farmer in the heart of the U.S. fit into this? He's the bottom link in the entire chain, the producer of a raw material for which global demand exists. Because his prices have been abandoned to globalization they must remain at rock-bottom to maintain U.S. competitiveness. Any shortfalls in farmer income must be subsidized by Washington because there is no alternative if production is to continue. And when the subsidies do not shore up a farmer's solvency, the farm operation consumes its own capital, then the strength and lives of its people.

This global network is one of the reasons why American industrial production has sagged dismally over the past two decades. Had anyone bothered to look, it is no secret that American output began to slide within a year of activation of this global network. As soon as the monetary systems of the world were linked to each other for instantaneous fund transfers, the U.S. simply ceased to be competitive because our prices were too high in terms of peasant labor forces available elsewhere, and too few American producers had access to this network.

These few paragraphs comprise the background to *Night Came to the Farms of the Great Plains*. In a way, the Great Plains examined here in detail are merely a metaphor for all of agriculture and manufacturing, and the spectacle of a Congress unable to balance a single budget in a non-parity year since 1929. The human dramas detailed here by Raymond D. North are more than an indictment. They are a crime, and a sorrow on the land. They rate a hearing because even Congressmen— who cannot handle the high-level abstractions that have created the debt malaise—can comprehend the human problem once it is reduced to a mundane business equation.

Night Came to the Farms of the Great Plains has its Greek tragedy opening. It tells a story much more poignant than Frank Popper's vision of returning the Great Plains to Buffalo Commons status. That tragedy must be expressed in exponential figures, for only then will those who replace the mediocrities now in office understand what ignorance has wrought.

—*Charles Walters Jr.*
Publisher, *Acres U.S.A.*

PROLOGUE

Minerva Lestikow was upset. The weather was rainy and the school bus had not run, so the children were home from school. It was one of those dreary days that occasionally hit the Great Plains, and she was concerned about her husband, Henry Lestikow. He too was upset.

She had seen something in him before their marriage that told her he was solid. She still believed that was the case, but she worried. He was not his usual self.

They had expanded their farm operation several years ago when times were good and now the payments on those debts were falling due. She knew that Henry did not like the loan officers at the federal land bank and at the Farmers Home Administration. He called them narodniks. She knew it was a Russian word, but she didn't understand it. She didn't like these loan officers, either. They were sassy and unkind. They parked their feet on top of their desks when they talked to Henry and her. They smoked big cigars and blew the smoke into their faces. They lied repeatedly. They scorned the farmer and his methods. But most of all they were snotty. She knew that the relationship between them and Henry had beem deteriorating for many months.

She worried about Henry. She often noticed that he sat and stared off into the distance without seeming to really see anything. When they talked, which was less than usual now, he talked about holding onto the land. He had a deep love for the land.

She didn't really know what to do. Then, on this dreary day, she heard a noise from outside the house, a sudden eruption, and she rushed to the window. She screamed. She had seen most of the things in life that her mother had seen before her, and her grandmother before that. But she had never seen this. In broad daylight, night came to the farms of the Great Plains. This is the story of how it happened.

NARRATIVE

1

THE GREAT PLAINS

The Great Plains is a relatively flat, treeless, dry, natural grassland located in Texas, Oklahoma, Kansas, Nebraska, South Dakota and North Dakota. It also extends well into Canada. Saying it is relatively flat does not mean that it lacks hills, but that is about all it means. There are no mountains worthy of the name, although the Ozarks Mountains of southern Missouri and Northern Arkansas extend well into eastern Oklahoma and southeastern Kansas. There is also a chain of mountains in southern Arkansas and southeastern Oklahoma called the Ouachita Mountains, the only mountain range in the Western Hemisphere that runs east and west. But these ranges are really rolling hills. Likewise, west of Enid, Oklahoma there is a small chain of hills known as the Glass Mountains, never more than a few hundred feet high and without peaks. The Black Hills of southwestern South Dakota are just what the name implies.

There are few trees as well. In western Kansas and Nebraska, it is possible to drive ten miles and never see a single tree. Creeks and rivers that cross the Great Plains have trees along their banks, often elm and cottonwood. Many of the villages and towns have annual tree planting days and after a century of cultivation they have created a fairly good tree cover. But the Great Plains will always be known as a place without trees. During the early days of American history, travelers crossing the Great Plains always reported back east that this land could never be settled because of the lack of water and trees. It was considered a desert.

Great Plains weather is remarkably similar throughout the area. The summers are long, hot and dry; temperatures over 100 degrees Fahrenheit are common and often persist for weeks on end. The winters are cold and the northern winds relentless. Amarillo, Texas, has more wind than any city in the nation, including Chicago. Dodge City, Kansas is second in windiness and Guymon, Oklahoma third. The constant wind, whether coming from the north in winter or the south in summer, dries out the land and can be quite monotonous to those of us who live on the Great Plains.

Temperatures below freezing may last for several months in the northern states. Winter storms in the southern states are mild by comparison, consisting of a very sharp cold snap before it warms up again.

Drought hits the area about every twenty-five years and creates vast social and financial dislocations. The 1850s were dry years in Kansas. Old John Brown lived through that drought, then went East and became the John Brown of Harper's Ferry. One can easily imagine how some of his wilder ideas were formed during that horrible drought.

The 1890s were also dry, so many farmers gave up and left for more wetter parts of the nation. When Jacob Sechler Coxey marched on Washington to demand relief in 1894, part of his contingent, the famous Coxey's Army, was recruited from the Great Plains. In South Dakota, Laura Ingalls Wilder and her husband Almanzo Wilder suffered greatly from the same drought and the constant crop failures it caused. They left in 1894, travelling by wagon to Mansfield, Missouri, where they established their new farm home. Laura became a good story-teller during her next forty years in the Ozarks, and at the age of sixty-five she wrote the first of her memorable *Little House on the Prairie* books, later a popular television series. Her daughter, Rose Wilder Lane, lived there for many years and developed into an artful storyteller as well. She commented that the valleys and flatlands raised good corn, whereas it took hills to raise men. This may be true, but she should have carried this thought one step further and noted that the Great Plains nurtured great women.

Whenever the Great Plains suffer an economic collapse such as the one we are now in the midst of, we go back to the basics—back to our women, and they nurture us through it. Our women hold us together. They are the greatest insurance policy we have on the Great Plains.

During the Dust Bowl days of the 1930s, the rain failed for almost an entire decade. There was no recorded moisture at all in the panhandle town of Guymon, Oklahoma during 1935. Its citizens were too poor to pay their taxes, so school didn't open that fall. In parts of Garfield County, Oklahoma, and up into the center of Kansas, there were only skiffs of snow in February 1938, and then no moisture at all until November. Trees died along the creek banks and wells dried up. Towns and cities had to ration water. A great exodus from the land emptied the countryside.

The drought of the 1950s was not as severe as the previous two. Still, many farmers gave up and left for the cities.

As I write, a drought has fastened itself upon parts of Nebraska, and all of South and North Dakota. The latter state has already endured over three years of drought. When I visited Bismarck, North Dakota in the summer of 1989, a dust storm raged with such blinding intensity that it was impossible to drive safely on the highway.

Kansas lost half of its wheat crop in 1989 to the drought in the western part of the state, and wheat production was sparse in the nearby Oklahoma and Texas Panhandles.

Cattle are an important facet of agriculture in all of the six states that comprise the classic Great Plains, as they account for a great deal of the farm and ranch income there. Wheat is the only cultivated crop of commercial significance in the Great Plains. It is grown all over the territory, from southern Texas to North Dakota and well into Canada. Because it is the principal cash crop of the Great Plains, the story about to unfold is essentially a story of wheat.

Some areas are known for producing a certain commodity, and derive much of their income from it. Cotton, for example, is grown in Texas and southern Oklahoma, but is seldom seen north of there. Flax, a common crop in the Dakotas, is a weed everywhere else. Soybeans are important in the three northern states, but something of an oddity elsewhere. Eastern Nebraska has plenty of corn, whereas Alfalfa County, Oklahoma couldn't come up with a single acre of corn even if all the sweet corn grown in backyard gardens was counted.

Wheat was one of the earliest imports into this continent after the first European settlements were founded. Native Americans already had corn, and they taught the white settlers how to grow it. Corn was on the table at the first Thanksgiving in 1621. But it wasn't long until the settlers demanded the fine bread that can only be made from wheat.

George Washington grew wheat, milled it into flour and sold it throughout Virginia. Much of his income came from such sales. Cotton didn't become a significant crop in the South until well after Eli Whitney invented the cotton gin in 1793, and Washington's soil yielded poor tobacco due to its high acidity. Wheat flour sales carried him through the Revolutionary War, a period during which the British weren't buying American tobacco anyway.

The people who settled the Great Plains after the Civil War brought corn with them, but it didn't do well because corn pollen hardens at 96 F, a common temperature in a Great Plains summer. Unless properly pollinated, a corn ear will not fill. Farmers call such a plant a "nubbin" because it has no grain.

A group of immigrants from southern Russia settled in McPherson, Kansas during the early 1870s. They were Mennonites, and legend has it that the womenfolk hid wheat in the seams of their underclothes to smuggle it out of Russia. This wheat was called Turkey Red, and all winter wheat now grown in the United States is a descendant of it. The Mennonites taught other pioneers to value wheat and grow it correctly. Other Germans from the Volga River Valley in Russia arrived in 1876, and in a few years the seventh and greatest breadbasket in world history was underway.

Winter wheat is the principal cash crop of the lower three Great Plains States—Kansas, Oklahoma, and Texas. The northern three Great Plains States also grow some winter wheat, though North and South Dakota mostly grow spring wheat.

A small genetic difference separates spring and winter wheat. Winter wheat is short a chromosome and must go through at least one hard freeze in order for the wheat stalk to develop. Otherwise it will remain grass. This characteristic, true to some degree in all kinds of wheat, explains why wheat is never found in the tropics.

Winter wheat is planted during September and October in the southern Great Plains. When it comes up, it makes good grazing forage for cattle. At 10 to 14 F, wheat freezes to the soil, and there is always at least one such freeze every winter. It comes up from its roots sometime between late February and late March, depending on the weather. After late May, when the crop in southern Texas matures, the harvest moves north up the Great Plains to northern Kansas, arriving there in late June. Therefore the long, hot, dry summer months of July and August do not affect winter wheat, a hard grain that eventually makes good bread.

Spring wheat, grown most often in Nebraska and the Dakotas, cannot stand much freezing. Since the soil in these states is often frozen all winter long, the crop is planted in late spring. Harvest time arrives in August and September. Softer than winter wheat, spring wheat makes good flour for pastries and pasta.

The Great Plains wheat industry is both a great national blessing and a grave national problem. Wheat production is abundant enough to satisfy all of our domestic needs with a great deal left over for export. A considerable part of this country's earnings from foreign trade is generated by the sale of wheat. When government programs, imports and market manipulation cause wheat to pile up in government warehouses, the inventory is used to feed the hungry populations of Third World countries. Famines in many parts of the world have been halted or averted with American wheat.

Government planners can always rely upon a plentiful supply of wheat, an advantage only four other countries in the world possess—Canada, Australia, Argentina and New Zealand. All other countries must constantly worry about their food supply. Japan and England, for example, have to import over one-half of their food. Their nation's planners must constantly concern themselves with this shortage. People stand for hours in food lines in Russia and other communist countries just to get a loaf of bread. Did you ever see a bread line in the United States? Of course not, and the reason for this is the abundance of wheat. You will see soup lines in the United States, and in the Great Plains, but that involves the soul of this nation, not the production of wheat.

But wheat also appears to bring abundant trouble. So much of it is grown, the authorities say, that the farmers cannot make money. Hunger, starvation and malnourishment exist throughout much of the Great Plains, and food pantries everywhere are at work to help the poor, many of whom are wheat farmers. When crops are poor and prices are low, wheat then is considered a curse on the farmer.

Many remedies were tried over the years to help the wheat farmer, and none really worked well. Probably the best were the parity and the "every normal granary" ideas of Henry A. Wallace, who served as Secretary of Agriculture from 1933 to 1940, and as vice-president during Franklin Roosevelt's third term. His plans restricted the planting of wheat and thus lowered production. *Any government plan or scheme that does not control the output of wheat is always doomed to early failure,* became the adage. Every subsequent generation of politicians in America has failed to learn this simple lesson of history. But the people of the Great Plains have always known why profligate wheat production brings plentiful hardship.

Kansas lost half of its 1989 wheat crop to drought, and the Oklahoma and Texas Panhandles were severely damaged as well. Wheat production also fell sharply in the Dakotas, as many farms only grew five to ten bushels an acre. Plants that would have been 30 inches tall in a good year were only six inches high. The heads of the wheat were about half an inch long when they should have been three inches, and combine sickles couldn't be set low enough to cut the grain.

Despite all this hardship, wheat supplies are still good, guaranteeing plenty of bread, pasta and pastry for all. Bread in my local stores is selling at ninety-nine cents for three large loaves. There is absolutely no excuse for hunger in America.

Drive a hundred miles any direction from Enid, Oklahoma, and all there is in cultivation is wheat. In western Kansas, a 2,000 acre wheat field is not uncommon. The Dakotas have even larger wheat fields. An ocean of wheat fills the horizon, yet farmers cannot make a profit. This is the basic economic situation on the Great Plains.

Misconduct by two government agencies and a badly misjudged national farm policy adversely affected agriculture in the 1950s, 1960s, 1970s and 1980s, bringing darkness to the farms of the Great Plains. This is the story of how it happened.

2

LAWS AND ECONOMIC IDEAS

There has always been a farm problem in the U.S. and the Great Plains. The English colonized Jamestown, Virginia in 1607, and established the first freely elected law-making body in the Western Hemisphere in 1619, the House of Burgesses. One of the first laws passed by this legislature in its first session was an act requiring farmers to plant grape vines. Our colonial fathers were interested in building up a local wine industry.

In the early 1790s, a drought moved President Washington to sign a bill into law appropriating money to help farmers buy seed. But Congress rarely acted on farm issues during this country's first 140 years, though occasionally a new administration would loose a flurry of new farm laws. One of the pivotal laws was passed under Abraham Lincoln in 1862, when Congress established a Department of Agriculture. A commissioner was appointed to administer it. Prior to this act farmers had been represented by a few agricultural clerks in the Patent Office. Congress upgraded the commissioner's post to a full Secretary in 1887, making him a member of the Cabinet.

The Morrill Act of 1862 gave 30,000 acres of land in the West to each state for each member of Congress it had, this to be used as an endowment for an agricultural and mechanical college. This resulted in the creation of more than fifty colleges, sometimes called the land grant colleges.

The Homestead Act, which Congress passed in 1862, provided 160 acres of land free of charge to a settler who stayed on it for five years. The only requirements were that the settler build some kind of dwelling and cultivate a certain number of acres. Credit was given for military service to satisfy the time requirement. Though the act never affected Texas because it joined the Union as an independent nation and thus had title to all of its public lands, the Homestead Act was a widely used settlement method in the other five Great Plains states.

The farm cooperative movement began in Denmark during the winter of 1881 and 1882, when a group of small farmers formed an organization to collectively market their butter. Farm co-ops quickly spread throughout the Scandinavian peninsula; they were formed to sell bacon, eggs and types of produce. Eventually the co-ops collectively purchased such farm necessities as fuel, fertilizer, and implements. They found that small farmers could improve their lot by gaining some control over the market where once they had none. Immigrants from Scandinavia brought their ideas to the Dakotas, and the Great Plains became the birthplace of the American farm co-op movement.

Congress responded by passing the Sherman Anti-trust Act in 1890, which prohibited restraint of trade and outlawed any group formed to restrain trade. In time this law was used against farm co-ops.

The Capper-Volstead Act, passed in 1924, gave farm co-ops, a reprieve, declaring their business activities not in violation of the Sherman Act, thus allowing them to operate. This legislation marks the real beginning of the co-op movement in the Great Plains. These units spread quickly. A co-op bank was set up to lend money to the local co-ops.

The other significant flurry of laws affecting agriculture were enacted during Woodrow Wilson's two terms in office. The Income Tax Amendment was added to the Constitution in 1913, making it only a matter of time before farmers were taxed under it. That year also saw the passage of the Federal Reserve Act, which created the Federal Reserve System. This act laid the groundwork for the system that governs the rationing of credit, and eventually had a strong adverse affect on the farm economy of the Great Plains.

Congress passed the Smith-Lever Act in 1914. It established the Extension Service and created a new government position, the county agent, who is empowered to instruct farmers in agricultural techniques and help solve their problems.

At about this time—1915—the U.S. became a creditor nation for the first time in its history, a position it enjoyed until 1984, at which time the U.S. became the biggest debtor nation in world history.

Government policy on matters of farm credit underwent its biggest change yet in 1916, when Congress passed the Federal Farm Loan Act. This bill set up twelve federal land banks across the country, and allowed the formation of federal land bank associations in rural towns. These banks also came to have a strong negative impact on the farmers of the Great Plains, and will be discussed in detail later. It was the first time in U.S. history that the federal government developed a policy designed to help farmers with farm credit.

Vocational agriculture education at the high school level was established by the Smith-Hughes Act, enacted in 1917. The idea was to teach modern farming techniques and the realties of modern farm life to rural boys and girls.

Henry C. Wallace of Iowa served as Secretary of Agriculture during the Harding administration and during part of the Coolidge administration. He convinced Congress to approve the McNary-Haugen Act of 1924, which provided a basis for two fixed prices for farm produce. The higher price applied to food sold for domestic consumption, and the lower one applied to agricultural exports. The bill contained no provisions for restricting the production of any particular crop. President Coolidge vetoed the measure, and this is the only time in history a president vetoed agricultural legislation passed by Congress at the request of his Secretary of Agriculture. This bill passed Congress twice and was vetoed twice.

Herbert Hoover, then Secretary of Commerce, predicted in 1926 that within a decade the U.S. would be an agriculturally deficient nation and forced to import most of its food.

Consequently, the Republican Party platform of 1928 promised higher tariffs to protect farmers. After taking office, President Hoover requested higher tariffs. Congress responded by passing the Smoot-Hawley Tariff Act of 1930. Though this Act went into effect months after the 1929 stock market crash, and could not have triggered the Great Depression, it became the favorite whipping boy for those who had achieved the breakdown of the American dollar and the globalization of American commodity prices.

About four months before the 1929 crash, Congress voted to set up a Federal Farm Board in the U.S. Department of Agriculture (USDA), and gave it a generous capital infusion of $500 million, and charged it with supporting the prices of farm produce. Farmers were then asked to *voluntarily* restrict the production of wheat and many other forms of production. They did not respond, because individual farmers do not have the financial reserves that would enable them to adapt flexibly to large economic forces. The Board spent most of its money on wheat and cotton, losing half of the $500 million on wheat alone. It bought a great deal of wheat it could not dispose of domestically, then sold the surplus to China and Germany, both of which paid for it with worthless bonds. Both sales were total losses. By the time it got out of the wheat business in 1931, the Board had done nothing to reduce wheat production. Even though it owned one-fourth of the world's wheat by then, it was helpless to stop farm prices from plummeting. Wheat fell to all time low of twenty-three cents per bushel in the Chicago grain market.

As American farmers mechanized their operations between 1920 and 1940, tractors replaced horses and many former horse pastures were plowed up and planted with wheat. This created an inventory buildup. Meanwhile, the collapse of speculative markets led to the collapse of commodity markets, and finally the collapse of the entire Hoover farm program. As the price of wheat fell, so did the price of farmland. The Depression deepened and misery spread across the Great Plains.

The defect in Herbert Hoover's agriculture policy was the lack of any strategy for controlling wheat production, and the shortfall of income to permit consumption. Though he had a few good ideas, he could not countenance the notion that a farmer should not be allowed to grow as much wheat as he wanted. Ezra Taft Benson, Eisenhower's Secretary of Agriculture, felt the same way and pushed for unlimited production in 1953. Richard Nixon's appointee, Earl Butz, advocated a similar lack of restrictions on production in 1971, as did Reagan's John Block in 1981. Each time, wheat prices collapsed due to inventory buildup, import invasion and general imbalance in domestically produced farm commodities.

Unless an effort is made to control wheat production, and to meet this country's red meat requirement entirely with domestic beef, the wheat problem is probably insoluble. When a new administration enters the White House, I always wait and see whether it advocates voluntary controls on wheat production. If it does, as the Eisenhower, Nixon and Reagan administrations did, I know that it cannot be taken seriously, and a wheat collapse will inevitably follow. Unfortunately, I've never been wrong.

The story of Henry Wallace is instructive. As the incoming Secretary of Agriculture in 1933, Wallace encouraged Congress to pass the Agricultural Adjustment Act, which came to be known as the Triple A. It mandated strict production controls on designated crops. For the farmers of the Great Plains, it meant that for the first time there were strict controls on the planting and harvesting of wheat. Acreage had to be taken out of production at a level calculated to ensure a steady supply for consumption, abolishing enormous surpluses.

This idea came from the Bible. When Joseph told the Pharaoh of the meaning of his dreams, the Egyptians "stored up grain for seven years and re-issued it during the seven bad years." Thus the ever-normal granary idea. The acres diverted from wheat production were planted with other crops, an action particularly helpful in accomplishing diversification for small farms.

The price of wheat was supported via a loan mechanism. A farmer could apply for a loan from the Commodity Credit Corporation, an agency within the USDA. If the market price of wheat did not rise to the support price by a designated time, the loan would be cancelled and the government became the owner of the stored wheat. If the price did rise above the government loan price, the farmer could redeem the wheat, sell it, pay off the government and keep the difference.

The cornbelt suffered from a great drought at the time this program went into effect. I've always been amazed at how droughts and depressions hit the farm economy at precisely the same time. But it always happens that way. In 1933 the government ordered a portion of the wheat and cotton crop plowed up to reduce production, and paid farmers to do it. The government bought piglets from farmers in the cornbelt because there wasn't enough corn to feed them to full butchering size. The USDA then had the small pigs butchered, canned and distributed it to the poor. An unbelievable political uproar ensued. Rebellious USDA employees, newspaper publishers and opportunistic politicos led a fierce attack against Wallace. When Roosevelt died in 1945—a dozen years after the hog canning event—one lady said she guessed she was sorry, but she would never forgive him for killing those little pigs.

Wallace's entire agriculture program was to be paid for by a tax on the processing and milling of farm products. The program was destroyed when the Supreme Court declared this tax unconstitutional in 1935. The Court also ruled that the federal government could not regulate agriculture. While the question of what the federal government should be allowed to do is always good fodder for debate, the argument advanced by Lincoln, Eisenhower and Hoover—that the federal government should do only those things that the individual cannot do, and not do what the individual can—is in my view faulty and rather immature. It is also historically incorrect and it meets no legal or constitutional test. A better criterion is whether the problem at hand is a national problem, thus requiring a national solution. Wheat over-production, for instance, is a national problem that screams for a national solution.

A wheat farmer cannot control production by himself. Yet Hoover and the Supreme Court said that the government could not act. The state and local governments could not act because the problem was national in scope. If Kansas, for instance, had set up a wheat program for its farmers, wheat would have poured across its borders in an ever-widening stream until the Kansas program collapsed, for the U.S. Constitution guarantees ingress and egress across a state line.

What the Supreme Court did was create a no-man's land in which no law operated. The wheat farmer over-produced in terms of domestic demand, and literally and figuratively starved. He couldn't act in his own best interest as an individual. The state governments couldn't act, and now neither could the federal government. Any time there is a no-man's land situation in law, massive injustices result.

The example of Judge Parker is instructive. When Congress set up the Oklahoma Indian Territory after the Civil War, it gave federal jurisdiction over the area to the Federal District Court at Fort Smith, Arkansas. A federal judge there by the name of Isaac C. Parker presided over it, and he quickly became known as the "hanging judge." He was a rabid believer in the death sentence. He indulged himself in hour-long harangues against the defendants during their jury trials. His closing statements on the law were ill-tempered and ill-considered. Many juries were inflamed by his rhetoric, and they convicted. Judge Parker's enthusiasm was such that he personally participated in the hangings.

During his twenty-one years on the bench in U.S. District Court, Fort Smith, Arkansas, 13,000 cases were tried by him. He pronounced the word, "I find the defendant guilty as charged" no less than 9,500 times. He sentenced 172 men to death, eighty-eight of whom were actually hanged. During his final seven years on the bench, he lost final jurisdiction over the cases he tried.

This deplorable situation was caused by a no-man's land that opened up because Congress neglected to provide an appeal out of Judge Parker's court when he was trying a case from the Indian lands. Cases from the western district of Arkansas, however, could be appealed, so no death sentences were carried out there. It took Congress almost thirty years, until 1896, to change the law, too late for the dozens of men Parker railroaded to the gallows. And all because of a legal situation in which no one could act.

Labor law contains another good example. Many years ago Congress passed a law regulating child labor. Businesses were not allowed to hire children in dangerous jobs, or work them long hours. The Supreme Court declared this law unconstitutional. State governments constructed their own versions of the law. Oregon played a particularly significant leadership role in the fight against child labor abuses. Then the Supreme Court declared the state laws unconstitutional because they violated a child's right to make a contract. Under state law, children didn't have the right to make a contract because they were minors, but the high court ignored this. Once more the door was opened to sweeping injustices because neither the state nor the federal government could act to rectify them. This represented a classic no-man's-land created by the courts.

The moral of the story is that if no one has the authority to act, then evil is empowered. There is no rule of thumb in legal history more important than the one prohibiting no-man's-lands within the law. The law, like gravity, should behave consistently.

When the Supreme Court created a no-man's land by declaring the first Triple A Act unconstitutional, many observers said that the laws of economics should be allowed to work. Inevitably, the farmers could not balance their end of the economy, and they brought poverty down on themselves.

One evil went largely unnoticed. For many years prior to 1937, when a certain party didn't like a federal law, he could—if he was wealthy enough—hire a battery of constitutional lawyers who would hatch a scheme to have the law declared unconstitutional. This is what happened to the first Triple A Act. A food processor who was having financial hard times filed for bankruptcy. In bankruptcy a receiver is appointed to hold and administer the property of the bankrupt party, and both parties hire attorney's to represent them. Since bankruptcy is a federal matter under Article 1, Section 8 of the constitution, they had no problem of getting this into federal court. The case also involved a federal tax.

Here is how the scheme developed. The attorney for the bankrupt and the attorney for the receiver each decided that they didn't like the Agricultural Adjustment Act of 1933 and wanted it declared unconstitutional. Then they maneuvered to get the case heard by a federal judge who agreed with them politically and ideologically. At the request of both defendants, this judge then declared the act unconstitutional. There was little or no debate over the decision's merits, and certainly no argument on behalf of Wallace's law. The use of wealthy litigants to fight the New Deal in the courts was widely invoked by Republicans in the 1930s.

Determined to reverse this tendency, Franklin D. Roosevelt sent a bill to Congress in 1937 asking that the number of judges on the Supreme Court be increased from nine to fifteen. The bill was quickly dubbed a court-packing plan, and it was hotly debated by members of Congress and the public. Most lawyers of the day had at least two distinct opinions on it. The Senate Judiciary Committee voted down the bill, but having lost the battle, Roosevelt went on to win the war. Congress was so fed up with the Supreme Court that for the first time in history it restricted the ability of the federal courts to declare a law unconstitutional by changing court procedure. Congress legislated that any challenge to the constitutionality of a federal statute, whether in federal or state court, must be made in writing. Once the challenge is made, the court must suspend its hearings and notify the Attorney General in writing, attaching copies of all relevant documents. The attorney general then has ninety days to make a decision. Generally, the Department of Justice will enter the case as a party litigant, file a brief and proceed with full arguments. Professional courtesy among attorneys also holds that a copy of the record shall be mailed to the local U.S. District Attorney. At any rate, gone are the days when two attorneys representing rich clients can shop around the federal courts until they find a friendly judge who will gladly toss out a law the three of them don't like.

Thus a problem in the farm belt changed the rights and responsibilities of the entire citizenry. This simple law changing the rules of how a court may proceed when attempting to declare a law unconstitutional had vast implications. *From 1937 to 1947, the Supreme Court of the U.S. reversed itself forty-seven times on major points of constitutional law.* Never before in world legal history was such a massive reversal of law been peacefully accomplished. Herbert Hoover stated, in 1937, that he wasn't too concerned about most of the New Deal legislation because the Supreme Court could declare it unconstitutional. After all, it was unwise from an economic standpoint. Apparently he never thought Congress would take away the power to declare legislation unconstitutional because it hurts someone's pocketbook.

Congress then passed a new Agriculture Adjustment Act, known as the Second Triple A. It contained some thoughtful and important changes. First, it didn't mention a tax, thereby staving off certain controversy over tax laws. Second, it granted crop subsidies and loans to farmers who restricted production. If a farmer would not restrict production, the government could prevent production by declaring an easement across his land. An easement is a well-established, centuries-old legal point that grants a legal right to do something on someone else's property. The electricity that lights your home, the natural gas that gives you heat, and the lines leading to your telephone are all brought across private property through the power to declare an easement.

So few constitutional arguments could be mounted against crop restriction. Most farmers of the 1930s lined up to comply with the restrictions and to get their subsidies, and many of them could not have stayed on the farms without those payments, which were a lifesaver. There is no record of anyone refusing the money. In the Oklahoma panhandle, government subsidies exceeded all other forms of farm income.

Aside from restricting production, the government didn't bother farmers too much during the New Deal. Farmers weren't told what to buy or whether to fertilize. But a key problem soon revealed itself. When the government ordered the restrictions, it would tell a farmer to take a certain percentage of his land out of wheat production, or whatever. If that farmer left 10% of his land out of wheat production, for instance, he diverted the worst 10% of his land, then carefully cultivated his remaining acres, adding more fertilizers. He also took other measures to ensure a good crop. Consequently, the overall drop in production was small. Later it developed that about 30% of the land had to be taken out of production to effect a significant reduction. But that kind of reduction hurt a lot of small farmers. A man with only ten acres to his name needed every penny he could get just to stay alive in those days. So an exception was made which allowed a small farmer to farm without losing benefits.

All the exception did, unfortunately, was help the wheat belt spread further into new territory. States such as Indiana and Ohio became major wheat producers. Gone are the cornfields once cultivated by Abraham Lincoln. Nowadays they're planted with wheat. Formerly well-diversified Illinois and Indiana farms changed over to wheat. Some of them even used to support flocks of sheep, now a memory along with domestic wool production. The U.S. today imports most of its wool from New Zealand.

Tucumcari, New Mexico is another place that comes to mind. When I passed through on a train about forty years ago, it was a great railroad town. Farmers in the area were usually beef ranchers, and there were plenty of them. Today, the railroad is gone, a large wheat elevator dominates the skyline, and the ranches have been plowed up and planted to wheat. And the farmers are losing money. Wheat has been a curse to the grass and cattle country surrounding Tucumcari, New Mexico.

Nor did wheat bring prosperity to Dalhart, Texas. Dalhart grew out of one of the divisions of the old XIT ranch, which was the largest ranch in the history of the world. Dalhart has a substantial wheat culture, but it is located in grass country. Let a drought develop and the soil blows away.

So the spread of the wheat industry can only be considered an economic curse when the wheat can't be sold. And it rarely can, because there are no markets for that much wheat inventory. This country can't consume all of the wheat it is capable of producing. A Nebraska wheat farmer once observed that this dilemma was the story of his life.

The major problem is that this country doesn't have a national land use policy. In fact, we have virtually no land use policy at all concerning farm land. Cities have zoning to regulate land use, but such regulations are unknown in rural areas, except in a very few states such as Wisconsin.

The New Deal farm program also disturbed traditional landlord-tenant relations. Because many landlords skilfully arranged to keep all the subsidy payments made under the Act for themselves, Congress passed the Bankhead Cotton Control program in 1934. It directed the USDA Secretary to make provisions for the protection of tenant farmers and sharecroppers. This was another historical first. Never before had the federal government undertaken a policy consciously designed to protect poor farmers from the economic ravages heaped upon them by wealthy farmers and plantation owners. A few criminal prosecutions of the rich men helped make the point that the poor were not to be kicked around. (When Eisenhower became president in 1953, one of the first things he did was abandon all efforts to protect the poor.) With similar goals in mind, the Southern Tenant Farmer's Union was formed in July 1934 at Tyronza, Arkansas, to fight for the rights of the sharecroppers under Triple A. Eleven whites and seven blacks organized the union. It was multiracial from the start, which was unheard of in 1934. It was never very big in the Great Plains, except in the cotton growing regions of Oklahoma and

Texas. The latter state is where it is strongest today.

Wheat farmers were allowed under New Deal farm programs to use their diverted acres to grow any other crop—oats, corn, maize, kaffir, or other sorghums—or put the lay-out land in hay or in soil-improving crops such as legumes. Overproduction was eventually brought under control by the second Triple A, which was a lifesaver for many of wheat farmers. The production controls were lifted during the WWII as part of the Lend-Lease program to aid the Allies, reinstated from 1945-50, then lifted again.

The 1930s was a time of great economic distress. Yet the deep economic crisis in Europe and the U.S. moved many economists to think boldly about their subject, and as a result economists in general made great progress during this decade.

One of them was the British theorist John Maynard Keynes, who published *The General Theory of Employment, Interest and Money* in 1936. This book came to be recognized by many economists as the most influential economic treatise of this century. In California a few years earlier, Dr. Francis Townsend advanced the idea that elderly people should be given a monthly pension. He recommended a pension of $200 per month, a considerable sum in those days, to be funded by a national sales tax. Though this notion remained a notion, it did help galvanize the Congress into passing the Social Security Act of 1935, which provided for more modest monthly pensions. The first pensions were only $15 per month when Dr. Townsend advocated $200. The Social Security program is paid for by a tax on payrolls and salaries and the employer and the employee pay the same amount. Later self-employed persons were covered.

Down in Louisiana, Huey Long proclaimed his Share the Wealth Program. In Michigan, a Catholic priest named Charles Coughlin labored to focus public attention on the plight of the needy and the elderly. In Washington, Roosevelt's Secretary of Labor, Frances Perkins, worked to implement pension programs, Social Security, and aid to the elderly, unemployed, dependent, blind, and neglected. She also encouraged Congress to pass the National Labor Relations Act, which protected laborers from various abuses on the part of their employers. Unions were granted the right to bargain collectively with employers, and Congress passed the Minimum Wage and Maximum Hours Act of 1938. Before the Frances Perkins era, there was no withholding from a salary or wage check. She revolutionized the economics of working people.

So to say the least, great economic decisions were made in the 1930s. Never before or since have diverse enonomic ideas been treated with so much spirited debate and discussion.

An equally passionate debate raged in the world of farming. While Henry Wallace preached controlled production, a farmer in Iowa named Carl H. Wilken became convinced that the Depression would never be truly resolved and future depressions could not be averted unless the farmer received a fair price on every commodity produced. Wilken noted that farming was the nations's largest industry and therefore what took place in farming had an enormous effect on the whole economy. Farming today is still the nation's largest business. Add food processing and food distribution, and it has an enormous impact on the economy. Wilken liked the idea of parity that George Peek preached. Parity was first the economic, then the legal concept of the farmer getting a fair price for his products. This fair price was determined by the cost of items the farmer had to buy from the other sectors of the economy. The concept of parity was based on the price relationship of 1910 to 1914. Because 1910-14 was an era in which unemployment figures were low, and price structures were not ruptured by import invasion, underconsumption or overproduction—all factors considered desirable norms—this time frame was cemented into place as base year "100."

Prices based on 1910-14 gave the farmer money to become a consumer again. He could buy the cars, clothes and other items that our economy could produce. If the farmer had no money, then he would be an economic exile, unable to buy the same things as the rest of society. Wilken concluded, soon enough, that overproduction was less a problem than underconsumption. His figures revealed that inventory buildups are a consequence of faltering parity, and not the cause. Furthermore, his studies proved that one dollar in farm income rippled through the economy and fed the multiplier until seven dollars in national income resulted. In other words, the key to unlimited prosperity lay in making sure that farmers had cash to spend.

Wilken put it this way. When a farmer produced a bushel of wheat and sold it for one dollar, that meant turning a gift of nature into new earned income. As that dollar flowed though the economy it created seven dollars of increased sales. But if that farmer could get three dollars for a bushel of wheat, this represented an increase of $21 in economic activity. However, if the price of wheat sank to twenty-five cents a bushel, the earned income at the national level fell to $1.75.

Many discussions of farm problems hinge on support prices that the farmer is to receive. However, the real goal should be to make it possible for the farmer to consume. He cannot consume if he has an inadequate income. Support prices should be high enough so he can be a good consumer.

Most historians don't like to suggest solutions to problems, but I disagree with that approach. I think there is an obvious solution to one of society's most vexing problems—the plight of disenfranchised minorities—and that the solution suggests an appropriate analogy to the idea of farm parity. Most citizens seem to agree that discrimination against American blacks and other minorities should be ended, and that segregation was too poor and stupid an idea to survive. Yet it is a defensible generalization to suggest that the current Supreme Court and President George Bush (the people's choice in 1988) are anti-Civil Rights. And during the Reagan years and afterward, Bush never opposed the trend toward breaking down worker wages by importing Mexican and Oriental nationals as cheap labor. It is a destructive practice not because it allows more people into the U.S., but because the underlying motive is to turn worker wages into mere costs, and then deny those same workers the purchasing power they need to live decently. If they had adequate income, they could fully participate in the economy as consumers, rather than scrape by as marginal members of society. Today they are on the outside looking into the economic bins, but not enjoying the fruits of this country's economy. We need minorities as consumers, not solely as the objects of non-discriminatory policies.

So it is with the farmer. The farmer needs a respectable income so he can be a good consumer. Carl Wilken started to popularize his ideas during the 1930s, and in time brought them to the attention of Homer Capehart's House Banking Committee. Parity for basic storable commodities was included in the War Stabilization Act of 1942. The agricultural component rested upon the Agricultural Adjustment Act of 1938. During 1942, Congress also passed the Steagall Amendment to the Stabilization Act. This Amendment established farm prices at 90 to 92.5% parity for semi-storable commodities such as pork bellies, eggs, poultry, milk, butterfat, dry peas of all kinds, soybeans, flaxseed, and many other items that had not been covered earlier. The prices were maintained through commodity loans. As a consequence, the American farm economy enjoyed real prosperity.

It must be noted, parenthetically at least, that the WWII stabilization measure was a money and banking bill, not a farm act. Its preamble called attention to language in the Constitution that requires Congress to create the national currency and "regulate the value thereof." When the law finally expired, Congressman Harold Cooley observed that the stabilization measure hadn't cost the government a dime—indeed, the procedure had resulted in a profit while maintaining the national income level so well that a 15% income tax would have paid for the war out of then-current income. Prices for farm commodities did not reach as high a level in WWII as they had during WWI. This fact is often forgotten. Wheat sold for $3.02 a bushel in 1918, yet during the WWII its highest price was only $2.82. But all prices were at parity and stabilized in the last case.

According to the Steagall Amendment, that price structure was to be abandoned two years after the end of WWII. It is not precisely clear why Congress boxes itself in with such constricting legal language, though procrastination fueled by fear must have something to do with it. All such limits accomplish is to postpone the day of reckoning when Congress must finally deal with an unpleasant situation whether it wants to or not. Congress recently inflicted a similar legal full-Nelson on itself with the staggeringly stupid Gramm-Rudman Act of 1985. Every year the law mandates a certain reduction in the deficit, and every year Congress engages in a ludicrous budget dance to avoid sequestration and huge automatic cuts. Temporary shutdowns of the government are now common around late September and early October as budget negotiations kick into high gear and go from frantic to frenzied. The brazen idiocy of the whole procedure, not to mention the twisted logic behind it, is all too self-evident.

Similarly, the Steagall Amendment locked Congress into an unwise course, that of terminating the price support system two years after the end of WWII. The law was written so that the war could be terminated by a Congressional action or a Presidential Proclamation. Truman, in fact, did proclaim the end of the war on December 31, 1946. Two years later, on the last day of 1948, the support system based on both the WWII stabilization measure and the Steagall Amendment had to be withdrawn.

The Republicans gained control of both houses in the November 1946 elections, and proceeded to gut as much of the New Deal and Fair Deal as they could. In 1948 the Republicans in the Senate forced though the Aiken bill, which provided for a sliding scale ranging between 60 and 90% of parity. This scale came to govern the profitability—or lack of same—of agriculture. It was the opening salvo in the fight to globalize commodity prices. Although the cant of "surpluses" rolled like thunder across the country, the fact was that for five years imports had created the surpluses. Locally and on the exchanges, the case could be made that surpluses created faltering parity when the exact opposite was true. As apparent surpluses grew, income supplied by programs fell—thus the name, "sliding parity."

The amount a farmer received depended largely on how much he produced. The House of Representatives passed a different version of the bill and a conference committee was appointed by both bodies to work out the differences. The representatives could not agree to the Aiken bill. Some members resigned from the Committee rather than endorse it. In time conferees decided to make the Aiken bill the controlling factor, but delayed its activation for one year. Though Truman reluctantly signed this compromise bill after it passed both houses, he made it his chief complaint against the Republicans in the 1948 election. In the farm belt Truman had his aides pass out sheets showing the prices of farm produce under the Democrats and what would happen to them under the Republicans. Then he said that the Republicans took a pitchfork and stuck it in the farmer's back. Most farmers got the point and Truman carried the farm states by a good margin, and the farm vote turned out to be the key factor in his re-election.

Then, in 1949, Congress passed a bill that postponed the sliding scale of parity for one year. Congress continued passing one-year extensions until USDA Secretary Ezra Taft Benson convinced Dwight D. Eisenhower not to allow any further postponement of the sliding scale. This ended basic parity at 90% for most farm commodities.

It's interesting to note that Truman was the only president since Coolidge who consistently balanced budgets. Four of the seven budgets he sent to Congress were balanced by raising income above expenses. Yet after the Steagall Amendment came to an end under Eisenhower, not a single Eisenhower budget was balanced, and the country went through three major recessions during his terms in office—the worst record in history. More farmers went broke and left the countryside under Eisenhower than in any other era. During the Depression years under Roosevelt and the Steagall Amendment years under Truman, more people returned to farming than the other way around.

During the Roosevelt and Truman years, most farmers went

into town to shop on Saturday afternoon, and you couldn't find a parking space within three blocks of the main street. Ever since the Eisenhower years, you can amble down the main streets of most towns and villages on Saturday afternoon and there is not a car in sight. American farmers are not consuming, and that has been their basic economic problem since 1953. Carl Wilken was right!

Kennedy, Nixon, Ford, Carter, Reagan and, as of 1990, Bush, have not turned in a single balanced budget. Lyndon Johnson balanced one budget by placing a 10% surcharge on all income taxes, and by inserting Social Security income, which the government only holds in trust, into the budget to simulate actual revenues. Otherwise, all of his budgets were in the red.

Another interesting contrast to the present is the fact that Henry Wallace, Dr. Townsend, and Carl Wilken were all liberal Republicans. Their heyday was the 1930s, when people were much less terrified of new ideas, and the Republican Party was animated by the continuous cut and thrust of intellectual debate. The politicians today lack a single voice to betray even a glimmer of economic sense. The Gramm-Rudman Act is a fraud, and so is supply-side economics. Increasing the supply of commodities and manufactured items without price will not increase economic activity, but precisely the opposite. While the economy sinks the present administration refuses to devise a single idea that might undo the damage done during the Reagan years, preferring to favor the rich with further tax cuts.

The life and times of Carl Wilken are chronicled in a book about his ideas, written by *Acres U.S.A.* editor-publisher Charles Walters Jr., and called *Unforgiven*. The title came from *The People*, a poem by Tomasso Campanella, about those who "own all things between earth and heaven / But this it knows not / and if one arise to tell this truth / it kills him unforgiven." It might have been titled *Unforgivable*, which is what the actions of the 80th Congress were.

A number of New Deal programs had considerable impact on the Great Plains, as they did much to create the social and economic tapestry later shredded by lesser policies. One of them was the Soil Conservation Act, passed in 1935. This program fought erosion by funding the construction of terraces to restrain flowing water, and providing for an extensive grass planting campaign. Its effect on the Great Plains is hard to underestimate if you didn't live through the Dust Bowl years. That same year, the Rural Electrification Act empowered farmers to set up co-ops for the purpose of generating and distributing electricity. The change wrought by this act was little short of miraculous. It brought thousands of rural Americans into the 20th century virtually overnight. In places like the Hill Country just west of Austin, Texas, the old-timers still speak of the day electricity came in awestruck tones. Both of these programs were crucial to establishing rural prosperity, and both are still in effect.

Aside from having no electricity and watching their topsoil blow away, Great Plains farmers of the early 1930s were critically underfinanced. It was hard for banks to lend money to farmers. On one hand, many farmers were earning little or no income, and had next to nothing to offer for collateral. On the other hand, banks were falling before the Depression's onslaught like sandcastles under a steamroller. During the first few years of the crisis in South Dakota, for example, over half of all commercial banks went under. So Congress, led by Roosevelt and his lieutenants, set up the production credit associations that made short-term loans to farmers. Still extant, the production credit associations are arranged in different districts than the federal land banks. Some of these associations are now in financial difficulty, but their troubles do not concern us here, as this book is basically a study of long-term credit needs of our farmers.

In 1933 Congress passed the Farm Security Administration, which was a program to work with small, poor farmers and with tenants. This program was phased out and the Farmers Home Administration was established to do essentially the same thing in 1946. Since this program has come to hurt farmers badly, it will be reviewed in detail in a later chapter.

Ezra Taft Benson, whom Eisenhower appointed as USDA

chief in 1952, was a graduate of the agricultural college at Ames, Iowa. There he received his master's degree in agricultural economics. He then became a county agent and taught farm economics in Idaho. In 1933 he went to Washington, where he became Executive Secretary of the National Council of Farmers Cooperatives, another way of saying he was paid to lobby against the New Deal. As executive secretary of that group, he spent twenty years conducting political guerrilla warfare against the New Deal and Fair Deal.

Benson totally opposed restrictions on crop production, insisting that any reduction in crops had to be voluntary. He is a perfect example of an American politician incapable of seeing that voluntary controls don't work. And Congress unfortunately went along with far too much of his program. After Benson convinced Eisenhower that the long postponed Aiken bill should be activated, the flexible price support program worked like this: a farmer had to restrict production to a minor extent, but his subsidy payment would be based on total production. As production increased, farmers received fewer subsidies. As production fell, the farmer received more subsidies. A sliding scale was devised to determine the amounts.

This program went into effect in the southern Great Plains in the fall of 1954. Good weather came along and farmers enjoyed bumper crops. Subsidy payments fell sharply. As farm prices fell, the farmer's ability to consume fell sharply. Economic activity in society as a whole declined, and the consumption of farm products fell sharply. Hence the recessions of the Eisenhower era—the Wilken rule at work.

By the spring of 1956 it was obvious that massive production of wheat was destroying the economic viability of many farmers, so Congress passed the Soil Bank Act. Under this law farmers were paid to take land out of production. The program's conservation features were emphasized to make it look less like something out of the New Deal. Yet it was about the same, though in some cases the farmer could take all of his land out of production and get paid for it. This led to national jokes about the farmer who went fishing all of the time and got paid for it. Under Henry Wallace's old Triple A, the farmer could be paid for taking only part of his land out of production. The Soil Bank lasted until 1961, when Congress phased it out of existence.

Also created by Congress in 1954 was the Food For Peace Program. Designed by a farmer, Gwynn Garnett of Arlington, Virginia, this act set up the mechanism by which surplus agriculture products sitting in the government warehouses with few immediate prospects of being sold could be sent overseas to countries afflicted by famines or food shortages. As a humanitarian measure, Food for Peace, still in operation, saves lives overseas and generates plenty of good will toward the U.S. However, it has not reduced the amount of food in storage by much. The bins are still glutted with wheat, dairy products, peanuts, corn and honey. You name it, the U.S. has plenty of it because farm production is not balanced to needs.

Subsidies were not the only financial link between the feds and farmers. Congress amended the Social Security Act in 1954 to include farmers and, except for doctors, most other self-employed persons in the system. Social Security is now the principal economic lifeline to farmers over sixty-five.

Benson was an interesting politician with an intriguing personality. He firmly believed that the sun would not rise in the east the next day if the government restricted crop production. He worked against crop restrictions tirelessly, even going so far as to make the existing program as unworkable as possible. Once he fined a small farmer, Stanley Yankus of Dowignac, Michigan, who fed all of his wheat to his chickens. The farmer fled to Australia. He could have easily waived the fine, but because the man was a small farmer, Benson set out to make an example out of him.

When he took office, Eisenhower looked over government policies and programs with an eye toward changing them, or, better yet, ending them. This activity came to be known as the "unleashing" policy, the name taken from cancellation of Navy patrols in the Strait of Formosa. Truman had ordered the patrols to prevent war between the Nationalist Chinese on Formosa and the Red Chinese on the mainland. Eisenhower explained that he was "unleashing" Chiang Kai-shek, hence the policy's name. It was an idiotic action in that it simply left the Nationalist Chinese open to military invasion by the Red Chinese. The Nationalist Chinese had no military capability whatsoever. Eisenhower then threatened the Chinese with atomic warfare to protect the islands of Matsu and Quemoy, two insignificant islands no one had ever heard of. Aside from threatening world peace, unleashing accomplished next to nothing.

Benson applied the unleashing policy at the USDA with a similar lack of success, or, if you prefer, total failure. By way of unleashing the federal land banks, in 1954 Benson persuaded Congress to make them an independent agency of the government. He then insisted that because the land bank was not controlled by Washington, its employees were not employees of the U. S. government, and he had them removed from the Civil Service Commission's pension rolls. The banks were thus unleashed. No immediate harm was done, but when the Farm Credit Act of 1971 was passed, all of Benson's notions came home to roost, badly hurting the wheat farmers of the Great Plains.

Bad as Benson's policies were, his personality was probably worse. Benson insisted that every meeting in his office open with prayers to the Almighty. With that bit of sanctimony out of the way, he immediately turned to shilling for the rich. This proclivity became quite a problem. When anyone suggested some way to solve a problem that didn't benefit the rich, Benson opposed it. He also hated to hear about any shortcomings of the department. He withdrew government protection of small and tenant farmers. Gone were the days when the USDA would investigate a landlord who ordered a tenant off the land so he could collect all of the government subsidies. Farmers hated him for it.

Benson also curtailed protection of migratory farm laborers. When I was such a laborer in the 1950s, I worked on farms in Illinois, Wisconsin, and Minnesota, and lived in the labor camps. At no time did the USDA under Benson take an interest in the plight of the migrant worker. They slept in barns, ate government commodities that the employer "snitched" from the USDA, used open fields as toilets, bathed in nearby streams. No provisions were made for medical or dental attention, and there was no laundry service. If a worker even mentioned a problem, he was fired. One migrant employer in Illinois combed the Chicago slums for winos to use as replacements for disagreeable workers. If a wino died on the job, there were no survivors to step forward and claim death benefits. Though continuously reminded of these conditions, Benson refused to act. I remember an incident in 1956 when threats were made on his life during a visit to Belvidere, Illinois. Nothing happened, but the ill feeling remained.

Benson was haughty, snotty, and anti-intellectual all at once. His policies were politically divisive to say the least, and he spoke all over the country in an effort to rally political support. It didn't work, because he usually seemed on the verge of rolling his eyes heavenward and bleating, "Oh, Dear God, why must I deal with such asses?" Wheat farmers resented his attitude, and virtually everyone loathed him with a ferocity rarely encountered in public life. I attended a meeting of the Senate Agricultural Committee in 1955 where for two days every witness bitterly recommended that Benson be fired. At the 1960 Republican national convention, Richard M. Nixon, the party's nominee for president, suggested that the Eisenhower Cabinet always stand in protocol order, placing Benson at the back of the line and as far from Nixon as possible. Coziness is not always a Republican attribute, but to repel Richard Nixon is surely some kind of distinction.

It is difficult to adequately convey the hostility Benson stirred up among farmers. They didn't even regard him as a public official, only a windy demagogue. Moreover, Benson apparently left a curse of sorts on the office of USDA Secretary. Every Ag Secretary since Benson has inspired hatred on the part of wheat farmers, and none have escaped career ruin. When a Secretary of Agriculture takes office, his political future is over. Benson vanished into his church. Orville Freeman, who served under Kennedy and Johnson, has never been heard from again. Clifford Hardin, Nixon's first appointee to the post, is utterly forgotten. Bob Bergland, who was appointed by Jimmy Carter, works in the private sector.

At least Earl Butz—Nixon and Ford's man from 1971-76— went down in rather spectacular flames. A racist joke he made during the 1976 presidential campaign caused an uproar and thoroughly embarrassed Gerald Ford, who made Butz resign. Subsequently jailed on tax evasion charges, Butz is now remembered, if at all, as a minor player of the Watergate era. John R. Block, like dozens of Reagan appointees to high office, left the government under a cloud of suspicion. In Block's case, though, there was a touch of poetic justice about his downfall, which came when his farm partner went broke and defaulted on a government loan. Since leaving office, Block has kept busy trying to stave off personal bankruptcy, much like thousands of ordinary farmers during his years in office.

This sorry record stands in vivid contrast to the era before Benson. Henry Wallace went on to become vice president during Roosevelt's third term, and later served as Secretary of Commerce. Clinton P. Anderson, who held the job under Harry Truman, went on to a distinguished career in the U.S. Senate. Going back to the 19th century, James Wilson served under McKinley, (Theodore) Roosevelt and Taft, longer than any other Secretary. He remained a respected public servant through it all. Sterling Morton, Secretary of Agriculture during Grover Cleveland's second term (1893-1897), was well-liked in and out of office. He established Arbor Day, the spring holiday dedicated to tree planting, and in 1937 the State of Nebraska placed a statue of him in Washington's Statuary Hall. He was the only Secretary of Agriculture to ever receive such acclaim and distinction.

Ezra Taft Benson's tenure in office was a watershed event in American politics. He did not make history so much as vandalize it. His career clearly demonstrates the lasting damage that can be done by one petty, abrasive personality in the wrong place at the wrong time. Early in 1989, George Bush named

Clayton Yeutter as his Secretary of Agriculture. I asked many of the farmers who came to my office for help in getting their income taxes prepared what they thought about the new man. A farmer from the Bison, Oklahoma area said he guessed that he liked him all right, "but give him ten minutes in office and I will hate the bastard." Think of it: the new Secretary had ten minutes of grace before hatred set in. Such is the legacy of Ezra Taft Benson.

John F. Kennedy's short term in office didn't produce much in the way of significant agricultural policy. Yet he signed a tax bill that had dire consequences for farmers down the line: the Investment Tax Credit Act of 1963. The law, which Kennedy's IRS Commissioner asked him not to support, provided that businesses and farms could receive a tax credit if they invested in new equipment. Some buildings such as granaries and feeding slabs in feedlots were also covered by the program, though many other farm buildings were not. This law turned out to be a tragic mistake.

The tax credit worked as follows. If a farmer bought a tractor for $10,000 (about what they cost in 1963), then depreciated it out by using it for seven or more years, he was given a credit of $700 on any income tax he owed the government. For example, if the farmer owed $1,000 in income taxes, he could use the $700 credit to reduce the actual tax to $300. He would still owe Social Security taxes, but overall the tax credit was a bargain. In time the law was changed to raise the credit up to 10%, and then was reduced as the Vietnam War gathered momentum.

When Congress passes a tax law, the average wheat farmer may not understand it well enough to take immediate advantage of it. So ten years passed before the Investment Tax Credit was used in a big way throughout the countryside. By 1981, many farmers were using the terms of Reagan's tax cuts to buy machinery like there was no tomorrow, a practice that led to insolvency (as later chapters will discuss). Farmers could built up huge tax credits, and by the end of the 1970s farmers who had $50,000 in unused tax credits were not uncommon.

When the farm economy began to collapse in 1981, the credits turned out to be worthless, because farmers were losing money and had no income taxes. Only people who make money have to pay income tax. In 1986 Congress repealed the Investment Tax Credit, and it is to be hoped that nothing like it is ever passed again. It wrecked too many farmers.

Shortly after taking office, Kennedy vastly expanded the food commodity program that Eisenhower's people had set up in a few parts of the country. Kennedy made much of the fact that Congress granted Eisenhower the power to eliminate hunger by enlarging this program, and he had refused. Under the program, the USDA processed some of its surplus food and distributed it to the poor. Commodity day was the first day of the month in most areas of the country.

The Nixon administration ended this program and readopted an old New Deal program—food stamps, financed by the USDA, but administered by state welfare officials. Under the still extant program, stamps are sold to the poor for a nominal sum—for instance, $50 worth of stamps for $5—or, in some cases, given away. The recipients then go to any cooperating store, buy the groceries they need, and pay for them with food stamps. Many observers think food stamps are superior to commodities because the poor are given a choice of foodstuffs. Under the commodity program, they received a lot of corn meal, flour, beans and peanut butter. One welfare mother explained it to me this way. "Kids get tired of those commodities and when they do you have to go and buy something they will eat, and there goes the last of the money." Food stamps are an improvement over commodities, proof that Nixon was capable of making an occasional good decision.

Lyndon Johnson made his major agricultural decision in 1966 when he instituted strict controls on the amount of money that could be lent to farmers through the FmHA and the federal land banks. The fallout from this policy will be discussed in detail in later chapters.

When Richard Nixon arrived in Washington in 1969 to take office, so did one of his old campaign managers, Henry L.

Bellmon, the new Senator from Oklahoma. Both men were ultra-conservatives and both wanted to cut taxes and "get government off the back of the farmers." Bellmon used the ploy that he was the only farmer in the U.S. Senate as his advertising gimmick. Unfortunately other senators listened to him too much. Bellmon had a long history of trouble with financing his Oklahoma farm operation. Once, during the 1964 elections, someone suggested that he repay his FmHA loan in full, because as governor of Oklahoma he had additional income that disqualified him for the loan. He had not only adequate but ample credit with a life insurance company. Bellmon, to put it mildly, grew quite irritated. He'd always wanted farm subsidies to go mainly to the rich, and never showed much support for small or impoverished farmers. He fathered the Farm Credit Act of 1971, which led directly to much of the financial grief that now plagues the farms of the Great Plains.

Congress limited subsidies in 1970 to $55,000 for each wheat, feed grain, or cotton crop. Its hand was forced by such glaring cases as that of Senator James Eastland, a Democrat from Mississippi and Senate Agriculture Committee member that received $164,048 for cotton that year. Of course, a farmer could still be paid $55,000 apiece for his wheat, cotton and feed grain crops, provided he raised a sufficient quantity of all three. The cotton belts of West Texas and Oklahoma were the only places in the Great Plains where such a combination was possible.

Whatever the merit, or lack thereof, of the policies he enacted during his first two years in office, Nixon must also bear the responsibility for ensuring ultimate disaster by appointing the worst secretary of agriculture in history. Clifford Hardin, a carryover from the Johnson era, resigned in 1971, and Nixon replaced him with Earl Butz, a man who'd spent his entire adult life sucking up to rich farm corporations. He served on the board of directors of several such corporations and owned stock in several more. His supporters advanced the ridiculous idea that he could moderate between rich and poor farmers. Some senators knew as much, and his appointment was only confirmed by a vote of fifty-one to forty-five, the closest any new USDA Secretary ever came to defeat.

Butz lived up to his reputation. Upon taking office, he advocated the full production of wheat, recommending that it be planted "fence-row to fence-row." The deed was done. By 1973, and from then on for about six years the farmers tried to work out from under this abundance.

The administration of President Gerald R. Ford (1974-1977) is not remembered as an originator of farm programs. Indeed, he initiated no new programs.

President Carter kept very strict controls on the subsidy programs. His biggest bill for subsidies was $4 billion. Under Reagan it reached $26 billion, the highest in history. This represented an increase of 650%.

There were still huge quantities of surplus grains left over from the Butz years. Carter would not agree to increased payments to the farmer. Bob Bergland, his secretary of agriculture, had been a congressman from Minnesota, and had always campaigned on the platform of giving the farmer full parity on his farm produce. Once in office, he reversed himself and refused further payment. Incidentally in the Congressional elections of 1954, Eisenhower made a speech in Minnesota in which he stated he was against 90% parity for farmers because he wanted 100% parity. He returned to Washington and stabbed the farmers in the back with 60% parity. Diabolical political switches such as this are never appreciated by wheat farmers.

A movement developed in Colorado and the Texas panhandle which came to be called the American Agricultural Movement. Farmers held tractorcades across the nation and spent several months in 1978 in Washington lobbying for higher subsidies. They requested a meeting with Secretary Bergland and when they arrived at USDA they found the doors locked and they were denied entry. They requested a meeting with President Carter and he refused. A number of congressman insisted that Carter should meet with members of the group. A meeting was set up and Carter "stacked" the meeting with spokesmen from the Farm Bureau and other conservative groups and gave them all except four minutes of the time to speak. The American Agricultural Movement got only four minutes to present its ideas. Carter lost every state in the Great Plains in his 1980 re-election bid.

Carter appointed Paul Volcker as chairman of the Federal Reserve System in 1979 and Volcker announced in October that the Fed would not pay any attention to interest rates but would concern itself with cash flow and bank reserves. This led to interest rates of 21.9% for prime customers, and since farmers are not prime customers, they paid even more. Why Carter allowed this to happen has never been explained.

Carter would not remove the appointees of the Nixon and Ford Administration from policy-making positions in the farm credit system of USDA, and particularly from the FmHA. When it was forcibly pointed out to him that conservative Republicans were holding onto these political positions and were extending vast amounts of credit, he did nothing. Gossip in the Democratic Party was that Carter did not want to remove them if they were doing a good job. Well they were doing a good job of throwing vast amounts of credit around and in general were financing a land boom unprecedented in American history. If that is good, they were doing a good job. But any casual observer knew that this was wrong, and when it was pointed out to Carter that he should stop this, he would only agree to check on it. In Oklahoma, he finally was forced to remove a holdover from the FmHA, but before doing so he had a new job of agricultural advisor created and appointed the retiring bureaucrat to that position at the cost to the taxpayers of over $50,000 a year. The adviser did nothing during the remainder of Carter's years. Carter was incapable of seeing that political appointments could be used to advance a political agenda. In many ways he did not have a political agenda. His statements of being a born-again Christian and that he had love in his heart for everyone can't remotely be considered a political agenda. He was ineffective in many ways. Had he fired those Republicans who were slinging credit around, he would have done a favor for the Great Plains for which no amount of thanks could have been adequate. However, he did nothing.

He also was not knowledgeable about American history. Both Democrat and Republican Presidents always embargoed items of export, and the effect has been minimal. Jefferson embargoed goods to Europe just before the War of 1812. At no time did any European power pay much attention to it. Lincoln embargoed goods from the South during the Civil War. Roosevelt embargoed goods to Japan before WWII. Nixon embargoed goods a number of times, including sales of grain to the Soviet Union in 1974. During the presidential campaign of 1976, Jimmy Carter railed against this embargo. He made several speeches against embargoes in the Great Plains, and these were popular. He carried Texas largely for this reason. Yet when he got into office he reversed himself and embargoed the sale of agricultural products to the Soviet Union after the Soviet Union invaded Afghanistan in 1979. The actual date of the embargo was January 4, 1980. Had Carter followed his own promise, a lot of political fodder would not have been chopped. Carter's embargo did have a good point. It put a floor price on the sale of wheat during the time that the embargo was in effect. If the price of wheat suffered as a result of the embargo, the government would intervene in the market and support the old higher price of wheat by buying up the same amount of wheat that the Soviet Union would have taken. During the embargo the export of wheat climbed sharply and so did the price. Exports were helped by drought and famine in many areas of the world. For example, while wheat was embargoed under Carter during the year of 1980, agricultural exports rose from $31 billion to over $40 billion, the largest increase in one year in history. *The Carter embargo did not hurt farm exports.* On April 23, 1981, Reagan lifted the grain embargo to the Soviet Union and in 1982 farm exports fell to $36 billion, the sharpest drop in history. If one fervently believes something, proof is not needed. Republicans believe the embargo hurt the farmers. They ignore all the observed facts of the situation.

The effect the government has on the wheat market is enormous. It is not necessary for the U.S. Government to buy up all wheat in order to affect the market price of wheat. The price is affected just as soon as grain dealers are aware of the fact that government traders have a power to act. When Carter announced that the government would intervene in the market to buy the same amount of grain the Soviets would have bought, this firmed up the market and held prices steady. Had a private buyer of wheat made this statement, it would have been meaningless.

A study of the prices of wheat reveals that wheat farmers did not suffer due to the embargo because the price activity by the government kept the price of wheat from falling. I think that this feature of the Carter embargo should be closely studied now and in the future, so if another embargo is deemed proper, Americans will not be hurt by it.

Unfortunately that is not the way it worked. In the presidential election of 1980, Ronald Reagan "railed" against Carter for the embargo just as Carter had "railed" against President Ford during the election of 1976. Had Reagan followed his own political rhetoric he would not have embargoed during his administration as he did. For example in December 1981, Reagan broke off negotiations with the Soviet Union for a long term grain deal to protest the imposition of martial law in Poland. Later he limited discussions to only one year. This is an embargo. Wheat farmers needs at least one year notice in order to rearrange their farming operation. A one year deal is of no use to a wheat farmer. It might be to a radish farmer. However, the Soviet Union does not import radishes. In 1981 and 1982 Reagan embargoed industrial items to the Soviet Union on a gas pipeline the Soviet Union was building to Western Europe. So there were several embargoes during the Reagan administration.

The Carter embargo had very little effect inside the Soviet Union. All it did was to cause the Soviet people to tighten their belts just a little more. Soviets are experts on belt tightening. Their's is a very poor country and belt tightening is a common practice. They have never known prosperity.

President Reagan often reminded those who would listen that the Carter embargo hurt the farmers. This is false. What hurt the farmer was the removal of the Carter embargo, because that act destroyed the farm price support for wheat that Carter had imposed. The economic effect was about the same as eliminating full parity price supports during the Eisenhower administration.

Whenever a price fixture is in place, it hurts badly to remove it all at once in any case. Perhaps what needs to be done is to remove it in stages, and over an extended period of time, if indeed, removal is indicated at all. This would allow the market time to adjust. During WWII, price ceilings on most items were in place. Richard M. Nixon worked as an attorney for the Office of Price Administration. This office held down some price increases and supported others. As a consequence, there was little inflation during the war. When the war was over, price ceilings were removed all at once, and prices went through the roof.

Without asking anyone's advice, Reagan removed and destroyed the price supports under wheat all at once and this started the economic collapse that caused night to come to the Great Plains.

When I talk about the price of wheat, it should be noted that the price varies greatly. The price a farmer would charge his neighbor for seed wheat is different from what those farmers would expect to get from the co-op elevator. That price in turn is different from the price a big grain elevator system would pay in such cities as Enid, Oklahoma, Hutchinson, Kansas, or Minneapolis, Minnesota. Those prices are different from the wheat price at ports with overseas shipping capabilities, such as Houston, Texas. The reason for much of this is the fact that a great deal of our wheat goes overseas and transportation to the water ports must be paid. So a bushel of wheat sold in Strasburg, North Dakota will be different from the price of a bushel of wheat sold at Cawker City, Kansas, which in turn is different from the price of a bushel of wheat sold at Keyes, Oklahoma. To compare the prices of wheat in various markets is often faulty and often leads to wrong conclusions. The Reagan administration manipulated these prices for all they were worth, and many people became honestly convinced that the Carter embargo hurt the wheat farmers. It did not.

I think that the best way to decide this is to look at the monthly average of wheat prices at the point of a water port. At that point, transportation charges have been equalized. I have taken the closing average monthly price of wheat from January 1979, which is a year before the start of the Carter embargo, through the end of December 1986. According to Reagan, et al., there was a sharp drop in the wheat price when the Carter embargo took effect on January 4, 1980. There was not. Reagan said there was a sharp rise in the wheat price after he removed the embargo on April 24, 1981. There was not. During the Carter embargo, the price of wheat increased from $4.68 a bushel at the Houston port in January 1980 to $5.10 in January 1981, when Carter left office—a price increase of 42 cents per bushel.

Reagan parroted falsehoods. When he destroyed the price floor in April 1981, wheat cost $4.89 at the Houston port. Then a slide in price developed and the utter collapse of wheat prices began. The price went to $2.77 in July 1986, which is the worst price of the Carter-Reagan years. This is a drop of over $2 per bushel of wheat. This is the largest drop in recorded history. This $2-plus drop in the price of wheat brought a complete economic collapse to the economy of the Great Plains. We have never recovered from it. There are constant government reports that it has bottomed out and the press picks up this propaganda and broadcasts it widely, but the collapse is still on. In the northern three Great Plains states, the collapse has been deepened by a great drought that has moved into the area. In the three southern Great Plains states, the collapse of the oil industry deepened the farm crisis.

As the price of wheat sank, so did the ability of farmers to consume. In 1988 I made out 300 tax returns for farmers. One farmer bought a used pickup and another bought a used car. The rest made do with their present vehicles. The farmers have failed to consume because of poor commodity prices. Here is the Wilken rule again.

I am going to set out, in full, the average monthly closing price of wheat from January 1979 to December 31, 1986, at the port of Houston, Texas. I will indicate by footnotes when an embargo was in place.

These prices are for the Port of Houston, Texas. They are not what the farmer receives at his village co-op elevator. There the price is much lower.

MONTHLY AVERAGE WHEAT PRICE

1979		1980	
January	3.75	January	4.68[1]
February	3.81	February	4.71
March	3.79	March	4.46
April	3.80	April	4.24
May	3.90	May	4.40
June	4.48	June	4.30
July	4.74	July	4.30
August	4.60	August	4.70
September	4.75	September	4.92
October	4.84	October	5.20
November	4.87	November	5.33
December	4.91	December	5.04

1981		1982	
January	5.10[2]	January	4.71
February	4.95	February	4.66
March	4.77	March	4.59
April	4.89[3]	April	4.61
May	4.69	May	4.53
June	4.57	June	4.24
July	4.57	July	4.10
August	4.61	August	4.12
September	4.65	September	4.16
October	4.63	October	4.04
November	4.85	November	4.23
December	4.69	December	4.23

1983		1984	
January	4.32	January	4.15
February	4.38	February	4.08
March	4.48	March	4.20
April	4.53	April	4.29
May	4.32	May	4.18
June	3.76	June	4.07
July	3.99	July	4.00
August	4.17	August	4.14
September	4.26	September	4.23
October	4.16	October	4.17
November	4.13	November	4.14
December	4.16	December	4.06
1985		**1986**	
January	4.05	January	3.59
February	4.02	February	3.53
March	3.94	March	3.66
April	3.93	April	3.60
May	3.69	May	3.24
June	3.45	June	2.86
July	3.49	July	2.77[4]
August	3.34	August	2.79
September	3.41	September	2.83
October	3.48	October	2.86
November	3.61	November	2.89
December	3.72	December	2.94

1. January 4, 1980, Carter imposed embargo and places price floor.
2. January 20, 1981, Carter leaves office.
3. April 24, 1981, Reagan lifts the embargo and destroys the price floor.
4. Low point of price of wheat of the Carter-Reagan years.

On August 31, 1989, the price of wheat at the Houston gulf port was $4.46. At Enid, Oklahoma it was $3.71, a spread of seventy-five cents. This spread in the two prices for wheat tends to be stable throughout the year and the decade. It involves transportation charges. The farmer did not get $4.68 at Enid, Oklahoma, which was the Gulf price in January, 1980, at the time of the Carter embargo. The farmer got seventy-five cents less or $3.93 per bushel. The low point of the price of wheat during the Carter-Reagan years was in July, 1986, five years after Reagan took office, at the Houston gulf port when the price was $2.77. This is not what a farmer got at Enid, Oklahoma. He got $2.02 per bushel, the difference of seventy-five cents being transportation charges. This price for wheat, namely $2.02, is less than the price of wheat in 1866. This drop in the price of wheat from $5.10 under Carter to $2.77 under Reagan is the whole story of the farm collapse. No matter how many times Reagan, et al., falsified this, the truth was still there. Reagan wrecked the wheat market.

When I got these figures at the Houston gulf port elevators, I was asked why I wanted them. I said I was writing a paper on agricultural economics and I had trouble in rationalizing the statements made by Reagan to other figures that I had developed. The man there told me that I was only the second person who ever asked about it. He told me that Reagan was wrong and was falsely propagandizing the American people. He had known about this falsehood for a long time. The press has continuously printed and broadcast Reagan's story and there was not a word of truth in it. Reagan used the press throughout his time in office to pass propaganda to the American people. The fact that Reagan makes up things is no reason for the press to print or broadcast it as the truth. Reagan's own children have written books about their father. They admit that he makes up things to justify what he wants to do. They say he is incapable of seeing himself as a source of falsehoods, but he is. This has to be the oddest and saddest presidential characteristic in history.

During the political campaign of 1984, Reagan went to New York and appeared at a housing project for the elderly, the handicapped and the impaired. He praised such projects in glowing term. Television news gave this wide coverage and gave great praise to Reagan for his enlightened humanitarian housing programs. The actual truth was the project was started and financed during the Carter years. Reagan had nothing to do with it. Further Reagan refused to allow the building of a single such project during his administration. Reagan has always been anti-public housing!

Let me give another example of this. In 1988, just a few days before the November election, Reagan presented figures that showed that the economy was moving ahead nicely providing jobs and essentials for all of our people. The television stations in Oklahoma City all presented this with glowing comments on how well all were doing. Had those television reporters in Oklahoma City looked out of their side windows of their cars when they drove to work that day, they would have noticed long lines of men, women and small children waiting to get into a dilapidated building to get a bowl of soup. Those lines were soup lines. There were no soup lines under Carter or prior presidents. All soup lines in the Great Plains developed under Reagan. Can a television news reporter actually keep a straight face knowing that there are such social conditions when they talk about Reagan's supposed successes? The press of this nation has done a miserable job in presenting the Reagan years. This nation has sent servicemen all over the world to fight, and die in towns and villages that are so strange and so far away that the serviceman cannot pronounce the names of them. They suffered and bled for freedom of the press. The survivors have come home to find that the press is prostituted with propaganda from the White House. Is it any wonder that cynicism is on the rise in this country?

Reagan's next great weakness was that he appointed John R. Block as Secretary of Agriculture. He was undoubtedly the second worst agricultural secretary in history, Earl Butz being the worst. Block was a graduate of West Point Military Academy and spent a number of years in the military and then went home to the family hog farm in Illinois and engaged in politics. I always had the uncomfortable feeling when he took over as secretary that he was an army barracks sergeant settling the new recruits into the training process. I used to be an army barracks sergeant and know the procedure by heart. He arrived in Washington with the idea that full crop production was what was needed and he encouraged the farmer to plant as much as they could. Here was this old theme again. The farmer had to be free to plant all he can. President Hoover had this idea. Benson had this idea. Butz worshipped at the shrine of full production.

By the end of 1982 even Secretary Block could see that his program would not work. So he asked farmers to *voluntarily* restrict planting of wheat by 15% and all other crops by 10%. Few farmers paid any attention. They needed cash to pay their bills and so one just planted more wheat in hope of earning more money. Block had stated that food was needed all over the world and that it was a great weapon for peace. Farmers planted widely and by December 1982 it could be seen that the whole pricing system was collapsing due to overproduction and imports, and Reagan's destruction of the price floor. By this time the Reagan budgets were so out of balance that many in the government did not want further expensive farm programs. So the USDA came up with the idea of returning the stored wheat to the farmer in lieu of higher subsidy payments. This program was developed from existing laws on the books. There are many agricultural laws on the federal books that are not being used and the Secretary of Agriculture and the President can trigger these into operation if certain criteria are met. That was the case here. The program was called Payment-In-Kind. It was given the initials of PIK (pronounced *pick*, like—pick up your toys).

If the winter wheat farmers would plow up certain amounts of his planted acres, or as in the case of the spring wheat, not plant it, he could and would receive a certain number of bushels of wheat in a designated elevator. In designating where the wheat was, the USDA tried to designate the elevator near the farmer, but in a big program such as this, that was not always possible. In one case a farmer near Garber, Oklahoma, had to go to Garden City, Kansas, 275 miles away, if he wanted to gain actual physical possession of the wheat. It was thought by the people who set up the program that if the farmer would take physical control of the wheat and truck it out to his farm, he might use the wheat as animal feed. This would get it out of the market. Actually few farmers ever took physical possession of their wheat. They received a colored certificate which stated the number of bushels of wheat that they were receiving as payment-in-kind or PIK. They sold the certificate to anyone who wanted to buy it. In general, the farmer could not get the market price for the wheat. He had to take a discount on it. This was called a "slide."

I have heard and documented the "slide" at $1.01 cents on the dollar to only eighty-nine cents on the dollar. It depended on where the wheat was, how many bushels there were, the market price of wheat and other factors. In time, these certificates were bought and sold and came to be owned by large grain dealers. Village elevators bought few or none, although they did provide storage for the new owners in many cases.

Isn't that a nice program? Well thought out and competently administered! Right? Actually it was the second most stupid blunder ever made in American agricultural policy.

First, the farmer did not get the amount of wheat as based on his county historical average. The county historical average is computed by the government and many farm programs are based on this average. It is supposed to be the historical average of what wheat makes per acre in that county over a period of years. Where the government gets some of these figures has always amazed many of us who are acquainted with wheat farming. Many of the averages are too high and others too low. For example, I live in Garfield County, Oklahoma, and we have a county average of twenty-eight bushels. Probably twenty-one bushels would cover it. In Alfalfa County, Oklahoma, which is one of the counties that we are going to investigate in depth in a later chapter, the average is thirty-one bushels per acre. I can't find a farmer in that county who thinks that is correct, and from what I know about the county, I'd say it is not. Anyway, the government has the averages, and these were used in the PIK program.

But the farmer did not get the county average. The thought as expressed by the government was that while the winter wheat farmers had already planted the crop, they would not have to further fertilize in the spring, no insect control would be needed, and no harvesting would be done. There could be a lesser payment because certain expenses would not have to be met by the farmers. Our county average was twenty-eight bushels per acre and so there would be a drop or a "dock" of 10% or 2.8 bushels with the farmer getting 25.2 bushel in PIK payments. Then he had to take the "slide," which we explained above and which in all too many cases was 10%. That in effect reduced the payment to 22.7 bushels per acre. This was not a good deal for the farmer. It took only one crop year for the farmer to see this. When this program was first announced in December 1982, wheat farmers flocked into government offices to sign up. Over seventy million acres were diverted. Reagan thus presided over the largest agricultural diversion program in history. He has never commented on this dubious distinction.

Block killed the program he created in another way. What happened is simple. There are a lot of farmers in the Great Plains who are not going to go along with the government when it is a matter of the rich vs. the poor, as Block predicated. Those farmers are not going to participate in any way to help the government give more to the rich. They will however always cooperate with the government when the program is lawful and done in the best interest of all. These people believe that the U.S. Government has a higher destiny in the world than feathering the nest of the rich. They absolutely refused to participate in PIK. By nightfall, this was known all over the small villages. "Old Joe over there says he ain't PIK'ing," was the way it was put.

The rains fell and the non-PIK'ers put on some more fertilizer and they grew a huge crop. Their wheat averaged thirty-eight bushels per acre in Garfield County, Oklahoma. The PIK'ers had destroyed much of their crop. They got a PIK payment of 22.7 bushel. The difference here was 15.3 bushels and the price in July 1983 was $4, giving non-PIK'ers a monetary advantage of $62.73 per acre. Multiply that by a hundred acres and it is not chicken feed. When this became known in the small villages, the PIK'ers were outraged. One farmer in northern Garfield County, Oklahoma, explained it this way: "PIK was the dumbest thing I ever did. I destroyed wheat that would have made forty-five bushels an acre and got back 22.7 bushel PIK payments. I will never PIK again." This was the end of PIK and the end of Block's political career.

When so much wheat land was taken out of production, there was a drop in wheat production, and in the case of PIK the price firmed some, and the non-PIK'ers benefited again. They had wheat to sell. But the price didn't go up very much. Large grain dealers imported low priced wheat into the U.S. and broke the market. Why the U.S. Government allows foreign imports of things that are in abundance here has never been explained to a rational and intelligent human being. Why our nation can't be self-sufficient in some things is ridiculous.

In the 1984 crop year, the program was re-offered to wheat growers and virtually no one signed up. This is sad because it can now be seen that this program would work best during years of crop failure. Such a situation exists now in the Dakotas and Nebraska where the wheat crop has failed due to drought. A PIK payment to those farmers would have been a great boost.

However it should be noted that PIK was never much of a success in reducing the abundance of wheat. The government gave the wheat to the farmer and he in turn sold it to large grain dealers who then owned the wheat. The wheat in most cases never left the local elevator and there was just as much wheat in those elevators after PIK as there was before. All PIK did was to take the wheat out of government ownership and transferred it through the wheat farmers to the ownership of large grain dealers. These dealers then had to dispose of it. That did not help the price very much. The wheat was still there—in storage. Wheat did not circulate under the PIK program. It was colored scraps of paper called certificates that circulated.

Another bad feature of this law was the disintegrating effect PIK had on local support businesses of wheat farmers. The local co-op elevators did not buy as much grain in the 1983 crop year. So its possibilities of profits were reduced. In the southern Great Plains, farmers normally top-dress their wheat, which is what an application of liquid nitrogen fertilizer is called. This is applied as the wheat greens up after the end of the winter freezes. This year they didn't do so. They PIK'ed their wheat. In the northern Great Plains, no fertilizer was applied at all. The local fertilizer dealers, including the local co-op elevators, were left with huge stocks of fertilizers that they had placed in inventory and which they could not sell. Local banks had fewer and smaller loans on wheat and were thus hurt. Local machinery dealers had a slump in sales because the farmer did not need new machinery. He was, in effect, not farming.

Many farmers in the Great Plains are stockholders in their local village co-op elevators. Suddenly these co-ops were losing money and in a few cases bankruptcy was filed. In virtually every case, they stopped paying patronage dividends to their customers. Some had long and enviable dividend paying records. For example, at the Douglas Co-op Elevator at Douglas, Oklahoma, where I marketed my wheat, the elevator was formed in 1924 and it paid its first dividends in 1926. It paid dividends all through the 1930s depression and on until 1984 when it passed a dividend for the first time in its history. It has not recovered from the Reagan disaster. This broke a fifty-eight year run of dividend payments. This record of paying dividends was better than that of most corporations listed on the New York Stock Exchange. The elevator has not paid a dividend since.

I doubt if 1% of these farm co-ops have paid any dividends at all since PIK. I notice that the farmer-customers of my tax service show no payments. I prepare the tax returns for about 300 farmers and only two farmers showed any patronage dividends at all in 1987. They had always appreciated and looked forward to getting these dividend checks. Now there were none because of PIK.

Another bad feature about PIK was the way Secretary of Agriculture John R. Block tried to and did manipulate the program for the benefit of the rich. He stated that if the large farmer could not go over the restriction of $55,000 limit on farm payments, which was imposed by Congress during the Nixon years, the large farmer would sue the government for discrimination or would not participate at all.

Where he got this idea I don't know. I have taken many trips across the Great Plains and I have talked to hundreds and hundreds of farmers, and to attorneys and to tax preparers, and they all have stated clearly that they never heard of any large or rich farmer making such a threat. It is not in the nature of a rich farmer to do such a thing. The average wheat farmer lives on his farm, or in the small village near his farm. He knows everybody and everyone knows him. Everyone goes to the same or similar churches. Their children attend the same schools. They are very close. Many of these villages are so tightly-knit that no adverse information about someone is ever given to an outsider. The idea of a rich farmer making such a threat is ridiculous and Block's statements were totally false. One farmer called it a bare-faced lie.

Block asked Congress to remove the spending limits in December 1982, and by January 1983 it was obvious that Congress would not do such a thing. Block had the attorneys in the USDA issue a legal opinion that the spending limit did not apply to PIK payments, but only to cash payments. To say that these lawyers were turned into professional prostitutes is to put it mildly. "I've got to do this, my lawyers tell me to do it." Isn't that the most feeble excuse ever devised? It is one of the oldest of all excuses. It is also the cheapest. What he should have done was to ask the Attorney General of the U.S. to issue an opinion as the chief legal officer of the government, or he could have gone into federal court and asked the courts to issue a declaratory judgment saying what the law was. He would have been fully covered. He elected not to do this. Many members of Congress were shocked by his deliberate disobedience of the law.

What is to be done when a cabinet officer deliberately flaunts the law? History speaks quite clearly on this point. The Secretary of War during the administration of President U. S. Grant was William W. Belknap, a Union general under Grant in the Civil War. The wife of Secretary Belknap died and he promptly married his wife's younger sister. It was the talk of

Washington. This second wife was supposed to have a business, but Secretary Belknap did not involve himself with it. One day a party came to the door where the Belknaps lived with some money. Only Secretary Belknap was at home. The visitor told him that some money was due to the second Mrs. Belknap. He agreed to and did make out a full receipt for this money. He gave the money to his new wife later in the day. This money was a bribe from post traders at Fort Sill in what is now Oklahoma and was paid to get Mrs. Belknap to convince her husband to give the tradeship to the visitor. Soon this came to be known all over Washington and President Grant heard about it, but he didn't do anything. Impeachment charges were instituted against Secretary Belknap and the House of Representatives, in fact, impeached him. President Grant called Secretary Belknap to the White House and demanded his resignation. Secretary Belknap thought he was being treated too roughly because he did not know what the money was for and only receipted for it. He never spent any of it. President Grant insisted and got his resignation. The case in the Senate against Secretary Belknap never went to trial because of the resignation; however, the Senate did pass a resolution that Secretary Belknap's removal was proper.

When a secretary in the President's cabinet deliberately flaunts the law, if the House of Representatives would impeach, I believe that would be a good lesson in citizenship for all. But Congress paralyzed itself and Block hurried out the PIK payments. He got what he wanted—he feathered the nests of rich farmers. This was a senseless churning of the rich vs. poor issue of our society. Rich farmers never asked for PIK. One farmer said, "Where there is a trough, the hogs will gather." But that comment overlooks the fact that the trough was there long before rich farmers got in line. Congress slammed the door on such further financial shenanigans by making future PIK restricted to the congressional limits.

This turned out to be a major political blunder of the Reagan years. The administrator of the PIK program was Everett G. Rank, a Reagan appointee and part-owner of the Cinco Farms,

Inc. of Huron, California. Rank got over $200,000 in fees and in payments from this farm since 1981, when he took office under Reagan and Block. The PIK payment to Cinco Farms, Inc. was $1,200,000. Under the law it should have been $55,000. In other words Secretary Block lifted the payment schedule and the first person to benefit was his appointee, Everett G. Rank. This went a long way in undermining the confidence of farmers in PIK. The Department of Justice investigated this, and during the Reagan years, a political factor called "sleaze" came into play. The Justice Department decided not to prosecute Rank because of "sleaze." It criticized him, but did nothing. The reason there was to be no prosecution was that Rank had not received legal and ethical advise on conflicts of interest. The USDA decided to hold classes on ethics and such employees as Rank were required to attend. One congressman exploded and said that he was sick and tired of fifty year old men in the Reagan Administration having to take on-the-job training in honesty.

What should have been done? The Justice Department should have asked the courts to appoint a special prosecutor.

After the lifting of the grain embargo by President Reagan on April 24, 1981, the Soviet Union did start to buy grain and in later years bought even more that contracted. At no time did these higher grain sales to the Soviet Union have any effect on the domestic price of wheat. In fact the price of wheat sank steadily. The Reagan Administration tried to justify this on the grounds that the U.S. was not a good supplier to the Soviet Union. The truth is the U.S. supplied more wheat than was contracted for.

Another bad feature of Reagan's tenure of office was his tax policies. He arrived in Washington fully convinced that taxes were too high, and he set about to cut them. He wanted a flat 30% cut in all income taxes. Congress passed a tax cut bill reducing taxes 5% the first year; 10% the second and third years, for a total reduction of 25%. When these tax cuts went into effect, soup lines started to form in the Great Plains. Prior to Reagan, there had been no soup lines in the Great Plains.

Every time one of his tax reductions went into effect, the soup lines lengthened. Many observers commented that it always seemed to work out this way.

The tax cuts applied to the wheat farmers as well as everyone else. It soon came to be noticed that most of the cuts went to the rich.

The Reagan administration kept up a barrage of propaganda that these tax cuts would stimulate the economy and make more jobs available. There is just enough truth in such a statement to make it misleading. In Enid, Oklahoma, a businessman got a tax cut of $19,000 per year. His secretary got a tax cut of twenty-two cents per week. You cannot convince her that this tax cut was fair. The businessman took his tax cut to Nevada and gambled it away on the strip. No one could see any increase in employment in these casinos. Nevada gambling casinos have an inherent ability to move money around so fast that they do not need to hire additional workers. As soon as some sucker walks through the door, employment is not affected. It's his money that is affected—it's gone.

A retired school teacher in southern Kansas became concerned about how the economy in the Great Plains was acting and she believed it would collapse as it did in the 1930s when she was young. Her concern was so great that she took the $2,000 that the tax cuts saved her, and other money that she could gather up, and sent the nest egg to banks in Switzerland. This did not create additional jobs. Moving money out of the economy of America and into the economy of Switzerland is a deflationary thing for America. A doctor in the Great Plains took $20,000 tax cut savings and bought a U.S. Treasury Note. This did not create jobs. Had the doctor paid taxes in accordance with his ability to pay, he would not have bought that instrument. This transaction did not create jobs. It only transferred wealth from the government to the doctor.

In none of these examples of spending the tax savings were jobs created. The best that can be said for Reagan's reasoning on job creation is that the secretary of the above businessman took her twenty-two cents per week tax cut, and bought a new toothbrush. Of these four examples, this is the only one that had any possibility of job creation. However toothbrushes are mass-produced and the average toothbrush company can leave its machines on another second or two to fill this purchase. It is doubtful that it would add jobs. It might have, but probably did not.

I remember addressing a high school political science class in 1984 when the election was on, and this point came up. I pointed out that I doubted if Reagan's job creation program was working at all. One girl in the back of the class burst out and said it was not. Her father had been out of work for two years and with all of Reagan's tax cuts and job creation programs her father still could not find a job. I sympathized with her.

So whether Reagan's tax cuts created jobs *depended entirely on what the taxpayer did with the money saved.* In the above four examples, three did not produce new jobs. The other might have, but probably did not.

Assuming that new jobs were created by these tax cuts, they did not help the Great Plains. Many of our businesses collapsed and many good jobs were lost. Banks closed their doors, savings and loan associations went bankrupt and farmers left the farms and crowded in the cities looking for work. Flipping pancakes at the local pancake parlor is a job, but it is not a good paying job. Take home pay on a minimum wage job is only $114 per week. It is hard for a husband and wife with four children to live on that.

Another feature of the Reagan tax program was the increase in depreciation rates for depreciable items of businesses and farmers. This increase in depreciation rates was called Accelerated Cost Recovery System (ACRS, pronounced *acres*). Prior to Reagan, a farmer would depreciate out a piece of machinery based on his historical average of use of a machine. If he bought a new tractor every ten years, this established his historical average and his depreciation rate would be 10% per year. In case of a farmer using a truck only five years, and he bought a new truck every five years, this would determine his depreciation rate on trucks, which would be 20% per year. In case of custom machine operators it would be possible for them to write off the cost of their machines in one year. In many cases they bought a new machine every year.

In general, if a farmer attempted to write off the cost of a machine in less than ten years, Internal Revenue Service was prone to audit that return to see if the farmer could justify or substantiate the shorter depreciation time. If he could, Internal Revenue would let him do so. I do not know of a single case in which Internal Revenue Service did not do this.

Many farmers and their tax preparers quickly learned of this attitude and would hold their depreciation time to not less than ten years. Few were ever audited on that.

Along came Reaganomics, and the farmer was required to write off the new machine in three years. This was the accelerated rate that was first used under Reagan in 1981. There are many annual tax seminars around the country on how to prepare tax returns. These are held in November and December of each year. Several are sponsored by extension services of the colleges of agriculture. Many times agents of Internal Revenue Service are asked to speak at these meetings. This gives the tax preparer an opportunity to see and meet these agents, and to learn of the attitudes of Internal Revenue Service on any problem that they consider important. These agents emphasized that the ACRS depreciation had to be used. Their attention was called to the fact that many farmers—particularly small and medium sized farmers—did not use their machines enough to justify a three year depreciation rate. These agents emphasized that Internal Revenue Service would expect ACRS to be used and probably an audit would develop if ACRS was not used. So ACRS was used.

What this did was to distort the expenses of the wheat farmer. *Reaganomics was actually a distortion of the accounting process to show that something was happening when it was not actually happening.* For example, a farmer buys a combine for $120,000. Under ACRS depreciation the time to depreciate is three years. Reagan was on television several times and always emphasized how important this was. He reasoned that it allowed the farmer, or businessman, to recover the cost quickly. But that is true *only if the farmer is making a profit to underwrite that cost*. If the farmer is suffering a loss, ACRS depreciation adds greatly to that loss, and there is no recovery.

If we use straight line depreciation based on the farmer's experience of wearing out or depreciating the above combine, the depreciation cost is $12,000 per year. But with Reagan's ACRS, it is $40,000 per year. The difference is $28,000, and this is nothing more than an accounting distortion.

In trying to explain this, I am often asked if there are other examples of distortion of the accounting process. The answer, unfortunately, is yes. Let me give you an example. Our states have boards and commissions at the state level whose job is to pass on requested rate increases of public utilities. They raise rates and in a few cases they cut the rates that the utility can charge. An electrical company had its case for a rate increase before one of these boards and was asking that electrical rates be increased because they were in the process of building a new generating station. It would take about eight more years for the station to be completed.

An elderly woman got up and gained the attention of the chairman of the commission, and made the remark that she was eighty-eight years old. "I will be dead and gone long before this power plant is generating electricity. Why do I have to help pay for something that I will never use," she exploded? So the commission, wanting to be fair and nice, decided to distort the accounting process of the utility. It required that the electrical company take all expenses related to the generating station and present them after the plant actually started to generate electricity. Since this would amount to a large amount of borrowed money the commission further provided that an Allowance for Funds Used During Construction (AFUDC) be made for the interest on that borrowed money. This allowance is shown in the consolidated statement of income under other income. It is shown as income and an asset of the utility. Actually it is an allowance for funds used and is thus a non-cash item. It does not contribute to current cash flows until the plant comes on-line and produces electricity. Yet it shows up as an earning per share income.

Let's take an example. A utility in Michigan shows income for the year of $3.12 per share of common stock. The Board of Directors is so delighted that they raised the dividends from $2.44 per share to $2.52 per share, an eight cent gain. This is spread out in four equal installments, payable once each quarter of the year. By traditional accounting standards, there is nothing wrong in this example. But a deeper and closer look shows the accounting distortion used. The company had been required to make an AFUDC allowance of $118,353,000. This is shown as income. Actually it is nothing. There is no cash in the bank. The utility never received a single penny, yet it is credited with earning an additional $118,353,000.

This company had 78,761,382 shares of stock outstanding. The AFUDC comes to $1.52 per share income. So the $3.12 per share of income should be reduced by $1.52 per share leaving an actual per cash share of income of only $1.60 per share. $1.60 per share is what went through the bank account. The company paid an increased dividend of $2.52, yet it had only $1.60 cash income per share to meet that dividend. This is a loss of ninety-two cents per share. If this actual cash loss per share of ninety-two cents had been before the Board of Directors, would they have increased dividends of eight cents per share? Probably not. In other words, due to this accounting distortion of income, the directors were misled as to what the company should have been paying in dividends. Most laymen looking at AFUDC income would think that the company is doing well. Actually here it was not making enough to pay the dividend. It could not afford its current dividend much less an increase in dividends.

But you say, this is only a hypothetical example. Actually it is a good example for leaving accounting standards alone by not creating a distortion in them. But also it is taken from the 1984 annual report of the Consumers Power Company of Jackson, Michigan, and is not a hypothetical example. It is a business corporation that was required to distort its income by AFUDC of $118 million and the mistake was made in its dividends and eventually the company had to stop paying dividends and be reorganized.

A change in accounting standards may be confusing a president of the U.S. at this time. George Bush recently announced that farming had turned around and the land banks were making money. This is true if—and only if—you believe that an accounting change made by Congress in 1987 was legitimate. Congress provided that the federal land banks need only write off 5% of their losses each year for the next twenty years. A loss of $100,000 shows up in the profits and loss statement as a $5,000 loss. The rest is passed on. So Bush is clearly mistaken. I have talked with a number of employees of the federal land banks and they too were dumbfounded that the president would make such a statement. The banks are actually losing money hand over fist.

Accounting standards should be left alone. Whenever you find a company that is required by law to distort its income, "sell out as fast as you can," would be good advice both on and off the New York Stock Exchange. Reaganomics and ACRS depreciation is a distortion of accounting principles. The average farmer has only his bank statements and his income tax returns for his financial records. *Any distortion in his income and expenses is often not understood.* Many farmers rushed out and bought a lot of new, expensive farm machinery, believing what their president told them—that there was a quick and easy way to recover the cost. In reality there was not.

When Reagan destroyed the price floor under wheat when he lifted the embargo to the Soviet Union, the price of wheat sank. A farmer pays taxes *when he makes a profit, not when he suffers a loss.* When the price of wheat sank, losses piled up on farmers. Many tax preparers have commented that fewer than 2% of their farmer tax clients could show a profit. Remember the statement that I made when I reviewed the achievement, or lack of achievements, that Carter made on farm policy. Remember how the American Agriculture Movement exploded with fast growth. The thing that caused this was the lack of profits that the wheat farmers were experiencing. Also, farmers had learned to use the Investment Tax Credit Act of the Kennedy years and so when they had a tax to pay, they would buy another piece of machinery and "eschew" the tax. Wheat farmers were using this in a big way when Reagan took office. So when Reagan's tax cuts took effect, it did not help many farmers on the Great Plains. They simply were not paying taxes anyway.

As the price of wheat sank under Reagan, so did the hope of ever paying for the huge investment some farmers made in machinery. They seldom consulted with their tax preparers about this. They listened to the president. It turned out to be a disaster for nearly every farmer who did this. About 10% of the wheat farmers of the Great Plains failed for this reason. A happy thought is that over 50% of farmers still in business have no debts at all, and are in fairly good shape. They will keep the wheat coming in the years ahead.

Farmers who bought their machinery are spending years paying out this machinery, and *never got a single cent in tax savings*. Many farmers built up huge investment tax credits against future tax bills by buying this machinery. Some have amounts as large as $45,000 and even $50,000. I know of one case where a farmer built up $75,000 in tax credit. He had no income taxes to off-set these credits and in 1986 Congress repealed the Investment Tax Credit Act of the Kennedy era, and started to phase out these tax credits. That can only be considered a plus.

Much of Reagan's tax program was geared to helping rich people. But on the farms of the Great Plains rich farmers did not profit much by it. I can document a case of a farm family that owns about sixty-five wheat farms. He can use a $120,000 tractor. Such a farmer is very careful to keep the tractor busy as much of the year as possible. That is the only way he can justify such a huge investment. He works it twenty-three hours a day, seven days a week. During much of the spring, summer and fall the tractor is in the field nearly every day. He will put in more hours of machine work in a week than the average farmer will put in on his tractor in an entire year. The large farmer will often wear out such a tractor in three years or even less. That is his new ACRS depreciation base and it was the old straight line depreciation base. So ACRS depreciation did not help the rich farmer. He went along and depreciated his equipment out the same before and after Reaganomics.

In time Congress and President Reagan could see that ACRS depreciation was a disaster. In 1985 Congress changed farm depreciation and this came to be called Modified Accelerated Cost Recovery Systems (MACRS, pronounced *makers*), and two years later an Alternate MACRES came into being. It came much too late to help the small and medium size farmer, and the larger farmers were not helped either. It too was a disaster. Congress thus developed three different depreciation systems in seven years. All proved to be disasters to wheat farmers.

It should be noted that ACRS depreciation caused the depreciation expense to be taken in the first few years, but the farmer may keep the tractor for many years. In these later years, he has no depreciation expense to deduct. Income tax rates hit him harder at that time. So Congress at the request of Reagan amended the tax codes to provide for a two tier tax rate, and one of the main reasons for this was the speed-up in depreciation. A more rational way of handling this problem would have been to keep to traditional accounting standards with straight line depreciation. Taxes should raise revenue for the government and not act as an economic stimulus to every Tom, Dick and Clara who thinks they should have one.

Another bad feature of ACRS depreciation is the fact that you can not explain it rationally to a bank loan officer. In making out farmers' tax returns, I often commented to them that ACRS distorted their expenses on the farm, and that they did not actually suffer the losses that showed up on their tax returns.

A farmer would go to the bank and try to get a loan. The bank required a financial statement and a copy of the last two years of his tax returns. He had lost his copies of the tax returns and so he went by his tax preparer's office and had photocopies made. The preparer mentioned that his losses were larger due to ACRS depreciation than it would have been if he could have stayed with straight line accounting rules. The farmer takes the papers to the bank and leaves them with the loan officer. He is instructed to come back in about two days, and he does so, at which point he is told by the loan officer that he cannot get a loan there. He asks why since he had banked there for over thirty years. The loan officer says that he cannot show a profit on his farm operation and in fact he has a loss of $52,500. This is much too much to qualify for a loan, he is told. The farmer remembers that his tax preparer said something about Reaganomics distorting expenses but he can't explain it. The loan officer knows nothing about this. The farmer says he will go to talk to this tax preparer and get back to the loan officer. He does so and the tax preparer calls for an appointment with the loan officer and they all meet at the bank the next day. The tax preparer has the tax file and they start through it. The farmer bought a tractor for $120,000 and a combine for $105,000 for a combined purchase of $225,000, all of which is bought on credit at the local farm dealer and the first payment is not due until the next harvest. A combine is a combination of machines, namely the binder or reaper invented by Cyrus McCormick and the threshing machine invented by Jerome Case. When these two machines were put together they became a combination of the two. The farmer shortened the name to "combine." It is a mechanical harvester that cuts, threshes, and cleans the wheat.

The tractor we mentioned above has to be depreciated out in three years under ACRS depreciation and this year's depreciation is $40,000. Under the old rules it would have been $12,000.

The combine costs $105,000, and under ACRS depreciation it must depreciated out in three years, and this is an expense of $35,000 a year. Under the old rules it would have been $10,500. Total depreciation is $75,000 under Reaganomics and $22,500 under the old straight line accounting rules.

This farmer had a profit of $24,000 on his farm operation before depreciation is considered.

When you subtract the depreciation figure under the old rules in the amount of $22,500 he has a profit of $1,500 but under Reaganomics and the new ACRS depreciation of $75,000 he has a loss of $52,500. The difference between $1,500 profit and $52,500 loss is nothing more than a distortion in the accounting process. ACRS speeded up the costs of depreciation. It did not increase the cash flow of the farmer a single cent. The farmer pays for his machinery from profits and cash flow, not from accounting distortions. *There is no fast recovery in the price of new machinery unless there was available profits to absorb the depreciation expense.* Reagan never understood this.

Let's see if we can put this in a small chart and make it easier to understand.

	Cost	Straight Line Depreciation	Reaganomics ACRS Depreciation
New Tractor	$120,000	$12,000	$40,000
New Combine	105,000	10,500	35,000
Total	$225,000	$22,500	$75,000
Farmer's profit before Depreciation		$24,000	
Less Straight Line Depreciation			22,500
Net farm **Profit**			$ 1,500
Farmer's profit before Depreciation		$24,000	
Less Reaganomics ACRS Depreciation			75,000
Net farm **Loss**			($52,500)

The difference between the net farm profit of $1,500 and the net farm loss of $52,500 is the difference between traditional straight line depreciation standards and Reaganomics ACRS depreciation. It is the same machinery and the same farmer, and he does not have a single penny in the bank. That is why he is in the bank trying to borrow money. The tax preparer explains all this to the bank loan officer and he says: "No one ever explained Reaganomics to me that way. As I heard it discussed on news reports, Reaganomics would be a great benefit to the farmers and other businessmen. Yet you show it here as a loss." He decides to take the figures to the bank's accountant and have him go over them. The tax preparer and the farmer adjourn and the bank accountant promises to call later. He does so in about a week and all "troupe" over to hear him.

He has had the bank attorney and the bank accountant to go over the farmer's figures and they agree that this farm operation could have made a profit of $1,500 or it could have suffered a loss of $52,500. It all depends on how you compute depreciation. The bank officer asks if the farmer has made any payments on the machinery. The answer is *no*, and that none are due until after harvest in about three months. Also no interest has been paid on this loan, and that will be due in June. The interest will be $31,500 and will increase farm expenses. The rate is 14%. To summarize, the loss of $52,500 will be a loss of $84,000 the following year due to the interest on the machinery loan, provided all other incomes and expenses are equal. The loan officer does not believe that the income will be equal, because the price of wheat has now dropped a dollar a bushel. If this holds there will be a further loss of income of $32,000 here alone. Add this to the above loss and you could expect a total loss of $116,000 next year. The only hope to offset this is if the yield of wheat goes up or if the farmer can reduce his expenses some way. Neither way looks hopeful.

The bank refused the loan. When you step aside and look at the position of the bank loan officer, he is not totally wrong. He must not loan the bank's money when there is no real way it can be repaid. This farmer eventually goes bankrupt with all the social, financial and emotional dislocations that can be caused to the farmer and his family. Had this farmer never heard of Ronald Reagan, he would have had a profit of $24,000. The farmer explained: "Reagan broke me, but he is such a nice guy." Wheat farmers are notorious for having an utter lack of political sophistication.

Even government loan officers could not understand the tragic distortion of farm expenses caused by Reaganomics. The local office of the FmHA in Alfalfa County, Oklahoma, once received loan applications from seventeen farmers and turned all of them down because of their huge losses. These losses were nothing more than excessive depreciation caused by ACRS. In 1985 Congress repassed the forbearance statute which I will discuss later. Many wheat farmers could not qualify because of the huge losses caused by ACRS depreciation. In 1986 Congress passed a new farm reorganization amendment to the bankruptcy code. Many wheat farmers could not qualify because of the huge losses caused by ACRS depreciation. The ACRS depreciation of Reaganomics is thus a terrible trap for farmers and accounted for the worst depreciation rates ever passed in the history of the cultivation of wheat.

This story can be repeated over and over again. One tax preparer in South Dakota told me that he felt that there was too much encouragement for the farmer to buy a lot of machinery and it could not be justified by the profitability of the farmer. "These farmers have a bigger electric bill for one month than my father had in income for the entire year when he was farming in the 1930s. No matter how you look at it, the farmers' expenses are just too high. That is the cause of much of the farm problem," he said.

You can talk with attorneys and tax preparers all across the Great Plains, and the basic causes, they will tell you, for the farm crisis are the collapse in the price of wheat, fast depreciation, and high interest cost. All of these problems came to a head in the administration of Ronald Reagan. Then night came to the farms of the Great Plains.

3

THE FEDERAL RESERVE SYSTEM

In 1907 the U.S. went through one of its periodic economic slumps. The trigger mechanism was the lack of credit. Investment houses in Wall Street, led by the House of Morgan, poured financial resources into the economy and this did have a good effect. However, it's impossible for a private business to act as a national bank. Congress studied the problem for almost five years.

In 1913 Congress set up the Federal Reserve System. The Fed, as it's usually known, is managed by a seven-member Board of Governors, each of whom serve one fourteen year term. A new board member is appointed every two years by the president and confirmed by the Senate. Their duty as the Brahmins of the Fed is to foster economic growth by regulating the flow of credit into the U.S. economy, ensure the stability of the dollar, and maintain balance in the country's system of overseas payments.

The 1913 Act made no specific provision for agriculture, which was the beginning of much agony for the wheat farmers of the Great Plains. It did establish twelve Federal Reserve Bank districts across the nation. A city was designated in the

Act as the location of that district bank and the various states were placed in a district.

Congress frequently takes action without giving much consideration to how local economies will be affected. It would be difficult to find a better example than the Federal Reserve Act (though the federal land bank system comes close). For geographic and political purposes, the Great Plains run north and south. Yet Federal Reserve Bank districts run east and west, cutting across the economy of the Great Plains in three different places. North and South Dakota share the bank district administered out of Minneapolis. Nebraska, Kansas and Oklahoma (except the southeast corner) belong to the Kansas City, Missouri district office, which also administers a portion of western Missouri. Texas and southeastern Oklahoma have a district of their own, administered out of Dallas.

The Fed's bank boundaries don't make much economic sense. Its standard procedures for dealing with the Great Plains farm economy make even less. For several decades, wheat has been the only commercial crop grown in all six Great Plains states. Astonishingly, the Fed does not employ a wheat specialist. Instead, each district bank gathers its own statistics on wheat production and farmland use, then promptly forwards them to Washington, where they are pigeonholed and forgotten. When asked what is being done, the district people say such problems are beyond the ability of one district to control. These problems must await a national solution, goes the litany.

I live in the district administered by the Fed's Kansas City office. After observing this bank for forty-five years and counting, I can't think of a single thing it's ever done for wheat farmers. Of course, it's commonplace to say that the Federal Reserve deals with banks, not farmers. Yet if that is true, then rural bankers on the local level should be able to cite something the Federal Reserve has done for them. If you talk to small town bankers regularly, as I do, you'll find they all agree: the Federal Reserve system has never done anything for wheat farmers *or* for small town banks.

The Fed's regional districts are governed by a nine member board, three of whom are also appointed by the President (the district chairman who serves on the main board in Washington is always one of these three). The remaining board members are selected by the the heads of member banks in that district. The membership of the Federal Reserve System comprises all nationally chartered banks and those state banks that qualify and purchase stock in the system. Most state banks are not members of the Federal Reserve system, and thus do not qualify for a vote on the election of the governors who operate the area Federal Reserve Bank.

There are about 14,500 banks in the United States. Of those, 4,700 are nationally chartered and thus members of the Federal Reserve System. There are 9,800 state chartered banks, of which only 1,100 are members of the Federal Reserve. Therefore about 8,700, or over half of the nation's banks are not members of the Federal Reserve System.

Hence most rural banks exercise no control nor influence over the Federal Reserve System banks. Thanks to their location, these banks are the ones wheat farmers tend to use. A few rural banks, such as those at the Oklahoma towns of Nash and Carmen, are nationally chartered. But most rural banks are chartered by the state government.

Another evil of the district Federal Reserve Bank is that the boards of governors are totally controlled by bankers in large cities such as Minneapolis, Omaha, Wichita, Oklahoma City and Dallas. Still another is that when the federal government sets up a national program and then designates area or local administrative control, inevitably the agencies fall into the hands of conservative rich people. This is a lesson from history that plagues and scandalizes this nation. Conservatives want local control over administration because they can control the program and manipulate it for their benefit. The best way to make government conservative and thus insensitive to people is to fragment political control and administration.

Where Congress set up district Federal Reserve Banks such as the one at Boston, where the economy of the district is compact and compatible, the system has worked fairly well. The ones in New York City and Philadelphia also work fairly well. A wheat farmer of the Great Plains is more likely to be affected by what is done by the bank in New York than he is by the one in Minneapolis. He is also more knowledgeable about what goes on in New York.

The area Federal Reserve Banks that cuts the Great Plains states east and west have little influence on credit events. Maybe they can't. For example, the bank at Minneapolis must deal with tree farmers in northern Michigan, dairy farmers of Wisconsin, diversified farmers in Minnesota, wheat farmers in North and South Dakota and beef cattle ranchers in Montana. This bank district sprawls across three time zones. To expect one bank to deal with all of these farm situations well is perhaps asking too much. It operates poorly. Congress could greatly improve this situation by making more banking districts, structured more compactly, and more compatible with the principal economic activity of that district.

The boards of the area Federal Reserve banks are unrepresentative of the area and people they serve. They are highly undemocratic. No true farmer or poor person has ever been on one of these boards. Rich people from the large cities get these appointments. Criticism of this reached a new high a number of years ago in the bank located at Kansas City, consequently an effort was made to appoint and select members from smaller cities. They selected the president of Oklahoma State University located at Stillwater, Oklahoma as a member. This university houses over 20,000 students located on its principal campus and thousands more elsewhere in satellite campuses. It controls and operates the extension service throughout the seventy-seven counties of the state and has major foreign involvement. How much time do you think that this busy university president could give to the management of the area Federal Reserve Bank?

He gave very little time to the bank. He tried to make the meetings on a fairly regular basis and gave assent to what the insiders of the bank wanted done and then departed immediately to his campus. You cannot imagine a worse system than this, but this is the system that is primarily involved with the credit of the farmers of the Great Plains.

Another major weakness of the Federal Reserve System is that it often just does not know what to do and so it does something, making a bad situation much worse. For example, the 1920s was a time of rampant inflation and wild speculation. People were more interested in the price of some stock than they were in the price of wheat. Everyone's eyes were glued to a ticker tape. Yet at the same time the 1920s was a time of political conservatism. Harding, Coolidge and Hoover can only be explained as conservatives. They refused to do anything about the stock market. Had they done something the Federal Reserve would have probably ignored them. Late in the term of Calvin Coolidge, the Federal Reserve Board decided to act—and did so by lowering interest rates—and this in turned further fueled a high on the stock market. What should have been done in Coolidge's term was to raise interest rates in order to dampen inflation. *In other words, the Federal Reserve did exactly the wrong thing.* The stock market built to a sensational high and then collapsed in 1929.

In 1979 the Federal Reserve announced that it would no longer be concerned with interest rates, but instead would govern cash flow and bank reserves. It pumped money and credit out of the system. Borrowers competed to get what little credit was available. This can only be considered a meat-ax approach to the problem. The Federal Reserve could have used all economic levers, rather that just this one.

Interest rates went to 21.9% under Carter and 22.9% under Reagan, the highest in U.S. history. Reagan and Bush have always accused the Democrats under Carter for the high interest of the period, but Reagan's record is far worse. However, that doesn't make Carter look like a saint. Carter is hard to categorize. As a youth he was brought up in a family in southern Georgia that voted and supported Republicans, but as an adult he joined the Democratic Party because that was the party you joined if you wanted to win a political office in

Georgia. He was educated as a naval officer and became an expert in nuclear energy. He demonstrated little or no knowledge of history. He should have known that the Democratic Party was the party of low interest. Had he followed this legacy, some of our economic grief would have been prevented.

Carter's ignorance about basic economic ideas could be startling at times. He kept telling Congress and the press that the trade deficit was inflationary and should be stopped. Actually a trade deficit is deflationary. Goods flow into the country and "sop" up money. There is less money available. This is deflationary. It is the injection of debt as a substitute that is the chief cause of inflation. Carter could never grasp this.

Reagan was just as ignorant, if more wilfully so. He believed a huge deficit was a good thing because it enticed foreigners to invest their money in America. He was wrong, of course. Foreigners are using the deficit to buy up America. Reagans failure to create authentic economic vitality was largely due to the debilitating impact of the huge trade deficit.

It is odd that two American presidents, one a Democrat and one a Republican, could be so ignorant of basic economic matters. For the Great Plains, their ignorance meant disaster, but there is hope for the future. Ignorance is a curable malady.

Another weakness of the Federal Reserve System is the fact that it often acts tyrannical and refuses to follow clearly designated mandates of Congress. In 1969 Congress gave the power to the Federal Reserve Board to control all credit allocations in the U.S. This included credit for farmland. The Federal Reserve did nothing.

Carter sent a letter to the Fed in 1979, insisting that they halt inflation in the price of farmland. The Fed refused, and land prices collapsed by 1983. Why should the Federal Reserve be allowed to ignore congressional and presidential directions? If everything the Federal Reserve did was perfect that would be different. But its record is covered with blotches. The stock market collapsed in 1929; the Great Plains real estate market collapsed by 1983. Later I am going to make political recommendations on what needs to be done and I will recommend that the Federal Reserve System be transformed into a national bank. After all, two booms and two busts in one lifetime is enough, to paraphrase Oliver Wendell Holmes, Jr. Under the Federal Reserve System, economic disasters are recurring nightmares.

Eventually Carter felt that the Federal Reserve had set interest rates too high, and he wanted them lowered. This was not done by the Fed. Reagan thought the Fed interest rates too high during his first term. Here the rates went to 22.9%, the highest in modern history. The Fed refused to lower them. In 1989 Bush felt that interest rates were too high. Several of his aides publicly mentioned that they should be lowered. One of the greatest evils of the Federal Reserve System has been its refusal to help the administration reach its economic goals. A true national bank never would do such a thing. Sweden, England, France and Italy all have a national bank. Those banks help the government. Our new national bank should do the same.

In each of these cases on lowering interest, I believe that these presidents were right. It was the Federal Reserve that was wrong. Yet none of these three presidents could do a single thing about interest rates. Yet all will be blamed for the economic slump. It is ironic that our nation renders political abuse to a president for trying to do the right thing while the Fed is doing the wrecking job. This is not political responsibility. A politician should be responsible for something such as the state of the economy and he should be held responsible for it. It is unwise to expect a president to do something when the power is located elsewhere, in an independent agency that is only accountable to itself.

Secrecy is a hallmark of the Federal Reserve System: all of its deliberations are held behind closed doors. The idea of seven men in dark suits, huddled around a table to decide the economic fate of a great nation, is profoundly discomforting. This feeling is not mere paranoia. The Fed helped assure Richard Nixon's re-election in 1972 by presiding over his silly wage and price control effort during 1971. Using the simplest panacea available, the Fed opened the spigot, flooding the country with money and credit to create the impression of great prosperity. There was never any prior public discussion of this policy, which led to the ruinous recession of 1973.

The imperious, incontestable announcement from on high is a cornerstone of Fed tradition. And the rules are changed as they go along. Late in 1979, for example, the Fed announced that money flow and bank revenues would be used to control inflation. Need I mention that there had been no public discussion of this? The policy went into effect. Interest rates soared.

Another weakness of the system is the fact that the Federal Reserve System has never controlled credit or credit transactions on land values, except for interest rates, even when directed by Congress and the president to do so. The Federal Reserve is ponderous, slow and inefficient. Traditionally it tries to stall or rally the economy through interest rates. This takes much too long to get results. They could do better if they used all levers of economic activity to control inflation or speed up economic recovery. They never do this. One can look long and hard before finding another government agency that has served us so poorly. As much as any other actor in the drama, the Federal Reserve System brought darkness to the farms of the Great Plains.

4

THE LAND BANK SYSTEM

By 1916 it was already clear that the Federal Reserve System was not working in the farm belt, so Congress passed the Federal Farm Loan Act. It established twelve federal land banks and designated their locations. The Great Plains land banks are currently located in St. Paul, Omaha, Wichita, and Austin. These four banks did great injury to the farmers of the Great Plains, and they will be reviewed in detail.

The federal land bank districts do not coincide with the Federal Reserve Bank districts. No valid reason exists for this discrepancy. For example, while North and South Dakota belong to the Federal Reserve Bank district headquartered at Minneapolis, the federal land bank splits them up. North Dakota belongs to the district administered out of St. Paul, but South Dakota belongs to the Omaha office. Because the Dakotas possess identical economies, separating them makes no sense at all.

The federal land bank for Missouri is located at St. Louis, whereas the Kansas bank is at Wichita, a hundred miles or so down the road from the Federal Reserve Bank in Kansas City. Confused? Hold on. Much of Oklahoma is under the jurisdiction of the federal lank bank at Wichita, but the Federal Reserve Bank district runs out of Dallas, which includes southeastern Oklahoma.

Taken as a whole, the overlapping districts make this system a confusing one. When you have a farm credit problem, you need to be an east coast economic geographer to figure out where to get help. For a lawyer, it is obviously important to know the law. But it is crucial that he knows where to get help for his client. A lawyer often is little more than a person who gets the client into the right government office, where a decision can be made.

Regrettably, the land banks are not identical to the Fed in generating consistent farm statistics. Hence they are of little value to policy planners in Washington.

Neither the government nor the private sector is capable of rationally addressing the problem of running things from east to west, even though this structural misconception has plagued the country for over 150 years. During the Civil War, Lincoln was amazed and distressed to find that the railroad system ran east and west, forcing Union troops to move south on foot. If history is inevitable, this may be one of the reasons.

In the early days, the land banks reported annually to the U.S. Treasury, which they also depended on for cash. They had nothing to do with the USDA, and their employees were protected by Civil Service guidlelines and received government pensions upon retirement. Then, in 1935, an obscure Senator from Missouri named Harry S Truman introduced a bill to amend the Federal Farm Loan Act so the land banks would be administered by the USDA. It was referred to the Committee on Banking and Currency, where it died. The land banks remained a part of Treasury, overseen by the same committee that killed Truman's bill.

Four years later, Franklin Roosevelt finished what Truman had started by transferring the land banks to the USDA (the Reorganization Act of 1939 vested him with the power to make the transfer). His stated reason for doing this was that he wanted the farmer to have one location where he could receive all information concerning farm activities, subsidy programs and governmental finances. "The farmer should not have to drive all over town to do this," he said.

However laudable Roosevelt's intention, the transfer was a terrible mistake. Henry Wallace publicly maintained that he was not informed about it in advance, and announced that the USDA wouldn't try to control the day-to-day affairs of the land banks.

Yet the transfer did not adversely affect the farmers of the Great Plains until 1971, when Congress passed that year's version of the Farm Credit Act. This bill visited financial agony on the wheat farmers of the Great Plain, and it is one of the principal causes of the economic collapse that hit the region like a thunderclap in 1981.

Ever since the land banks were created in 1916, concerned parties have argued over whether the banks are private or public in nature, whether they fall under federal or state law. According to the original enabling legislation, the land banks were supposed to raise their own money. This makes them look private to many observers. However, Congress appropriated money to start them: of the original $9 million used to capitalize the banks, $8,392,130 came from congressional appropriation. This gives them a definite federal tinge. Also, they were placed under the Treasury Department, where they were governed by the Farm Loan Board. And the president of the United States obviously has no transfer power over private businesses.

Twice Congress had to appropriate additional money to the land banks, once in 1933 to help them through the Great Depression, and again in 1984 to guarantee certain bonds the banks had issued. These actions tend to bolster the federal agency argument. On the other hand, the start-up and Great Depression appropriations were repaid. Nothing has been repaid on the 1984 appropriations (nor on others made since then).

The land banks generated all other monies from their own operations. More important still, in terms of amounts, are the sums the system has borrowed from private money markets. In 1954 the Eisenhower administration "unleashed" the banks. This meant that they were farm cooperatives and nothing would be done to try to regulate them. In 1958 their employees were removed from the Civil Service protection as to political hirings and firings, and they were removed from the pension rolls of the government.

Making the farm credit system an independent agency of the government was an idea that sounded good and was politically popular. Here the activities of Secretary of Agriculture Ezra Taft Benson were scarcely altruistic because he had been executive secretary of the National Council of Farmers Cooperatives. He was just favoring his former employer by increasing the farm co-op movement.

If an agency of government is truly independent then it can truly be responsible to no one. That is what happened during Nixon's term when the farm credit system decided to socialize the long term credit system of farmers. There has never been public discussion on this. The biggest failure of an independent agency of government is the fact that they became doctrinaire and wholly unpredictable.

This would make the banks appear to be private banks. Their bonds are not required to be listed with the Securities and Exchange Commission since they are a federal agency. State security commissions have uniformly refused to require listings because of the federal nature. In other words, speaking biologically, not financially, the banks are mules. That is the way one of its loan officers explained it to me. What, may we ask, is a mule? It is a hybrid caused by breeding a female horse to a male ass. When I review the activities of these banks in the various county courthouses across the Great Plains, I see that this is correct.

Actually there has always been a point of legal contention on this, but it did not become material until 1981, at which point the farm economy started its final collapse. The reason for this is the fact that banks were well run and lawsuits did not develop. After 1981, a multiplicity of law suits developed, and lawyers everywhere started to question the legal status of the banks.

Actually from day one the federal land banks have used the argument that they are private *when they want a benefit provided by state law*, but that they are a federal instrumentality *when they want a benefit provided only by federal law*.

These banks are poorly capitalized. Over the years, earnings were used to support the system. Then any left over was returned to the farmer-borrower as a patronage dividend and little or none was kept by the banks. It is noteworthy that for decades farmers received tax forms from the bank at the end of every year showing patronage dividends. The farmer then reported this on his income tax return on Schedule F. He paid income taxes on it, if he earned enough income to be legally required to pay, and in addition he paid Social Security taxes on it. Since the banks distributed most of their earnings to their customers, they have very few financial reserves. When the crunch came, the reserves of the banks proved inadequate.

This is different from how commercial banks operate. If a commercial bank makes money, it will invariably hold onto some of the earnings and place them in the capital structure of the bank. This strengthens the financial condition of the bank. This money that commercial banks earn cannot be rebated to their customers. Federal and state law prohibit commercial banks from doing this. Also a commercial bank must increase its capital accounts as the bank grows and does more business. The commercial banks may and often do pay dividends to their stockholders; however, before doing so they must notify state or federal regulatory agencies—depending on which government chartered them—and get permission for payment of the dividend.

But these laws do not apply to the federal land banks because they are private businesses. Note how the reasoning switched. They are now private.

Another weakness inherent in the capital structures of these banks is the fact that *they exist on borrowed money*. When a farmer wants a loan, the bank uses only borrowed money to fill his need.

Each of the twelve federal land banks is expected to raise its operating money outside of the federal budget. They do this by selling bonds in the private financial markets, which is another way of saying that they sell them through Wall Street. The bonds are then resold to anyone—or to businesses across the nation—that wants to invest in them.

Who owns these bonds? It is estimated that 1,200 banks across the nation had officers who were stupid enough to buy these junk bonds. Also some state and local governments have a lot of them in the retirement pension plans of their employees. If Congress lets these banks collapse, which would be the best thing to do, then Congress would be bailing out the commercial banks the way it is now bailing out the savings and loan industry. So support the federal land banks, this reasoning goes. Actually there is another side to this argument. It is a grave sign of moral aimlessness for someone to argue that we have to do this because it will in time cause a bigger economic mess. What can be wrong with trying to do the right thing economically for just once? In the name of Aunt Sadie's sacred garter belt, what is wrong with trying to do the right thing?

Many people have the mistaken idea that these bonds are guaranteed by the U.S. Treasury. In general they are not. But a few bonds have been guaranteed in some way by the government. The interest on some of the bonds issued during the 1930s was guaranteed by the government. That is, the bonds were not guaranteed, but the interest was. Some of the bonds issued in 1984 and thereafter have certain guarantees by the government. But in general the bonds are not guaranteed. Some believe that the income from the bonds is not taxable on one's income tax returns. The bond interest is exempt from state and local taxation, and this is one of the features that makes them attractive to some investors. Some taxpayers have purchased these bonds solely because they do not have to pay state income taxes, or federal and state inheritance taxes on them. But in general all income from the bonds is taxable to the federal government since the banks are "instrumentalities" of the federal government. Note how the legal existence of the banks has shifted back to federal existence.

At no time has Congress ever let these bondholders suffer due to their bad investment. Nothing would make the banks responsible faster than for Congress to let these bondholders hold an empty bag.

These banks take the borrowed money that they get from selling the bonds and loan it to the farmers. This borrowed money is the Achilles' heel of the farm credit system as represented by these banks. These banks do not have capital accounts or deposits, as do commercial banks. Commercial banks get most of their lendable money from deposits made by their customers.

These land banks also differ greatly from insurance companies. For example, let's say an insurance company sells a life insurance policy on a day old baby. In theory that baby will live seventy-two years or more. Of course the baby could die young, but actuarially speaking that is not likely to happen. Insurance premium rates are geared to cover such unhappy eventualities. The premiums paid on the policy can be used by the insurance company for many years. The first premium can be used for seventy-two years. The insurance company accumulates the premiums from many policyholders. It has cash in the bank when a farmer applies for a loan. It does not go out and borrow it. This is the great difference between how an insurance company operates as compared to the federal land banks. The insurance company has money to loan. It will not need it for years.

When the farm economy collapsed in 1981, the federal land banks *were operating almost totally on borrowed money*. Wall Street and its many investors wanted the interest on the bonds and the principal as the bonds matured, and under the law they certainly were entitled to that. But the federal land banks could not get it from the farmers who couldn't pay. So they resorted to strong-arm tactics against the wheat farmers: another principal cause of the devastation that hit the farms of the Great Plains.

If the federal land banks had reserve funds, they could have carried the farmers through the economic collapse as the insurance companies had done before.

In 1916 when Congress set up the land bank system, it provided that on each loan made by the bank, the bank was to sell stock equal to 5% of the loan and this money was to *increase the capital reserves of the bank*. If this had been done properly, the banks would have plenty of reserves today. In the Farm Credit Act of 1971 Congress repeated that the farmer must invest in stock in the farm credit system. Sec. 1.16 of the Act reads as follows: "Stock shall be paid for in cash at the time the loan is closed." Congress mandated that this stock investment be paid for in cash *in order to build up the banks' cash reserves*. But this was not done properly. I am unable to find just when the intent of Congress was bent, prostituted and made ineffective. Most of the earlier loan closing documents have long since disappeared, but I believe that it was some time in the early 1970s. In any event the federal land banks developed and concocted a method of avoiding or eschewing what Congress has twice directed.

Here is how the scam worked. Let's say that a wheat farmer wanted a loan of $90,000, and this is the amount that he applied for. He should pay $4,500 *in cash* to buy stock to build up the reserves of the bank. This loan application was made to the local federal land bank *association*, not the central bank, say, at Wichita, Kansas. The federal land bank of Wichita, Kansas would then "boost" this loan up to $100,000. Then that bank would draft a check to the farmer for $5,000 which was the 5% surcharge to build up the capital reserves of the bank. This is on the $100,000 "boosted" loan, not the $90,000 the farmer wanted. In theory this check went to the farmer. At least it was made out to him. In actual practice the check was mailed to the loan office located in the local federal land bank association, not to the farmer. The farmer would come by the office and endorse the check to the federal land bank association, which then would give him $5,000 in stock of the local federal land bank association, not in the federal land bank in

Wichita. The federal land bank association deposited the endorsed check in its account and then wrote out a check to the federal land bank of Wichita for $5,000, which put it back into its checking account.

The federal land bank of Wichita would then issue $5,000 worth of its stock in the name of the local federal land bank association, not the farmer. The federal land bank of Wichita got the money from the association, not the farmer. Does this build up the capital reserves of the federal land bank as Congress has twice directed? The answer is no. Let's look at a hypothetical checking account of the federal land bank for a week and see. On the date the check for $5,000 was made out the bank received a loan payment from Farmer Cooper in Kansas for $20,000 and another check from a Wall Street bonding firm for $1,000,000 for sale of bonds. It received a check for $14,000 from Farmer Dykes of Oklahoma and a check for the same amount from Farmer Jones in New Mexico. It wrote a check to Farmer Smith to close a loan of $120,000. It received a check for $5,000 from the federal land bank association down in Oklahoma on the original farm loan. All of these transactions flowed through the checking account of the federal land bank in Wichita. It is very easy to miss the point that no increase was made in the bank reserves. As far as I know, no other writer on this subject has ever mentioned this. It is important to understand this fact in order to comprehend why the banks have depleted reserves and how they collapse so easily.

Let's see if I can illustrate this. First I will eliminate all cash transactions from the hypothetical checking account of the federal land bank except for those that involve this loan.

The final figure is precisely the same amount that was in the bank's checking account before it made the loan for stock. Neither the bank's cash nor its reserves registers an increase or a decrease.

The federal land bank has a bank account of	$100,000
The bank makes a loan to a farmer for	-5,000
The federal land bank checking account now contains	$95,000
The farmer endorses the check to federal land bank *association* and sends federal land bank	5,000
The federal land bank deposits the check and now has a checking account of	$100,000

Several people who have read this manuscript have commented that the $5,000 is actually in the coffers of the federal land bank association, because the farmer gave the $5,000 check to the association after endorsing it. Correct, but the money did not build up the system's reserves because the association immediately made out a check for $5,000 to the land bank proper and sent it to them.

To illustrate my point:

Federal land bank *association* has a checking account balance of	$0
Federal land bank association receives an endorsed check from the farmer and deposits it	$5,000
Thus the association has a cash balance of	$5,000
The federal land bank association writes a check and mails it to the federal land bank at Wichita to pay for the stock	-$5,000
The federal land bank association has a bank account of	$0

Everything is exactly the same as before the loan. In time, the federal land banks became so brazen that they didn't even write the checks. Only a debit and credit entry appeared on the loan closing statement.

When a commercial bank wants to build up its reserves it does this by issuing common or preferred stock AND IT WILL NOT MAKE A LOAN TO PURCHASE THE STOCK. Because such a loan does not increase the reserves. Each new stock owner is required to have the money, or borrow it elsewhere. At the present time, there are a number of commercial banks that are in very poor financial condition, and the federal comptroller of the currency who regulates national banks, or the state banking commissioners who regulate state banks, will issue an order for the bank to get new money and build up its reserves. The bank issues preferred stock. *The bank will not make a loan to buy this new stock.* It can't do this and build up its reserves at the same time.

When the federal land banks got into financial trouble in 1984 and asked for a bailout from Congress, many people wanted to know why they didn't use the money they got on the sale of stock to farmers. The reason is plain to see. The banks never got cash for these stock sales. These sales were on credit. There was nothing in reserves to fall back on. Second, this stock is now generally considered to be absolutely worthless and most of it is. In 1986 the author of the Farm Credit Act of 1971, Henry L. Bellmon of Oklahoma, ran for governor. His federal land bank loans, all made after the passing of the 1971 Act that he sponsored, became a bone of contention in the political campaign. When asked how he felt about it, Bellmon replied in this manner: "I have over $50,000 of that stock. I guess that it's not worth much now. I'm not proud of it." This should tell you what it's worth.

Since 1971 the federal land banks consistently used this stock as come-on to get farmers to take loans. Private insurance companies, by way of contrast, do not use a stock transaction as a gimmick to lure farmers. Nor do they require that the farmer buy life insurance on the loan. But the federal land banks tell farmers that they can lend money cheaper than other lenders because they are the government (here is the federal instrumentality theory at work). They then tell the farmer that this stock will be very valuable in the future, that it's a good investment. One farmer near Lamont, Oklahoma was told that he should buy the stock and hold onto it because it would be worth a great deal when his children went to college and he would be able to use the proceeds from its sale to cover their tuition.

Thus the federal land bank induced farmers to borrow from it rather than the private insurance companies. Land bank stock has been worthless since 1984 because the whole federal land bank system is broke and depends on Congress just to stay open. All loans made by the federal land bank system since 1984 have sold this worthless stock *and the bank officers responsible for doing it knew it was worthless.* If this had been a private business, they would have been indicted for violating the securities laws of the U.S. government. Such laws prohibit the sale of all unlicensed and worthless securities, and each company that sells securities must abide by these laws. At the same time that the federal land bank in Wichita was conducting its affairs in this disgraceful fashion, the Kansas Gas and Electric Company—headquartered in Wichita—made certain that all of its stocks and bonds met the minimum requirement of the federal and state securities laws as required. KG&E, as this electrical company is known, hired a battery of attorneys and accountants who make certain that the company complied with all securities laws. Anyone who invests in Kansas Gas and Electric Company will reap good income, yet anyone who invests in the stock of the federal land bank of Wichita will reap nothing.

I can find no case where they ever alerted the farmer that it was worthless. When I get to the county courthouses and look at a series of cases, I find that some federal land banks have in general refused to give the farmer anything for his stock because of its worthlessness. Farmers have been refused anything for this stock in several of the banks, and in at least one case the federal land bank of Wichita, Kansas, simply cancelled the stock. The farmer got nothing even though his loan was paid in full. State law required that this stock be sold at a sheriff's sale after being advertised and the farmer notified that the sale would be held. This was not done. Anywhere else this would have been considered theft. It is also an abuse of the judicial process.

Third, this stock transfer is nothing but a legal scam. It causes the farmer to pay interest on an amount of money that he never received. When the loan in the above example was closed, the farmer would sign a mortgage for $100,000; however he would be given a check for only $95,000. This increased the interest expense to the farmer and it increased the interest income to the federal land bank. This has caused bad effects. First it created funds which allowed the federal land banks to build huge buildings for their operations. The bank at Wichita, Kansas is so plush that it is fit for a Roman emperor, not a wheat farmer. It has rugs in it that are luxurious. Its interior and exterior are plush beyond any necessity. The bank is losing money hand over fist, as a farmer would say. The associations have likewise over-built. For example the federal land bank association at Pratt, Kansas is so large that the cars of the officers and employees are parked under a car port so that they can come and go without getting their little or big feet wet during storms. All of this has to be paid for by the farmers. The association building at Enid, Oklahoma is plush beyond reason. It is built one and a half blocks from the most expensive private residence ever built in northwest Oklahoma. This is the Champlin mansion built by the late H.H. Champlin of the oil fortune. This mansion was built in the 1930s when labor was cheap, and it was built to provide jobs for unemployed people. It is on a through street of the city and is possibly one of the busiest streets on the Great Plains. Why the land bank would build there is anyone's guess, but a former employee said it was because they wanted to get as close to the Champlin mansion as they could. In other words the association building was built where it is for the snob appeal. The officers could sell this facility and relocate elsewhere in cheaper quarters, but they refuse because they can always get all of the money they want from the federal government.

In Wichita, Kansas the federal land bank building is just a short distance from the modest headquarters building of the Kansas Gas and Electric Company, which makes money. The federal land bank association building at Yankton, South Dakota is plush beyond words. It is losing money hand over fist. Yet a few blocks away is the building that houses the Gurney Seed and Nursery Company, which is the largest seed and garden company on the Great Plains. The Gurney building was built in four different sections at four different times. The company would build a section at a time and when it outgrew the facility, it would build an extension. This continued as they outgrew it again and again. There are three different kinds and colors of bricks in the building and one extension is a modern pre-fab. It gives an odd appearance to the building. They have outgrown the entire building and yet they stay put. The company is making good profits.

The federal land bank association building at Aberdeen, South Dakota is located in the northwest section of the city, which is the richest and most exclusive area. Most businesses here are housed in newly constructed buildings. This federal land bank association building is equipped with solar heating devices. Solar heating works well in hot desert regions such as El Paso, Texas and Albuquerque, New Mexico. It is useless and worthless in South Dakota, where the winters are long and cold. It is common for the temperature to stay below freezing for several months in these northern areas. During the summer the weather is hot and dry. Solar heating is useless because air conditioning is the main factor.

The federal land bank association building in Marysville, Kansas is the plushest thing in town. At Ponca City, Oklahoma will be found the most expensive private residence ever built on the Great Plains. It was build by the governor and oilman, the late E.W. Marland. The Marland mansion cost $5.5 million dollars in the 1920s. Today it would cost about $100 million to replace it. The Ponca City federal land bank association building is just down the road a few blocks. There is a consistent pattern of placing these bank buildings just as close to the richest part of town as is possible. This is not what a wheat farmer needs. But he is paying for it. Any one of the federal land banks and their associations can be housed cheaper almost anywhere else.

The only place where I found a federal land bank trying to live within its income was at North Platte, Nebraska. Here the local association moved out of a newly constructed, expensive shopping mall to cheaper quarters.

These banks started to collapse in 1984. They have had six

years to economize. But they have refused. The only way I know that this can be stopped is to cut off the money from the government and abolish the system.

This interest scam has been used in states such as Oklahoma, which used to have very strict laws on what a financial institution could charge for interest. Charging interest on $100,000— but actually loaning out only $95,000—gives an economic advantage to the federal land bank over commercial banks and insurance companies that could not and did not engage in such activity. Land banks can escape the effects of state laws on usury. Here is how this system works: any ten or more farmers can meet and set up a federal land bank *association*. This would be the governing body in their neighborhood. It would be officered by them. They would hire or fire any employee of the association. The association would be local. It would not be in a distant city. Here I must clearly distinguish between the federal land bank and the federal land bank associations. The banks in the Great Plains are in Minneapolis, Omaha, Wichita and Austin. The associations are in such cities as Ponca City, Enid, Clinton and Weatherford, Oklahoma; Pratt and Maryville, Kansas; North Platte, Nebraska; Yankton and Aberdeen, South Dakota; Bismarck, North Dakota; and, Perryton, Texas, to name a few. If a member wants a loan, he applies to the association, not the federal land bank. The local association has a committee that interviews the farmer and writes up the loan application. This committee decides whether the loan is good or bad, or whether it should even be made. Prior to 1971 the local committee knew every loan applicant because the association was in a small village. They knew what kind of farmer the applicant was. They knew whether he beat his wife or not, and whether he drank, and if so, how much. You cannot imagine how much the residents of our small villages know about each other. Let me illustrate this by recounting an event that I once experienced. I was born and reared near the small village of Douglas, Oklahoma. Our people lived there and we knew everybody—and where every nickel was. The town was home to about seventy-five souls. One local wag counted them and observed, "There are seventy-two people, two bears and a fox."

At that time the town had an elderly couple living there with the last name of Bear and an elderly lady there by the name of Fox. Hence the two Bears and a Fox. I had some tax business with a lady in the town and drove out to see her. Let's call her Mrs. Tarker. When I got to Mrs. Tarker's home, I discovered she was not there. I drove on to the local filling station. In the big city this is called the service station. In the small villages there is a vocabulary that goes with the village. What people in Kansas City call a service station, the people down home call a filling station. In Kansas City, there is a rail center. In Chicago, there is a rail terminal. Down in Douglas, they call it the depot. And so on.

So I drove to the filling station. The attendant came out to the car with a big grin on his face. He's married to my fifth cousin. "Hi, Ray. How are you?" he asked. I said fine and we caught up on family news and gossip. Then I asked about Mrs. Tarker.

"Oh, she ain't home, but you can get her over to Bownings," he said.

"What is she doing over there?" I asked.

"Oh, she just went over there to be sociable. They're having tea and sugar cookies. Go on over, they'd be glad to see you."

"When did she go over there?"

"About ten minutes ago."

So it goes in a Great Plains village. A lady goes to visit another person in town and less than ten minutes later everyone knows about it. They know it's a social, not a business visit, they even know what kind of cookies are eaten. Not only that, this expert extended an invitation for me to visit another person in her private home. Such is life in a small village. Can you imagine anyone in New York City knowing or caring about what a neighbor does or eats?

So when a farmer went to his local federal land bank association, the committee knew a great deal about him. This is important in understanding how these associations worked and why they failed after 1971. The Farm Credit Act gave the district federal land banks more control over the local associations. Believing that bigger is always better, the federal land banks forced all of the small associations out of the system. Before 1971 there were over 800 associations across the country. A few years after 1971 about 380 have survived. They are too large for good credit work.

The original act of Congress in 1916 provided that when a farmer borrowed money from his local federal land bank association, he JOINTLY AND SEVERALLY GUARANTEED all loans that were on the books and all that would be made thereafter. "Jointly and severally" means that the federal land bank can move against the assets of one farmer to pay the debts of another farmer.

For example:

Farmer White borrows	$100,000
Farmer Green borrows	100,000
Farmer Black borrows	50,000
Total borrowed	$250,000

An ordinary person would take this to mean that Farmer Black owes $50,000. But according to the federal land bank documents the farmer signed when he closed his loan, he is responsible for the repayment of $250,000. This is one of the clubs the federal land banks use to beat the farmers. This wasn't true before 1971, because the committees that operated the small federal land bank associations knew all of their borrowers and turned down bad loans. If the loan applicant was a drunk, they knew it and turned him down. They didn't want to be held liable for the debts of their local drunks. If a farmer couldn't hang onto his money, his loan application met the same fate. It was a virtually foolproof system. Some of their records are truly amazing.

For example, remember the federal land bank association in Mansfield, Missouri that was formed in 1917, and never had a loan loss until it was consolidated into a larger unit. From 1917 to 1932 it employed the same office secretary. She went over all loan applications and ran the office in an old building on Main Street where the rent was cheap and her books balanced to the penny. Neither her handling of the money nor her collection tactics were ever questioned. There were no questionable entries on her ledgers. She loaned out millions of dollars, and there was never a farm foreclosure nor a lawsuit over a loan she made. Her name was Laura Ingalls Wilder. She rode a hack down from South Dakota in 1894, during a decade of hard times. She had a fourth grade education, all of it from frontier schools, and she was never taught by a licensed, degree-holding teacher. Yet she ran the system properly and profitably.

Now contrast that with the performance of college trained loan officers who operated the system there after 1971. The federal land bank association of Mansfield, Missouri has been consolidated into a larger unit, and guess what—it is losing money like there's no tomorrow. And there wouldn't be if Congress wasn't propping up the system with new money.

Here is another example. The federal land bank association at Jet, Oklahoma operated profitably from the day it was opened until it was consolidated into a four county district, head-quartered in Enid, Oklahoma, in the 1970s. This local association was so small, it did not even have an office. When a meeting was necessary, they met in the community room of the local bank, at a cafe or in one of the churches. They never lost a penny. How well have things worked out for this new, larger association? It's lost money by the crateful. It can't make a profit and it can't operate properly. It oppresses the local farmers.

The local failure of the farm credit system as owned and operated by the federal government is recasting these federal land bank associations into large geographical units in which the loan officers and others do not know the farmers they're dealing with. Also it can be noted that some of these college trained loan officers bled the system of cash by using various scams, but I will get to that later.

When these larger associations were formed, the officers and committees were called upon to evaluate the credit worthiness of each loan applicant, and in many cases credit was extended when little or nothing was known about the applicant. When I was in a filling station one day in Douglas, my cousin told me that Aunt Pearl's "swinging rib" seemed to be doing a little better and Uncle Bill's kidney seemed to be worse. Do you think you could get that information as a stranger? Do you think a loan officer could? Of course not.

So when a loan officer based in a large city of the merged associations goes out to the countryside to see what the farmers are up to, the visit will not yield a great deal of information, and nothing that's derogatory to local farmers. If the loan officer asked whether a farmer drank too much, he would probably be told that no one knows what the man would do if he smelled the cap of a beer can. Nor will any light be shed on the farmer's operating methods. The loan officer can only get back into his expensive imported car and depart in a cloud of dust.

Every foreclosed farm loan in Alfalfa County, Oklahoma was made after the passage of the Farm Credit Act of 1971 and the forced mergers of the small local federal land bank associations with urban land banks. Every farm loan was made by an officer who didn't really know what was going on, or who he was dealing with.

An outsider is just not going to get the truth. For instance, once a regional welfare case worker drove into one such village to check out the welfare application of a resident. The case worker called on one of the town Moms. She stated her business and asked about the drinking habits of Old Jim. The Mom said she couldn't really say whether he drank or not. Probably he did drink, but if he did he was awful quiet about it because she never caught wind of it. There were no noise episodes or fights or anything like that. The case worker decided that there didn't seem to be a serious problem. What was the truth? Well, Old Jim was the town drunk. He scarcely drew a sober breath and everyone in town knew it. But an outsider is just not going to get that information. Old Jim got his welfare checks and drank them up.

Problems with the buying and selling of farmland also rose up to plague the system. Usually the auction system is employed. The seller retains an auctioneer to sell some farmland at a preset commission, usually 2 to 5% of the gross sales price. The two agree on a sale date and place an advertisement in the local weekly newspaper, plus at least one in the Sunday paper of the nearest large city. A leaflet is mailed to all post office boxes in the surrounding villages. By 1975, as the profit in farming disappeared, farmland went for a lot of money, so the land was sold and bought mostly by farmers. Most doctors and lawyers had vanished into their offices long before, then refusing to pay the enormous land prices. Most, but not all.

When the sale date arrives, a small crowd gathers at the designated spot. A few women show up, but most of the people in the crowd are men. If the sale is to take up most of the day, lunch will be served on the grounds, sponsored by a women's group. The sale always halts for lunch.

The auctioneer arrives at the sale at least thirty minutes before starting time, so he can work the crowd. Let's call him Wayne. Wayne goes around and visits with everyone. Failure to meet and give a friendly greeting to all would be an unforgivable breach of village etiquette. "Hi Joe, how are you. I haven't seen you in ages. What are you doing to keep yourself off the street," Wayne's senseless banter would go. On and on the chatter flows. An auctioneer is known by the flow of his chatter. One farmer observes: "Wayne is sure full of it today."

Wayne chatters on. "Bert, It's good to see you. I haven't seen you since I went to see your mama and she was making that mulberry jam. Oh, was that good. My teeth fought to get closer to that bread and jam. My-oh-my was it good." This will go on until the time of the sale. The auctioneer will then call everyone's attention to the cloud of dust that is approaching. He opines that it is the loan man from the federal land bank. A short wait occurs as the imported sedan screeches to a stop. Yep, the auctioneer guessed right, it is the loan man from the local federal land bank association. Let's call him Jim. He is dressed in the latest business suit and is wearing T-Texas cowboy boots and a large western hat. He can strut sitting down.

"Okay, boys," Wayne sings, "let's get this started. First, I want all of you to meet the owner, Miss Mandy. As you know Miss Mandy lost Jake last year and she's decided to move to town, and so she has put these two farms up for sale. Miss Mandy come on up and let everyone see you." She does and they do. She bites back a tear as she is introduced. The children of the late Jake and Miss Mandy are introduced, if they have any. It has always escaped me why an auctioneer can call a seventy-year-old woman, who was married over fifty years and has four children "Miss," but who am I to ask impertinent questions. It's the system I hate, not the people in it.

"Now boys," the auctioneer says, "this is good wheat land that we are selling here today. Jake and Miss Mandy made a good living on it. They lived here forty-five years and that will tell you how long you have to wait before another opportunity like this comes along. About forty-five years," he says, answering himself. "So if you want a chance to farm this land in your lifetime, buy today. Boys, that's the way it is." He pauses.

"Oh, wait a minute. You boys back there, step right up here. We want you in this. Don't wait back there. Boys, just step right up here," he cajoles. I wish someone would explain to me why an auctioneer calls men twice his age "you boys," but they all do. Probably it's a subtle form of intimidation, a reminder of the farmers' place in the scheme of things.

The "boys" step up and the auctioneer resumes his senseless chatter.

"Now boys, let's sell this farm where we are. It is a one hundred sixty acre farm and one hundred fifty-nine is in wheat, and one acre is where these here buildings are. It's a good loose loam soil and wheat grows well here. All minerals go with the land." This is important in the three southern Great Plains states, which have a lot of oil and gas production.

"Now boys, what am I bid on this land?"

He tries for $60,000. No one responds and so he goes to $50,000 and then to $40,000 before he receives the first bid.

The auctioneer's brain finally catches up with his mouth.

"Boys, if it's money, I want to introduce the loan officer of the federal land bank. He's got the money that you might need to buy this. Jim, come on up here. This is Jim, and I bet he wants to talk to any buyer here today." Jim agrees that is his mission here. He's got money to loan and lots of it. He wants to "hep" the farmer.

"Okay boys, let's get to going," the auctioneer cries. The bidding goes up to $50,000 and stalls. The auctioneer always brings a sidekick whose job is to work the crowd, scout for bids. "Loran, check with the man."

The sidekick goes over to one of the men who has dropped out asks why he is not bidding. The man says he is not certain that he has the money and he is not certain the land is worth over $50,000.

"Not worth it, are you kidding?" the sidekick says, feigning astonishment. "They ain't making no mo' land. This is all there is. If you want mo' farm land you will get it by buying it. I tell you what, you bid $52,000 and if you get the land and are still not satisfied with the price, I will give you $1,000 and take the land myself. In other words, you'll get $1,000 for your effort and I'll own the land."

"Okay," the farmer says, his voice not quite sure.

"Yipe," the sidekick yelps to the auctioneer, "I got a bid for $52,000 right here." This practice is called "pickin' a bid out of thin air." It's dishonest, yet practiced by scores of auctioneers and their sidekicks from Texas to North Dakota. In fact, many of these auctions are only one step away from outright fraud.

The auctioneer looks at the previous bidder, who bids it up to $53,000. The sidekick goes to another bidder who has long since dropped out and asked for him a bid. The farmer shakes his head *no*. The sidekick asks if it is money and the farmer shakes his head *yes*.

"Don't you remember," the sidekick badgers him, "Wayne told you at the start that the loan man from the federal land bank is here and that if you needed money Jim would get it for you. In fact, I suggest that you bid $55,000 and if you get it and the federal land bank won't loan you the money, I'll take it and give you $1,000 for your time."

"Do you really think the federal land bank will loan the money?" the farmer asks.

"Oh, yes, they will," says the sidekick, "95% of all farm loans today are made by the federal land bank." The man bids $55,000.

"Yipe, $55,000," the sidekick barks.

"And who will give me $60,000," the auctioneer wants to know. The sidekick works the crowd for another bid. There are none. The auctioneer speaks. His voice is grave and paternal.

"Now boys, we ain't goin' to let this land go for $55,000. That would be stealing it, not selling it. I said this land was to be sold, not stole'd, and I am not going to let anyone steal this land. Now boys, I'll tell you what I am going to do. I'm going to turn this squawk box [megaphone] off and let's visit about this. Then we will come back and sell the land, but it won't be for $55,000." The squawk box is turned off and the loan officer of the local federal land bank association steps forward to ply his dubious trade.

By then there are only two serious bidders. He visits with both of them.

"This land is worth a lot more than the bid is here," he tells the first bidder. "If you want the land, the federal land bank will loan you the money for it. I believe I can get you 100% financing."

"Are you sure you can finance me?" the farmer asks.

"Oh, sure," says the loan man. "Look, if you want this land, bid it on up and I'll approve your loan before I leave here today. You have credit with the federal land bank," he adds. "We'll back you. Isn't that fair enough?"

The farmer grins a grin as wide as the Mississippi River. All of his life he's said he could do better if he had a line of credit and now this nice man Jim is telling him just what he's always wanted to hear. "You may see me bidding a little faster," he says. "Good boy," the federal land bank man says. That word again. Here is a college graduate who cannot properly address another human being and falls into the evil habit of calling grown men, in this case a seventy-two-year-old, "boy."

The land bank man goes to the second bidder and talks with him. Jim asks if he needs credit. The farmer said probably not. His wife just inherited some money from a great aunt back in Pennsylvania, so he has most of the money he needs.

"Good, but if you need any, will you let us finance it? You have credit with us," the land bank operator says, and I mean operator the way it was meant in old gangster movies.

"I'll see what I can do," the farmer replies.

Now, consider what is going on here. The loan officer eagerly agrees to finance both bidders so they can purchase this property. Note that he doesn't even know their names. The loan committee knew everyone in the days of the small associations, but this loan officer is going out of his way to lend money to people whose names he doesn't know, whose credit worthiness is a complete mystery to him. Here the system reveals one of its major evils. By agreeing to finance each bidder as they bid against each other, the land bank officer drives the price of land upward, floating on a cushion of his own hot air. No representatives of insurance companies or commercial banks ever conduct themselves this way.

Once the land bank man is through working the two bidders, the auctioneer turns on his squawk box and the bidding resumes. They quickly bid the farm up to $100,000, and it sells to the first farmer.

The land bank officer and the auctioneer's sidekick rush over to congratulate the buyer. The auctioneer then calls for the sale of the second farm and uses exactly the same stunts to double its price.

The federal land bank officer approves both loan applications for the sale and purchase of the land before he leaves the sale grounds. No credit checks are run, no income taxes monitored to see if the farmer's operation is profitable. Knowing next to nothing about the farmers, the federal land bank contracts to lend them a total of $200,000. The farmers put up no cash to close the sales.

Why do loan officers of the federal land bank system conduct themselves in such a disgraceful fashion? One thing the Farm Credit Act of 1971 stated was that the system should be independent of all other federal departments. Consequently, the men who ran the system decided to crowd out other lenders by socializing the long-term credit system used by farmers. To make their loan officers more aggressive, the federal land bank system offered its loan officers commissions based on both the number and the size of the loans they made. Further augmenting the loan officers' strategy were fringe benefits: free trips to Reno, vacations in Hawaii, Bermuda and other garden spots. Some of these loan officers played the field so skilfully that they became quite well-to-do. Many of them still have their jobs. They constantly call on Congress for more money. The system is incapable of correcting itself.

The 1916 legislation that set up the federal land banks allowed them to lend only up to 50% of the land's appraised value. Congress raised the figure to 65% in 1946, and made loans from the Veterans Administration available to ex-G.I.s who wished to buy farms and farmhouses. Under the Farm Credit Act of 1971, loans could be made up to 85% of the appraised value. This last increase flooded the countryside with excessive credit.

By 1987, the federal land banks had foreclosed on considerable amounts of land, leaving a big backlog of farms they couldn't sell. Congress meekly raised the lending power of the banks to 97% of the appraised price. And because Congress had established in 1971 that the appraisal price of such property was whatever the banks wanted it to be, the land banks didn't have to follow state or federal laws, or real estate trade practices when deciding the value of land. Congress handed the land bank officers a very large cookie jar, and they proceeded to raid it of every crumb.

Over the decades the term "appraised price" has acquired a definite legal meaning. It means the best price that can be received for the land. Appraisers determine the figure by researching the price of similar land in the area, adding or subtracting as needed for improvements such as fences and buildings, soil specifics, whether it is terraced or not, and so on.

When the farms sold at the auction described above went for $100,000 apiece, this tended to adjust the appraised price of other farms in the area upward, where the federal land bankers apparently want them. But should that have happened? The fair market value of the land was actually $50,000 apiece. Remember how the bidding rose to $50,000 and stalled: because the fair market value of this land actually *was* $50,000. Clearly the auctioneer's sidekick and the land bank loan operator kited up the sales price. The latter was willing to finance all bidders, and no loan officers from other institutions even appeared. The insurance companies that traditionally made long term loans to farmers have long since removed themselves from competition. The federal land bank and only the federal land bank now gets the action.

The insurance companies fled the scene because they were not about to lend money on farms bearing artifically inflated price tags. A farmer from Garber, Oklahoma told me that his grandfather, father and himself had borrowed money from life insurance companies for over sixty years. All of a sudden in the early 1970s, they refused him a loan, and he never really knew why. They simply decided not to lend to farmers anymore. It happened all over the Great Plains. I asked a vice-president of one of the larger insurance companies why his company left, and he said there was a move on by the federal government to take over the long term farm credit system, and the feds wanted the insurance men out. "They'll bid up their loans to farmers and we're not going to get involved. When this boom that they're financing goes bust, we won't be there holding the bag."

Most of these companies' loans have been paid down and the small remaining balances are very well secured. Because they never kited up the sales price on a parcel of land, their customers remained loyal to them. And they've also remained solvent. It's important to remember that Congress never voted to socialize the farm credit system. It was the slick operators in the federal land banks who decided to take the matter into their own hands.

With their faked appraisals and their ability to attract huge sums of money to the system via tax exemptions, the land banks could afford to outbid the insurance companies. So they cornered the market on long term farm credit. The whole sorry mess makes a good case for never granting a federal agency that much independence. The likelihood that it will veer sharply away from general government policy is simply too great. Had the federal land bank system been audited and supervised by the Secretary of Agriculture, events probably wouldn't have spun so out of control. But we'll never know.

There is further tragedy in the way crucial lessons of history were ignored. During the New Deal, Frances Perkins was Secretary of Labor. She repeatedly warned against creating an independent government agency. She said that every agency must answer to someone who answers to the American people. She taught that responsibility is the key to good government.

Ezra Taft Benson was in Washington during all of the New Deal, and he had to know of Frances Perkins' views. Yet when he became top dog at USDA in 1953, one of the first things he did was to push legislation through Congress that made the federal land bank system an independent agency. He gave the land bank system a way of working outside the traditional channels of government. No audits would be run on its records. No inquiries would be made.

Benson's mind was totally closed on the subject, and a closed mind is the worst thing you can turn loose inside government. A closed mind can do far more damage than any terrorist.

As long as Benson was in office, however, nothing much went wrong. The same holds true for the Kennedy and Johnson years. But the chickens came home to roost when Richard Nixon took office, and federal dominance of farm credit is one of his most enduring and questionable legacies.

Until 1916, long term farm credit was totally a capitalistic system, and it was not working well. The land bank and mixed long term credit systems devised under Woodrow Wilson served the farmers and the nation fairly well. Under Franklin Roosevelt and Harry Truman, small impoverished farmers and tenant farmers were brought into the system. Then the Nixon administration, without consulting anyone, allowed this independent agency to engage in a crude form of socialism, and the system failed in every way.

Any system that is socialized along Stalinist lines becomes cumbersome, burdensome, and irrational. It loses touch with the people it serves, and has no feeling for them. It manifests concern only for itself and its economic privileges. It turns bureaucratic, snotty, and domineering. Bureaucrats by definition have a vested interest in protecting the failed policies of the past. They won't admit to making errors, and if left unchecked they're always ready to spend more money. Once entrenched, they will not surrender their economic privileges without a protracted struggle.

The system as it now stands forces farmers into a corner. That is the reason so many of them have committed suicide in the past decade. The system should make a farmer anxious to pay. Instead, it crushes him.

Here is how the racket works. After the sale described above, the loan officer went back to his office and pulled files on loan requests. He noticed that Old Jed talked to him several weeks ago about buying some more land, but both agreed then that he had no equity in his land and thus could not qualify for another loan. Now the loan officer gave him a call.

"Jed, there was a sale yesterday at Miss Mandy's place and guess what that farm sold for—$100,000." Then he notices that Jed's farm has better soil than Miss Mandy's, and so he adds $10,000 to the appraised price of Jed's farm. Notice how the appraised value has jumped from $50,000 to $110,000 in one day. No one did a thing to justify such an increase. The farmer certainly did nothing to earn the increased appraisal. The profitability of wheat certainly hadn't gone up. The land's value floated ever upward on a cushion of hot air from the loan officer's mouth. The new appraisal was based on a false sales price, not intrinsic worth.

Under the Farm Credit Act, the bank can now loan 85% of the appraisal. Now that Jed's farm is worth $110,000, this means a loan of $93,000 is possible. Jed can now buy another farm if he so desires. Sure enough, several weeks later there is a farm sale down the road. He bids the price up to $125,000 with the same loan officer standing at his side whooping him on. Jed pays nothing down and takes out a mortgage on his home place and the new land. A few weeks later, he buys two more farms for $150,000 each. Now he has four farms, each with an appraised value of $150,000, for a total of $600,000. He owes the federal land bank $425,000. With interest on the loan at 8%, Jed will owe $41,920 in interest for the first year.

But this is not the end of Old Jed's agony. When the federal land bank system became insolvent in 1984 and turned to Congress for financing, the federal land bank association increased Old Jed's interest rates from 8% to 13.75%. Old Jed now owed $58,437 per year in interest, rather than $41,920. Meanwhile, the price of wheat collapsed, leaving Old Jed with less money than ever to meet his increased interest costs. Under circumstances like these, it's a small wonder that so many farmers fell into chronic depression, or turned a gun on themselves. Suicide is now the most prevalent cause of death among wheat farmers.

Insurance companies never made the mistake of recklessly inflating the value of land. It's impossible to document a single case of an insurance company or private bank anywhere on the Great Plains engaging in such misconduct. Yet the federal land bank at Wichita, Kansas pulled these shenanigans a dozen times a day at the height of the land boom in the late 1970s and early 1980s. A loan officer at that bank once said to me, "You'll never live long enough to see wheat land go below $1,000 per acre."

Nowadays you can buy wheat land all over the Great Plains for less than $400 per acre, except for irrigated land, which is about $750. The idea that land prices would never come down was just not true, but loan officers repeatedly used it as a talking point to convince farmers to plunge helplessly and hopelessly into debt. I have documented the sale of a wheat farm in 1970 for $60,000; in 1980 the same farm sold for $240,000. In terms of price increases, the land boom of the 1970s was the largest in world history. The federal land banks bear sole responsibility for bringing it on. Since the federal government was behind the boom and the resulting collapse, I think it is only fair for it to help the farmers out of this disaster.

On a more positive note, at least half of America's remaining farmers have never done business with the federal land bank system and never will. Only about 30% of them used that system as their loan company, and they're the ones in trouble. There's an old saying, "What goes around, comes around." Payments on these ludicrously high farm loans have come around, and of course farmers can't pay them.

I attended a sale near Goltry, Oklahoma several years ago. An old Mennonite was sitting there, taking in the scene. He'd obviously seen the snow of many, many winters. After the sale I talked to him. He knew what the auctioneer's sidekick and the loan officer were up to. He'd been to many sales and he'd seen many bids picked out of thin air. He summed it up by saying, "It makes one wonder who is trying to skin whom."

It's an interesting point. Many farmers were greedy enough to participate in the scam (as I've heard it described a thousand times). The loan officers were certainly greedy for larger fees and commissions, and therefore willing to throw caution to the stiff prairie winds. The sidekicks worked for greedy auctioneers, who received higher commissions on larger sales.

This whole system stinks to high heaven, and screams for a solution. None has appeared. Washington has yet to penetrate the fraud, and Congress dutifully passes laws that make more money available to prop up the system, never stopping to ask what in hell is going on here.

Congress changed the accounting rules of the system in 1987. It was decided that the federal land bank system only had to write off 5% of its losses in any one year. Say that the federal land bank of Wichita lost $100,000 in one week. (I assure you that in some weeks it's lost a great deal more than that. Once it lost $1.8 million in a single day.) It writes off $5,000 as an operating expense. The rest of the loss is then held and written off in the succeeding nineteen years, assuming farmers are stupid enough to deal with this system in the future. Future farmers will have to pay for all current and past losses. This amounts to a built-in Sword of Damocles hanging over the necks of my farmer friends.

A few farmers were using government money to tie up the economic resources of the Great Plains—namely farmland—and hold it outside the traditional channels of commerce, in order to deprive their more cautious neighbors of more land. The government could best serve all by not serving anyone.

Is land valuable because of the misbehavior of some loan officers? Absolutely not. Land is valuable *because of what you do on it*. Let me give an example of this. At the north edge of Oklahoma City, there used to be some rough grassland owned by cattle farmers. This land was too poor to grow wheat. It was not worth over $300 an acre. A businessman bought some of it at $400 an acre. Everyone who knew of the sale thought this was too high and told him so. The businessman said, "No, I did not pay too much for this land. I will not graze cattle on it. I will build a huge shopping mall on it." He executed his plan. The land is easily worth a million dollars an acre today. Why this difference between $400 an acre and a million dollars an acre? It is the same land. The difference is what he did with the land. When Miss Mandy sold the land, she was selling wheat land. That is what she and her late husband did with the land. They grew wheat. What will the new owner do with this farm? He will grow wheat. He cannot justify the higher price he paid for the land because he is not changing the use of the land. This point is never remembered at farm auctions when loan officers and sidekicks are manipulating the crowds.

What we have here is a government agent—namely the loan officer of the federal land bank—going out to the countryside and talking the farmer into an irrational, uneconomical, unconscionable and stupid course of action. Let's forget the noise that occasionally emits from the plush halls of the federal land banks *that they are private*. They are not private. For some time I have mentioned this dispute on whether these banks are private or public. I have not fully answered and have let the reader use his own imagination. Now it's time to answer this question. These banks are owned, operated and financed by the U.S. government. The fact that they raise most of their money from private sources is not material. The Panama Canal Company raises most of its money privately. So does the Tennessee Valley Authority. So do many of the merchant marine shipping companies. So does the Post Office. That does not make them private.

The federal land banks are government agencies. The federal courts have this point of law before them repeatedly and have always ruled that the federal land bank system is an instrumentality of the U.S. government. The Farm Credit Act of 1971 states that these banks are federal instrumentalities and as such they need not pay local or state taxes, except for land taxes on their buildings. They are exempt from local government taxes because they are part of the U.S. Government. Yet, the government lets their officers go out into the countryside and talk the farmers into an irrational course of action.

In the history of the world, I know of only one other such instance. During the 1860s, when the U.S. was divided and fighting a Civil War over the slave question, Russia was thrown into turmoil because the Czar ordered freedom for the farmers. The Czar paid the landowners for their land and then sold the land to the peasants, taking long term mortgages. The peasant had to pay for the land that he and his family worked for centuries. This did not seem fair. A group of people in the cities went out into the countryside and talked to the peasants about this. They made continuous trips and spent years selling the peasants on the unfairness of it all. This helped undermine the confidence and trust that the peasant had in his government. These people in Russia who did this helped set the stage for the revolution that came in 1917, at which time the communists took over. Such agitators are called *narodniks* (pronounced *naw-*

rod-niks) in the Soviet Union.

That is what was done by loan officers of the federal land banks. They went out into the countryside and talked the farmers into bidding against each other, promised them huge loans, and in general encouraged some of our best farmers to plunge helplessly into debt. They are American *narodniks*.

The loan officers of the insurance companies and the small commercial banks did not participate in this tawdry practice. In fact, they abandoned the field. When I get to a review of certain counties in succeeding chapters, it will be noted that insurance companies did not compete for the farmer's business, but instead they let the federal government have the whole thing. In 1971 the Farm Credit Act was signed into law by President Nixon, and this is the year insurance companies quit loaning to farmers. From that point on the federal land banks and the FmHA totally socialized long term farm credit.

What is in the Farm Credit Act of 1971?

Among other things, this measure allowed the consolidation of the small federal land bank associations into larger geographical units, and it vastly increased the lending power of banks. There used to be a $200,000 limit on loans to a farmer, but this was removed, and the banks could loan any amount of money. Many loans in the millions have been made.

The federal land banks were allowed to make loans in towns and cities of less than 6,000 population. They could also loan to non-farmers. They were allowed to loan money to the fishing industry, which is the reason for the insolvency of the federal land bank at Seattle, Washington. The 1971 Act provided for the Fed to buy bonds and debts of the entire farm credit system. The United States Treasury was ordered to bail out the system when necessary. The Act provided that all loans should be over five years in duration, hence the system was kept out of the short term farm credit system. This is also the definition of long term credit in this book as opposed to short term of less than five years. I do not like this definition because commercial banks limit short term debts to not over one year. However, I will use the definition of *long term* of over five years as stated in the 1971 Act.

The Act also stated that all appraisal standards *shall be prescribed by the bank*, not by traditional standards under state or other national laws or the real estate industry. This is the way the system got the power to manipulate appraisals and kite them upward. A public figure in South Dakota told me that the appraisal practice was the key to the corruption of the system in South Dakota. Most of the loans the system made were on farm land that was not remotely worth what the federal land bank appraised it for. In Nebraska, an auctioneer told me that the federal land bank worked appraisals higher than any economic justification could account for. In Oklahoma, a former employee of the federal land bank stated that officials had so kited the appraisal that the bank would collapse if honest accounting and real estate standards were used. He quit the bank and took a lower paying job so that he would be in an honest environment. The idea that honesty always pays is not true. Honesty did not pay here, but he felt much better about his lower wages. His wife had to take a job to help meet family expenses.

The Farm Credit Act also provided that any member of the system could get a loan for "agricultural purposes and *other credit needs of the applicant*." Loans could now be made for rural housing, fishing gear, pool halls, bowling alleys and even a house of prostitution. You name it, they loaned on it. I will document cases in which lawyers and dentists got loans, not so they could go into farming, but so they could ride their investments in farm land into a personal fortune. Many borrowers were greedy. Many loans were made on farm land when that farm land could not gross enough to pay the interest much less other operating expenses. These operatives were making loans without the slightest reference to how they were to be repaid. The federal land banks threw money around like popcorn. And yet all of these loan officers were college graduates. It has been preached for fifty years that education is the key to solving most problems. This has not been proved to be true in this lending system.

I know of one case in which a lawyer got so many bad loans with the federal land bank of Wichita that he cost that bank over $800,000. A dentist slammed the bank with $50,000 in losses. Another lawyer cost the bank over a million dollars in losses. These people had nothing to do with farming, but they each applied for a loan and got it because he would agree to buy stock in the federal land bank on credit and thus become a member of the system. Recently a federal land bank association in Oklahoma loaned over a million dollars to a doctor on city property. This loan is now in foreclosure. This has nothing to do with farming. But it illustrates why the system is corrupt beyond redemption. And yet this is the system that brought massive amounts of credit to the wheat farmers of the high plains.

The Farm Credit Act was widely discussed in Congress between 1969 and 1971, the year it was passed. One provision speeded up the process by having a local attorney do the legal work rather then sending paperwork to the bank attorney.

These local attorneys all over the Great Plains were selected, not because they were knowledgeable about farm problems, but because they were ignorant of farm matters. Most of them knew nothing about the profitability of wheat or which end of a cow furnished the milk. They thought eggs originated in a supermarket. In one case the local manager of the federal land bank was asked why he selected a certain lawyer to represent the association since that attorney did not have a farm background and did not major in agricultural sciences. The manager said the attorney was hand-picked because he was stupid in farm matters and he was wimp enough to keep his mouth shut. This association lost money hand over fist. One of the attorneys was asked in court to state how much cash the farmer used to buy the stock in the system, and that attorney said in effect: "Why get excited about that. A farmer never uses cash. He always uses credit from the bank to buy the stock." This is in direct violation of the Farm Acts of 1916 and 1971. Yet that attorney was retained because he would go along with such foul play. He wouldn't stop these sales of stock on credit, and he wouldn't face down any other illegal or bad practices in the system. One has to conclude, sadly, that the legal profession, as hired by the federal land bank system, was for all practical purposes totally ineffective in the larger scheme of things.

As soon as this law was on the books, the farm credit system in the USDA went to work to vastly expand credit to the farmers. Any loan officer in the FmHA and the federal land bank systems who would not agree to make fast loans was encouraged to retire. If the officer failed to comply, removal became the next step. Many had criminal audits made of their management practices. Many took the hint and left. Many of these old managers were good managers. For example in Alfalfa County, Oklahoma—during the previous fifty years—the federal land bank never foreclosed a single farmer. In 1985 that bank foreclosed nineteen farmers on loans made after 1971.

Older competent loan officers were replaced by college graduates who held degrees chiefly in the field of agricultural economics. Most of these men were about twenty-two years of age. All were Republicans and from Republican families perceived to be ultra conservative. A liberal Republican was not even considered for employment. All came from farms where their fathers believed that they could make more money if they had better lines of credit, or if they got bigger. And so these young men went along with the federal land banks in the effort to vastly expand credit to farmers. The first thing that they did was to drive out all competition in the long-term credit system. Insurance companies held about 35% of the long-term farm debt in 1971. They soon found that their loans were being undermined with vast amounts of credit from the federal land banks and FmHA. This led to a high rate of defaults. As a consequence, insurance companies elected to stop loaning money to farmers. This trend was set in motion when the Farm Credit Act of 1971 was being debated in Congress. One insurance vice-president stated it this way: "There is absolutely no way that you can safely loan more than about $60,000 per one hundred sixty acres to wheat farmers. If you loan more than that, the farmer can't make money because his interest is so high. He defaults on the loan and the insurance company has no good way to get the money back. So it sues, and this makes for bad public relations. Everyone loses. The U.S. government is now going to loan many hundreds of thousands of dollars to farmers on one hundred sixty acre farms and all that they are going to have is a lot of financial losses. We will just sit back and let the government write off the losses during the next depression." And that is exactly what has happened.

The Farm Credit Act of 1971 is absolutely the worst piece of farm legislation ever to pass the U.S. Congress, if the Aiken bill that struck down parity is to be excepted. It financed a land boom unprecedented in the history of the world. It failed the wheat farmers in every way.

Its sponsor, Senator Bellmon, never borrowed from the federal land bank before 1971. But in the first year the Farm Credit Act of 1971 was in existence, he got four loans. In time he came to have over $2 million in credit from the federal land bank in Wichita. Some of these loan papers were signed in the halls of Congress itself. They were not signed in Oklahoma, where Bellmon lived and where he bought additional land.

A major problem here is that Congress is an 18th century institution, governed by an 18th century document, and uses and is governed by 18th century rules. It has fragmented its power into an 18th century committee system and in general acts like it is still in the 18th century. Its members should have fought and destroyed the Farm Credit Act of 1971. Instead they sat there with their minds on "hold" and let it pass. This represented a political compromise, and it was wrong.

The farm crisis of the 1980s became a crisis of credit and lending because no one in Congress faced up the the fact that world prices were half high enough to sustain a debt-free agriculture. It was not a crisis of crop failures. Wheat did not fail us. It was the substitution of debt for earnings that failed. The socialized financial systems of the federal government failed us, and night came to the farms of the Great Plains.

5

THE FmHA

In 1933 Congress set up the Farm Security Administration (FSA). This program was to work with poor, small farmers. It was to make loans to tenant farmers, to reduce farm tenancy, to resettle farmers and make loans to farmers when they could not get credit at any other place.

The Farm Bureau fought this measure from the start. In 1941, the U.S. went to war with Japan, Italy and Germany. The Farm Bureau used the opportunity to wage war against the Farm Security Administration. When the budget came up for review in Congress, Farm Bureau had its lobbyists attack it. They finally got the agency's employees dropped from the Civil Service system.

In 1942 the Farm Bureau renewed its attack against the system. It listed nine charges against the FSA. All of them were false. One of the charges was that the administration burdened the borrower with massive debts. This was not true then, but in the 1970s, when the Farm Credit Act and the Economy Emergency Loan Program were passed, rich farmers could borrow from FmHA and become hopelessly mired in debt. Charges leveled against FSA weren't valid then, but thirty-six years later they were on target. By that time they fit FmHA.

Another Farm Bureau charge was that the FSA used renewal notes and payment plans to disguise the fact that little or nothing was being paid on existing loans. That too was false then, but is exactly what happened in the 1970s and the 1980s. When I got to the county courthouses, I could see this clearly. The FmHA in the 1970s designed a scheme called cafeteria credit. Farmers could get as much credit as they wanted. This money would be loaned largely so that farmers could make payments at the federal land bank and mask the greater public policy being used to empty the countryside.

Another charge in the 1930s was that the program was communist dominated. The Farm Bureau may have found a sympathizer in some nook or cranny, but no one involved was ever identified as a communist. However, the charge was enough to get Congress to end the program in 1943 by refusing to appropriate money for it. Most of the staffers left for war factory jobs. This was McCarthyism before McCarthy. It shows clearly that when political mud is thrown, some of it sticks.

The Farm Bureau is a farm organization that caters to wealthy farmers and industrial counterparts. It has very high annual dues to keep out small farmers. The Farm Bureau has fought every attempt to restrict farm programs to the financial needs of agriculture. They want the wealthiest farmers to get the most from the public trough. This organization has not had a new idea in sixty-five years, and it has not been of any help to the wheat farmers of the Great Plains.

This problem illustrates the situation politicians constantly face. If a government program is restricted to people on the basis of financial need, there is little or no political support for it. But the cost is small and so it is not hard to finance. A good example is the welfare system. Few people qualify for welfare, and it has no political constituency. No one supports welfare. It is subject to constant attack. In 1970, President Nixon wanted Congress to reform the welfare system. His program was called Workfare. He tried to sell Workfare to Congress as a program that would get the "bums" and "cheats" off the welfare system. When he did this, he had on his desk a number of government investigative reports that clearly showed that most people on welfare were truly indigent, and that citizens seldom lied to get onto a program that paid a measly $135 per month, or less. Right wing fantasies of poor people in shiny new Cadillacs cruising by the welfare office notwithstanding, the overwhelming majority of welfare recipients actually need it.

Yet any program that essentially offers free money to large segments of the population soon grows extremely expensive and becomes a burden on the taxpayers. The Nixon administration allowed the FmHA to lend money, any amount of money, to farmers. These loans were available *to any farmer who claimed he had trouble getting credit elsewhere*. The policy was politically popular, of course, yet because of the sheer enormity of the sums involved, it became difficult to finance. The government constantly faces the same dilemma with Social Security. Intended for all citizens, this creation of the New Deal is enormously expensive. Generally it provides pensions for anyone over sixty-five without regard to financial need. Down the street a father and mother and their four children don't have enough to eat. What does the government do? It responds to lobbyists from retiree pressure groups, and though many older Americans legitimately need help, the current structure also doles out benefits to well-to-do elderly. Needy children must rely on a welfare system so restrictive that it works to discourage self-advancement. The contradictory values at the heart of this dilemma reflect a basic confusion in American life which must be resolved. It hinders the politicians' ability to govern, and it hurts a lot of decent people.

During Lyndon Johnson's escalation of the Vietnam War between 1964 and 1968, he placed limits on the FmHA's lending power. This was an administrative restriction, not a law. Loans were restricted to $25,000, with a few exceptions in cases of extraordinary need. As soon as Nixon took office, he lifted the ban, and farmers could borrow as much money as Congress was willing to appropriate.

When the FSA was set up under the New Deal so that benefits were limited to small or impoverished poor farmers, wealthy farmers, true to form, attacked it. Nevertheless the program did go ahead. The FSA helped farmers whose operations averaged about ten acres, providing them money to build a house and repay the loan on a long term basis. The FSA encouraged these farmers to grow all or most of their own food. One such project at Dyess, Arkansas gave a homestead to the father of singer Johnny Cash, who was raised on the farm FSA money built, like thousands of his peers. Farm camps were developed by the FSA in an effort to get migratory workers and destitute people off the streets. Showers and lodging were provided. For a good picture of life in such camps, think back to the Joad family in John Steinbeck's *The Grapes of Wrath*.

Congress officially abolished the FSA in 1943 and replaced it with the Farmers Home Administration (FmHA) in 1946. The FmHA was charged with lending money to small farmers, including tenant farmers. *No one could qualify for these loans unless he could get no credit elsewhere.* This policy excluded the wealthy farmers, who naturally waged another guerrilla war against the program, with the Farm Bureau leading the attack. Then, in 1971, the Nixon administration changed things around, announcing that it was finally okay for the FmHA to lend money to wealthy farmers, as long as they said they couldn't get credit elsewhere. If you're looking for a single distinct moment when darkness began to descend on the farms of the Great Plains, here it is.

The FmHA's enabling legislation stipulated that returning veterans must be given priority for jobs in the new agency. Though reasonable on its surface, this maneuver had the effect of excluding many former FSA employees who took jobs in the war factories. This is important to bear in mind as this account progesses. If and when the government makes a serious effort to remedy the farm crisis, the federal land bank system and the FmHA will have to be abolished; it is absolutely crucial that former employees of these agencies be barred from working in agencies that replace them. The reasons for this will be addressed later, although it doesn't require a crystal ball to know that wasted tax dollars are a large factor.

The FmHA was managed carefully during the Truman, Eisenhower, Kennedy and Johnson administrations. All of them strictly adhered to the rule that only poor and small farmers would receive loans, and that any farmer who could get any type of credit elsewhere would not get it through FmHA. WWII veterans hired to staff the FmHA, much as everyone else in the country, mainly wanted to get on with working and raising families. They did a good job.

Hindsight reveals that 1971 was a watershed year in the history of farm lending policies. Nixon and his minions crowded out the old managers. Civil Service rules offered scant protection against the ugly tactics employed by tricky Dick's henchmen. Audits were run on the offices of veteran staffers who wanted to stay, and criminal charges were threatened when the inevitable, and undoubtedly planted, irregularities turned up. Many of the older employees took the hint and retired. Many of them had accumulated over thirty years toward their pensions, since military service in WWII counted as government work in the eyes of the Civil Service. This made retirement especially attractive when compared to the prospect of continued hostility and abuse from the Nixonites.

Many of my good friends remain unhappy with Nixon over his crimes connected with the Watergate affair. They should save a few tears for the way Nixon prostituted the long-term farm credit system.

John Nance Garner, Roosevelt's vice president until 1941, used to say that a good law could be made bad by its administration, and a bad law could be made good by its administration. In other words, how a law is administered is often more important than the law itself. The FmHA's abuses of farm credit under Nixon proved this legal rule of thumb time and again. The rules were relaxed to the point where any farmer, rich or poor, sober or drunk, single or married, fatherless or fathered, drug-addicted or not, could walk into an FmHA office and get just about any amount of credit.

Moreover, loans were available for things that had little or nothing to do with farming. In Oklahoma, the FmHA gave out a loan for a pool hall. In another case it made a loan on a bowling alley. In still another case it was on a golf course. Money was doled out for a swanky housing complex in Red Willow County, Nebraska. A typical farmer, of course, could never meet the payments on such a mortgage. Only the wealthy benefited.

Appropriations for the system ballooned, and over the next few years the system grew by leaps and bounds. Bear in mind that as a division of the USDA, the FmHA enjoys the protection of the departmental umbrella from above and the Civil Service system from below. Though the Civil Service system is ordinarily thought of as a great government achievement, it was under Civil Service that the FmHA loan operators were hired. They did their dirty work under that system, and now they are protected by it. Sometimes the Civil Service only shields incompetent public office holders.

After the passage of the Farm Credit Act of 1971 and the federal land banks decided to socialize the long-term credit system available to farmers, and the new *narodiks* in the FmHA went right along with it and fell instantly into step. The FmHA is the agency that prepared the financial sledgehammer that put the insurance companies out of business. Until this basic trend developed the federal land banks were unable to drive the insurance companies out of the business.

Here is how this corrupt system developed. Insurance companies were financing the long-term credit needs of farmer-borrowers. The relationship was mutually profitable to both. Along came the federal land bank system. It decided it wanted the farmers' business. Land banks agreed to drop their interest rates half a percentage point below what insurance companies offered. The insurance companies retaliated by dropping their rate a full percentage point. The farmers stayed with the insurance people. There was no way the federal land bank system could get to the farmer except to pay off the insurance company and take a first mortgage on the farmer's land as required by the act of Congress of 1916.

In politics, what goes on in the halls of Congress or the state legislature is important, but what goes on in the corridors is of far greater importance. The same can be said of the courtroom. What goes on there is important, but what goes on in the corridors of the courthouse is often of much greater importance.

Somewhere between the federal land bank system and the county office of the FmHA, a scheme was concocted whereby the FmHA would "overdose" the farmer with credit. This would destroy the mortgages of the insurance firms. To do this the FmHA developed the idea that the farmer knows best how much credit he needs and others should not attempt to dictate to him what he needs. Parenthetically, it must be noted that any screwball scheme for papering over faltering parity was acceptable in academic circles. Professors and extension personnel iterated and reiterated to farmers the necessity to get big or get out. None of the great minds accepted the fact that international prices were too low, therefore the problem had to be credit supported cash flow. Therefore the idea of cafeteria credit came into being.

In a food cafeteria, the customer takes the food he wants and leaves the rest. The farmer, like the cafeteria customer, could look around and take the credit he wanted and leave the rest. In practice this meant the farmer could go to FmHA and get a line of credit. He could then draw on it to his heart's content. When he was totally obligated to the FmHA, that agency stepped in and demanded that all of the money received from the sales of crops be brought to its office so that FmHA could manage his financial affairs.

It is a crime to avoid paying the FmHA by spending the money elsewhere. This crime is called *illegal diversion of assets*. Insurance companies can't charge crime if their loans are not repaid. Once the FmHA got all of the farmer's income into its office, payments were stopped to the insurance company, and the insurance company then was presented with a number of very bad options. It could do nothing, and the state insurance commissioner would begin to see that the company had a lot of bad investments. The insurance commissioner could increase the reserves that the company was required to post. The insurance company could sue the farmer and this would make the farmer and his friends mad. They, in turn, would never consider buying insurance from that company. This company got a bad reputation with the public. Or, the insurance company could get out of the field of long-term credit to farmers.

Every insurance company opted out. *They simply left the field.* This left only the federal land bank system and the FmHA.

A stark lesson remains. No one should be given credit beyond the ability to pay. Before that time comes, credit extensions should stop. However, FmHA did not have to raise money outside of the congressionally approved budgets, and so it could lend and lend and lend. I clocked one farmer getting $575,000 on one 160 acre farm. This represents a debt of $3,593 per acre based on a third mortgage. An insurance company would not have loaned over $350 per acre, which is less than one-tenth as much, and would have insisted on a first mortgage. When the government raised interest rates on this farmer up to 11%, the interest bill for one year was $63,250. This farm had about thirty acres of fairly good wheat land and thirty acres of the sorriest land you can imagine and one hundred acres in grass. The grass was not very good. Two big creeks ran through the farm, which made it expensive to fence. High waters during rainstorms would wash out the fences. This farmer could not gross over $6000 on this farm. His interest expense alone was $63,250 each year. Each bushel of wheat this farmer produced cost the taxpayers over $65.

How does such a farmer live? He can't. He vegetates.

Cafeteria credit has been used all over the Great Plains. It has impoverished farmers more rapidly than the international prices that govern trade channels. Thus it appears that the government has violated the spirit of one of its own criminal laws, namely the law against peonage.

After the Civil War, the 13th Amendment was passed. It prohibited slavery, and it immediately was ratified by the states and became a part of the Constitution. One of its sections held that Congress could pass appropriate legislation to enforce the amendment. Congress made it a crime to hold or use a slave. The South was utterly prostrated by the Civil War and after freedom came the slaves left the plantation en mass. Often the former slave had no place to go and nothing to live on. In time the South developed the share-tenancy system. The landlord or former slaveowner would rent land to a former slave and take one-third of the crop for this use of the land. The renter or former slave would get one-third for his labor. The other third would go to either the former slave owner or to the black depending on who furnished machinery, seeds, the horse or mule to power the operation.

The share-tenancy system fastened itself quickly on the South and it became a great evil. The former slave was often in debt to the landowner for food, and clothing, and rent on the cabin while the crop was growing. After harvest, the former slave would settle up with the landlord. Frequently, his bills at the plantation store exceeded the value of his share of the crop. At times the tenant would settle this matter by moving out in the night. Often settlement day was also moving day.

In time southern legislatures provided that one could not leave the employment of another if a debt was owed. These laws were called Black Codes, and they went a long way towards the reintroduction of slavery. Actual ownership was not involved, but the black would be faced with criminal charges if he left the plantation. Federal courts overturned these laws and Congress made it a crime to hold another human in peonage if a debt was owed. But the share-tenancy system continued. The old plantation owner would follow the black to his new home and visit with the landowner. Often the black would find it difficult to get more land to farm.

President Harry S Truman was a good student of history. He understood the evils of the share-tenancy system. He believed that the federal government could have prevented a century of abuse and suffering by both the ex-slave and the ex-slave owner if the government helped both to get started at the end of the Civil War. After WWII, when friends and ex-enemies were prostrated in Europe, Truman did not allow that mistake to be repeated. His administration set up the Marshall Plan. History does not repeat itself when a student of history leads the nation. History repeats itself only when political leaders are illiterate about history.

After the Civil War the federal government made an effort to protect the black, but the economics of cotton growing was not too profitable and the landlord also had his problems. The government tried to investigate complaints, but there was no person or agency detailed to handle the job until 1908, at which time Theodore Roosevelt formed the Federal Bureau of Investigation. Its task was to investigate the complaints of the black to see if they were held in economic peonage. In time peonage was stopped.

Now the federal government is doing what the old ex-slave owner did. Perhaps the federal government is not in violation of its anti-peonage laws because that law was directed against private individuals. However, that does not make present acts of federal officials desirable or moral. The borrower from the FmHA is required to take all of his income to the local county office of the system, and there the local county supervisor or his employee will decide what is to be paid. The government is paid first. The rest, if any, is then used to pay other bills and to support the farmer. There is often not enough to go around. When this is the case, the farmer is faced with a difficult economic choice. He can pay some and forget the rest. The farmer has a saying for this: "Put the grease on the wheel that squeaks the loudest." If a creditor is hollering loudly, the farmer gives him a payment.

The annual settlement day of the FmHA reminds one of the annual settlement day in the South after the Civil War. The old black man stood in the plantation store, cap in hand, while the owner figured up his bills. The black man was short-changed many times. In many cases he was robbed. Interest was often 50%. The same is now going on in the local offices of the FmHA.

Interest on the FmHA debt can be changed at the whim of

the person who operates the system. The farmer has nothing to say about it. The FmHA computes the interest and sees to it that the agency is paid first. Often little or nothing is left for the farmer and his family to live on, or to get the crop out the next year. There have been so many complaints that the FmHA has created an appeals system whereby a creditor of the farmer is given a short hearing before the county supervisor. If he does not get a proper payment on his bill, the creditor can appeal to the state office of the FmHA. There he is given even less consideration. In twenty years I have never seen a small businessman get anything. FmHA always advises the businessman that he can bring his attorney to these hearings, but employees of the system warn that it has a "chilling effect" on the claim if an attorney actually appears. FmHA simply refuses all bills presented by a creditor of a farmer.

I was at a farm institute at Oklahoma City in the summer of 1989, and I mentioned to about twelve other practitioners in the field that I never saw a bill paid through the FmHA appeals system, and they all agreed that they had not either. After a sale, FmHA has the farmer's money and it is not going to give it up. The appeal system is a legal sham. I also mentioned that a bill of $400 owed by the farmer to a village blacksmith was an important item in the life of the blacksmith and they all agree that such a bill is important. But he is never paid.

Creditors in the small village where the farmer lives often do not get paid, and they are concerned about how far they can take collection remedies against the federal government. Since they are not paid they retaliate by refusing further credit to the farmer. The farmer then loses credit for fuel for the tractor and truck, and gone is the credit for blacksmithing and welding. Lost is the credit for fertilizers.

FmHA requires all wheat be taken to the nearest elevator and stored in the name of the farmer. It cannot be sold without prior permission from the FmHA. There is thus no seed for the farmer to put in another crop. Even if the farmer gets seed credit for a year or two, FmHA takes all of the crop income. Sooner or later credit dries up, and the farmer gets no seed to put in another crop.

Meetings sometimes are held in the county offices of the FmHA, and the farmer may get a small dribble of money to buy repairs for his machinery. Because he can't get help from his local suppliers he has to go to the next village. There he is not welcome because businessmen know that he would not be there if he properly used credit in his home village. And so the work is not done and the supplies, fuel, and seed are not sold to him until there is cash on the counter. The farmer then has the increased cost of transporting himself and the seed, fuel, etc., from the distant village to his farm. In parts of the western Great Plains, the next village may be forty miles away.

The farmer and his family experience sickness, much like anyone else. FmHA does not want the farmer to spend money on medical bills if by doing so he becomes delinquent in paying the agency. So the farmer goes to a doctor and hospital and gets treatment, and the bill is charged. When the doctor and hospital want to be paid, the farmer in effect says, "I can't. The FmHA has me tied up." The doctor and hospital mildly but firmly suggest that the farmer take his medical business elsewhere, and he does so. In time he comes to owe many doctors and hospitals and lawsuits are filed against him. They want payment, but here comes the FmHA to threaten criminal action if anyone bothers its security. The mortgage papers cover everything, including the farmer's clothes, pots and pans.

The local office of the FmHA at Guthrie, Oklahoma once asked the Attorney General of the U.S. to sue hospitals and doctors who wanted and needed to be paid. If the hospital is in a rural area, it may be offered loans from the FmHA. Then the FmHA may refuse to allow the farmer to pay his bills to that hospital. Rural hospitals are closing all over the Great Plains. One of the reasons for this is that the farmer is so deeply in debt to the FmHA he can't pay the hospital, and by law he is required to pay only the FmHA. In turn the hospital cannot repay the FmHA. The whole thing goes round and round and round, like characters in a Marx Brothers movie. Rural areas are losing hospitals and doctors at an alarming rate. If this is not stopped, very shortly the federal government is going to own most of the rural hospitals in the high plains. We will have a fully socialized health care system in rural areas without public discussion.

FmHA can bring criminal charges against a farmer if he does not cooperate in every way. No private business or insurance company can field such collection tactics.

One farm wife near Ringwood, Oklahoma, explained it this way: "We get $200 a month to live on. All the rest is taken by the FmHA. How can a man and wife and three children live on $200 per month. Our house rent alone is $175 a month. They just want us to do something crooked so they can throw my husband in jail." This marriage ended in divorce because the wife had to get free. She filed bankruptcy and now is the sole support of the three children. She works in a school lunch room.

In another case in South Dakota the farmer was given $150 per month to live on by the FmHA. The fuel bill during the winter was more than this. The wife is working somewhere and my informant did not want me to probe further because if it got back to the FmHA, they would take her salary. I agreed to not probe further.

One farm wife near McCook, Nebraska, explained it to me this way: "The FmHA just loves to get the farmer and his family by the hangyank, and take his money. We are secretly getting food supplies from the local food bank at the church. They don't know this and please don't tell." I won't.

A farmer near Strasburg, North Dakota, told me that his brother had a FmHA loan and the only way he could get loose was to file bankruptcy. The brother is now supporting his family by doing odd jobs in town.

A farmer near Harper, Kansas told me that the FmHA loved to get the farmer on a treadmill and then keep him there. The family of this farmer was forced to take food to him. A book could be written about the evil that the FmHA has used against its borrowers.

In spite of this, a greater evil is the guerrilla war that the

FmHA has conducted against small rural banks. These banks are owned by someone in the village and often the banker's entire property is tied up in the bank. The bank cannot be moved. Many of the villages across the Great Plains have suffered declining population for more than fifty years, and the local banks are trying to do just about everything to hold people in town. If anyone needs credit at the local bank, he could probably get it—that is until the FmHA started to lend. The bank and the FmHA then try to compete for the business of the farmer. FmHA wins most of these contests. Many village bankers have learned the hard way that it is not profitable for them to lend to a farmer who is also a customer of the FmHA. MANY VILLAGE BANKERS HAVE A POLICY THAT THEY WILL NOT LEND TO A FARMER WHO GETS CREDIT FROM THE FmHA, and this leads to a drying up of credit for the farmer. Once he gets credit from the FmHA, he is there from then on. The local banker won't have anything to do with him.

One banker in Nebraska explained that when he loaned money to a farmer, along came the FmHA and made a loan to the same farmer. The bank lost out. "We will not loan to a farmer who deals with the FmHA," he said.

I should note, nevertheless, that the farmer who deals with the FmHA is often referred to that office by someone. In about 40% of the cases, he is referred to the FmHA by an employee of the federal land bank system, and in 40% of the cases a small town banker refers him there, and in 20% of the cases he is referred by a neighbor or relative.

But in at least 40% of the cases, I believe, he is referred by the village banker who is mad at the FmHA over some loss the bank experienced a few months ago. The banker knows everybody in town. He knows where every nickel is hidden. He knows that this farmer drinks too much, won't pay his bills, beats his wife, makes over a red-haired divorcee down the street, won't go to church, and in general he is a big loser. The banker deliberately refers him to the FmHA and then laughs his fool head off when the losses pour in on the government people. All of this would be funny except that you and I as taxpayers are paying the interest on the national debt from which appropriations are made to support FmHA. We are not paying for the money the FmHA loses because the government is going into debt for that amount, but we are paying the interest on the national debt. This should be enough to stop us from laughing. But why is this system allowed to operate? I suggest that the only way to improve this system is to abolish the FmHA.

In the early days, the FmHA could deal with a farmer only if he could not find credit elsewhere. This is now a standing joke because the loan shills took over during the Nixon administration. Under these *narodniks*, almost anyone could get a loan from the FmHA. I documented a case in Oklahoma where a farmer got a million dollar loan from the FmHA. He was the owner of twenty-three wheat farms.

In another case in Oklahoma, a man (notice I said man) in the eastern part of the state got a loan from the FmHA for over $7.3 million on 1,000 acres, which means each acre was mortgaged for over $7,300. At 11% interest, each acre had an annual interest cost of over $803. This land was too poor to grow wheat and had a fair market value of only $100 per acre, or one-eighth of its annual interest cost. This case is in federal court at Muskogee, Oklahoma and the man wants to pay $107,720 and get a full release from the government on a scaledown as required by the Farm Credit Act of 1987. Notice I said *man*. This person is a former state legislator. He is also an attorney who is trying to gamble his way into a fortune. He is not a farmer.

You can also get a loan if you have suffered a natural disaster. Due to a drought, every farmer in North Dakota and much of South Dakota and Nebraska can qualify for a loan from the FmHA. Nevertheless, 50% of the farmers still in business have no debts at all. An additional 25% will not have anything to do with the FmHA even if they qualify. This leaves only about 25% of our farmers who are in trouble. Still, this is a human disaster beyond comprehension.

A farm wife near Blackwell, Oklahoma said she honestly

believes that the federal government is making it as hard as possible for farmers. She also said that she knows the county supervisor of the FmHA, and that he was solely interested in helping himself to a large salary and other perks. A federal job on the Great Plains pays much more than private industry. Many of the officers of the FmHA have this attitude. Some few do not. In South Dakota one county supervisor of FmHA became so distressed over what was being done to the farmers that he killed his wife and children, and then drove to his office and committed suicide. But such official concern is rare. Misery and death flicker across the Great Plains in the wake of the collection tactics of the FmHA. Death by farm accidents is no longer the leading cause of a violent end among Oklahoma farmers. Suicide is now the leading cause. Such deaths are not reported in the newspapers as suicides. Usually the papers report that the farmer was thirty-one and that he died suddenly and unexpectedly. Technically, this is correct, but it does not tell the whole story.

I heard of one case in Oklahoma but refused to investigate it. The rumor mill had it that a farmer went to welfare and got food stamps. He sold them to his mother who was drawing Social Security to get money to pay utility bills and then went to a food bank at a church and got food for his family. This can only be labeled a rumor because I refused to investigate it. The federal government has a law that makes it a crime to know of a crime and not report it. This is called the "snitch" law. I don't know that a crime has been committed, but then I don't want to know. So this is a rumor. I never checked it out.

In Kingfisher County, Oklahoma, a young farmer went to the FmHA and got a loan for $110,000 to buy a farm that was all in grass. There was no wheat land on it because the soil was too poor to grow wheat. The interest rate was 5 1/4%. When FmHA started having collection problems and loan losses in about 1983, the agency raised the interest rates on many of the farm loans. His interest rate was raised to 11%, or more than double the old rate. The farmer could not pay. Harassing tactics became so stressful that his wife took their child and left. They now live in a distant state. This marriage was destroyed by the collection tactics of the federal government. The farmer refused to pay anything and refused to work. FmHA is thus presented with a sit-down strike. Only farm foreclosure by the FmHA can settle this case. This farmer was able to and did make the payments when the interest was low, but not when it was doubled.

The list of hardships I have checked into is endless. The rule that only FmHA can tell the farmer where his money goes must be stopped. Our government is impoverishing a generation of farmers. A private insurance company or a commercial bank cannot do any of these things. They are required to follow state laws which provide protection for the debtor, but these laws do not apply to the federal government.

Another bad feature of the policies and practices of the FmHA is the fact that the agency will always support the federal land bank system in collecting from farmers. If a farmer cannot pay these banks, he is encouraged by bank officials to go to the FmHA and get a loan to pay the banks. This lending policy continues until someone up in the USDA squeals and stops it in the case of that particular farmer. What such loans do is to transfer the financial liability for loans made by the shills in the banks to the federal taxpayers. We should always remember that most of the money that the federal land bank uses is raised privately through Wall Street. Little comes from the federal treasury. In the case of FmHA, the treasury is financing loans, and this money then goes to the banks. There it is wasted on riotous business overhead, including imported limousines for officers and attorneys. Some, of course, goes to repay the bondholders of the federal land bank system. It is unsound credit and banking practice to borrow money to cover an annual payment, and this is a sure sign of a serious financial problem. These bankers and the FmHA ignore sound credit and banking practices. This can last only as long as the government is willing to underwrite the system. Good business people cannot operate in such a financial climate.

Another bad feature of loans from the FmHA is that they let

a farmer make a purchase of land when he does not qualify for a loan from that bank. Likely, the farmer is so deeply in debt he cannot come up with the 15% downstroke equity required.

Remember, the federal land bank system was restricted by Congress to loans of not more the 85% of appraised value in 1971, and many times the farmer cannot come up with the 15% he has to have to complete the loan. The banks would send that farmer to FmHA for the down payment. In effect, this farmer buys a farm with no cash of his own. He has 100% financing by the government. Many such loans are now in default.

FmHA also encouraged the farmer to buy expensive machinery and registered cattle. Many of these loans were made in excess of any possibility of repayment. Loan officers would drive out into the countryside to see the farmer. They encouraged him to think big, to borrow big and to plunge into debt. In far too many cases farmers did just that. They plunged. I have documented a case in which a farmer was making a fairly good living growing wheat by using old machinery. His cattle operation involved grade cattle rather than registered. He made money every year. The flim-flam con artist from the FmHA encouraged him to go into debt to the tune of $475,000. A complete new line of machinery was purchased. All his Okie cattle were sold for hamburger and registered animals were bought to replace them. The loan officer believed that this was the correct management technique. This farmer went bankrupt. A better and more sensible plan would have been to loan this farmer a strictly limited amount of money such as, say, $25,000, which was the limit during much of Lyndon Johnson's administration. The farmer could have bought a good registered bull and several registered mother cows from another herd. In a period of seven to ten years, this farmer could have changed his operation from a grade or cull line of cattle to a registered herd. At the same time he could have made enough to repay the government on the loan of $25,000 and keep enough for a decent living for his family. But the loan shills would not do this. They always insisted on the best—the best machinery, the best cattle, whatever. They wanted to make the loan for a huge operation. A farmer could get credit to buy one hundred cows, but not for five.

I discussed this with a tax counselor in Howard, South Dakota one day, and he said the worst problem of the government around there was loaning huge sums of money to young farmers. This was done several times. Sums of $500,000 and even more were loaned. A young wheat farmer would buy one hundred milk cows, build a new milking barn and lavishly equip it and start out as a dairy farmer. Our nation is producing too much milk as it is, at least in terms of the colored water and 2% milk we drink, and so he would be producing a product that others will not want or cannot consume. Also as a wheat farmer, he knew little or nothing about dairying. He never once doctored a sick milk cow through a bad case of mastitis.

A farmer is a person with a collection of many skills. He is a mechanic, financial expert, seedman, repairman, handyman, animal doctor, etc. But many of our wheat farmers have no skills in doctoring dairy cattle. So he calls the veterinarian and runs up huge bills. Dairy farmers work very hard. There is no such thing as a vacation. They must be present to milk the cows twice a day about twelve hours apart. Then the barn and the milk shed have to be cleaned and sterilized. Flies and other insects must be kept out at all times. Why loan half of a million dollars to such a young farmer who does not know what he is getting into? It would be much better to loan $25,000 and let him buy six milk cows and gradually build up the herd as he learns the trade of a dairyman. But our advisors are incapable of thinking small. Only the big will survive, the college experts say. This has been preached for fifty years, even though it is clearly wrong. The big are not doing well on the Great Plains either.

If this current financial crisis on the farms means anything it is the bankruptcy of USDA policy to the effect that only big is best. For example, I documented the cases of all wheat farmers in a federal land bank association in Oklahoma, people who owned twenty or more wheat farms. There were four such farmers in 1981. Today there are only two and one is struggling to stay afloat financially. The other two have filed bankruptcy. This represents a financial casualty rate of 50%. Our medium-size and small farmers are not suffering such a high rate of loss. So big is not necessarily better or more likely to survive. Big may be an early skid into financial oblivion. But still the government favors the big operator.

The government will loan one farmer $500,000 but refuses to loan another $15,000. This is wrong. The object of FmHA between 1946 to 1971 was to help the small, helpless and poor farmer, particularly the tenant. Rich and big farmers were expected to get their financing from private enterprise. They did not have their front feet in every government trough in existence. When we go back to that original program, we will find that it still works.

At Glen Elder, Kansas, I visited with a farmer who said that the big problem there was the government loaning large sums of money to farmers who wanted to get their sons into the business of farming. The government would pour out the money and the farmer and his sons went broke. I know of a heart-breaking case in Oklahoma. I played basketball and baseball against this farmer in the 1940s when we went to adjoining high schools. He married soon after leaving school in 1950 and started to grow wheat. He accumulated one farm while I was in the army during the Korean War and another by the time I was out of college. Then starting in 1975 he bought three more farms using loans from the federal land bank system and the FmHA. These loans totaled more than a million dollars. He did this to help his sons get started in farming. He and his sons are all broke today and this farmer has only the clothes on his back to show for thirty-nine years of day and night toil on a wheat farm.

I have documented a case near Jet, Oklahoma where a father retired at age sixty-five in 1975 and turned the wheat farming operation over to his son. The son started to borrow from the FmHA and the federal land bank, and is broke and in bankruptcy today. The old farmer, at seventy-nine years of age, came out of retirement and is back operating his wheat farms, using the old equipment and machinery that he had when he retired about fifteen years earlier, and he is making money. The money is given to the son to use for support for his children. The old farmer is making money and is supporting the next two generations of his family. He and his wife live on Social Security. No one would listen to his story and so I recorded it so you can hear him.

The federal land bank and the FmHA would loan money to a wheat farmer to build a mansion, but not a cent for a modest but comfortable home. A farmer in Oklahoma inherited a farm and the federal land bank loaned him $175,000 to build a mansion. It was a six bedroom house plush in every respect. This farmer wanted to invite all of his friends and neighbors in to see this but he did not want them to see the old family couch. He wanted something fancier. So this young wheat farmer borrowed $22,000 from a small loan company that loans money on nothing but furniture. At the house-warming party everyone marveled over the farmer's good fortune. Less than a year later, he started to borrow money from the FmHA.

A few miles away, a young wheat farmer needed a decent house for his family. He and his wife shared their lives with four children, and they were uncomfortable in their one bedroom shack. The young farmer went to his father and told him about the situation. The father agreed to give him an acre of land upon which to build a new house. The farmer, his three brothers and their father tore down several old buildings and got most of the lumber that they needed to build the new house. They spent several weeks pulling nails and placing the various sizes of lumber in appropriate stacks at the new location. The word soon got around in the small village that this young farmer was going to build a house for his family. On the day the foundation was to be dug, over thirty men from the local church showed up and helped. Their labor was donated. They charged nothing and the young farmer got the benefit of their labor. On the first day they dug the foundation, set up forms, mixed the concrete and poured the foundation. When one worker tired on the job, two more were there to take his place. At the end of three weeks the house was build and completed except for laying carpets inside and doing some trim work. The loan shill from FmHA came out several times during the three week period, and was he unhappy. The young farmer limited his cash outlays to not over $15,000. This young FmHA shill wanted him to build a five bedroom house, with sauna, steam bath, a hot tub, and outdoor swimming pool. The latter would be disguised in government reports as a fire prevention device.

The young farmer stuck to his guns. He could not pay for extravagances and in the end he used only $11,000 of the $15,000 allocated. To say that this loan shill was in a "backslide" condition is to put it too mildly. He was outraged that this farmer would not plunge further into debt. But the young farmer absolutely refused. His new house was a sturdily constructed home, the type that wheat farmers can afford and can pay for. The whole community around him got involved in the project. The women in the church served dinner on the grounds each work day.

Which of these two farmers do you think paid for his home? The young farmer who borrowed $175,000 to build a mansion, or the farmer who borrowed $11,000? Of course this is easy to answer. The farmer with the modest home has long since paid for it. The other farmer went to the FmHA the first year after he build his mansion because he could not meet the first payment to the federal land bank. He borrowed over $575,000 from FmHA and has been in bankruptcy for several years. He and his family are huddled in a one bedroom shack in an adjoining village and live on food stamps and hand outs from a church.

This is the way our government runs its financial business. Is there any reason to wonder why night came to the farms of the Great Plains?

INTERLUDE

INTERLUDE

AS NIGHT CAME TO THE FARMERS of the Great Plains, and farmers sought to maintain cash flow with borrowed money, unseen forces moved obliquely in the background as if to make wheat farming a sunset operation. Volga German wheat farmers in Kansas once called Woodrow Wilson *der schlechte* Wilson— "the evil Wilson"—because many of them understood that for 100 years the nation would suffer the consequences attached to an income tax, lowered tariffs, a Federal Reserve, a foundation plaything for the rich, and other assaults on the Constitution.

For mischief that is certain to haunt the American nation until well after 2050, one has to examine the Truman administration. Truman supported and signed the Administration Procedures Act during his first term. This law absolved Congress from handling the real job of governing. Henceforth the elected officials had only to pass enabling legislation and hand off to bureau people the task of creating rules and regulations, which they have done ever since, not by the page, but by the pound and ton.

The single action taken by Truman that will haunt his name for all time was the creation in the U.S. of an entity now known as the GATT negotiations (General Agreement on Tariffs and Trade). Its function—as far as agriculture is concerned—is to remove parity from the lexicon of acceptable economic thought, and to install diplomatic or commercial leverage as the real government for international trade. Farm organizations have never understood the grammar of the subject, and lawmakers have remained largely ignorant of how Truman was ill served by certain advisors.

To understand all this, one must go back to the end of WWII. The stabilization measure that governed WWII was written so that it would expire two years after the end of the war. The war could be declared over either by Congress or by Presidential Proclamation. Truman in fact took that step that ended the war on the last day of 1946. This meant that Congress had to face the knotty problem of parity because the WWII loan measure would expire at the end of 1948.

It was known, of course, that parity prices cost nothing. Because of the multiplier that stood between parity prices and national income, maintenance of farm prices at 100% of parity not only cost nothing, it supported the national earned income, and it did not increase the percentage of income spent on food during the decade of the 1940s.

Unfortunately the experts who wiggled their way into government had other visions. They were promoting a world wheat agreement which would establish a floor at $1.10 a bushel at the end of five years. This $1.10 price was approximately 50% of parity. Implemented, it would cut farm income in half and drop national earned income on a ratio 1:7, and open the nation to fantastic debt expansion.

Visiting with Harry Truman during his post-presidential years, the publisher of *Acres U.S.A.* and this book established that Truman understood all of this, but was fenced in by a constant threat of his vetoes being over-ridden in 1948. By June of that year it had become apparent that the Agriculture Committee of the House would not report out a long-range farm program. It became the judgment of the Committee, Chairman Hope said, to report out a bill that continued 90% price supports through loans, purchases and methods other than direct payments to farmers. And the House voted to accept this judgment with no more than three Representatives on record against the measure.

Then came the Aiken bill out of the Senate with its provision for 60 to 90% of parity for agriculture. The measure was written so that it would not go into effect for eighteen months, or until January 1, 1950. The time table became all important. A Republican convention had been scheduled for Philadelphia, June 20. And the Republicans dominating the 80th Congress had promised a long-range farm program, a point that stuck like undigested bone in the throats of the weary lawmakers. But the conferees refused to agree "under any circumstances" to a long-range program, any part of which would take effect as early as January 1, 1949.

That is why the Senate passed a bill that called for 60 to 90% of parity. As a sop to get House members to go along, the bill would not take effect immediately. House members could vote for it, and in turn have full parity accepted for the next year.

The conferees, Democrats and Republicans alike, Congressman Harold Cooley noted, objected to "having the measure rammed down our throats." So when the conferees found the bill too obnoxious, the politicians became horrified. "After secret meetings, and no doubt because of one member's unwillingness to surrender his convictions or to compromise his conscientious views, Congressman Reid F. Murray of Wisconsin resigned and another was appointed in his place."

Congressman Steven Pace of Georgia objected to the Aiken bill's ten year moving average. He objected to this obvious move to abandon the parity principle. "When the Aiken bill becomes effective a year and a half hence, the farmer will suffer a reduction in his support price. Therefore he will be hit twice." Nevertheless the question was taken, and the conference report was agreed to, 147 to 70 upon division of the House.

Two additional developments backgrounded the arrival of GATT. Franklin D. Roosevelt did not trust the Council on

Foreign Relations, and during his term of office he allowed few CFR members into his administration. When Truman took office, the gate was kicked wide open. CFR members were literally "gifted" the government, and they have been there in force ever since, and now exercise proprietorship over the presidency. Their bag—since the CFR was founded during the Wilson era— was free international trade.

Thus the seeming contradiction of the Aiken bill on the books and an administration dedicated to the proposition that the measure should not take effect. This dilemma was solved when USDA Secretary Charles E. Brannan appeared before a joint meeting of the Senate and House Agriculture Committees on April 7, 1949 to tell how Truman's promise could be kept and the CFR types made happy at the same time. And with that appearance, the Brannan Plan came into being. Briefly, the idea was for the government to pay in cash what the internationally manipulated market failed to provide. Unstated was the fact that an agency under the protective wing of the presidency would proceed to dismantle government subsidies via international agreement, thus burning down any retreat to parity, even if farmers and the nation woke up. That agency is now known as GATT.

It has always been realized that the harsh realities of free international trade cannot be endured without complaint by the farmers and workers involved. Always, there have been efforts to buffer the effects of debilitating foreign trade. Except during the Irish potato famine of 1846-1848, the British were not so hard hearted that they would endure mass starvation in homage to free trade, hence the corn laws and the countless measures invoked to alleviate the worst effects of a bankrupt idea.

The annihilation of American parity made it politically necessary to buffer the effects for the immediate future. Thus the hodge-podge of subsidy programs that came to punctuate the death rattle of the American farm. All the post-Eisenhower programs were invoked to keep outmigration just low enough and just high enough to keep revolution from breaking out in the countryside.

But the authors of public policy—that is, the shills for the international traders—never once abandoned their objective, namely reducing the buying power of the American dollar so that world disparities could be played off against each other to enrich the favored few.

GATT was set up in 1948, the very year Congress passed its pilot parity-breaking farm bill, the Aiken measure. In time twenty-three nations joined this program for the purpose of impoverishing the world for the benefit of a few, namely lenders hard on the hunt for great debt potentials. The immediate objective of GATT was to remove the buffers against instant economic relief by annihilating all of the steps individual nations might take to protect their own from the ravages of trade flow. This trade flow was based on the lowest common denominator price available in trade channels. Usually it meant six to ten cent an hour labor. Ultimately, by treaty, the several GATT rounds hoped to take away from Congress the right to set farm policy.

GATT's leaders have not had an easy time of it, even though U.S. presidents and USDA secretaries have been willing to sell their clients down the river. Except for Texas, not one State Department of Agriculture has even tried to inform its farmers of the consequences inherent in successes of the GATT rounds.

Understandably, the nations of Europe balked at the GATT equation for free international trade. Farmers have demonstrated effectively against the nostrums of the annointed undertakers for American agriculture. The Europeans see their own agriculture debased and killed off under GATT auspices. They see their food supply in the hands of foreign sources—ironically, also in the hands of starving Third World nations. They recall how The Netherlands suffered starvation during the last months of WWII because too much of the food supply was imported. They do not want to paint their countries into that same corner again.

It is the above climate of opinion GATT seeks to overcome so that the free international trade theory period can enjoy its finest hour. This "finest hour" is being presented as a self-evident truth, always without a single reference to the observed facts of the situation.

GATT business and rule making is done through multinational negotiations called "rounds." The current round, styled the Uruguay Round, began in 1986 at Punta del Este, Uruguay. The agenda includes further reduction of trade barriers and expansion of GATT rules to cover an additional fifteen trade categories (including agriculture, trade in services, intellectual property rights and trade related investment measures) and new rules for settling trade disputes.

In fact GATT is a Trojan horse. Presidents from Kennedy on forward to Bush have viewed GATT as a mechanism for making an end run around a more sensitive Congress. The GATT promoters remember how Franklin D. Roosevelt upgraded Woodrow Wilson's "freedom of the high seas" euphemism into Reciprocal Trade Agreements. Using this new nomenclature, Roosevelt was able to elude the Constitutional requirement for Senate ratification of treaties. GATT is more ambitious. It relies on ratification by a subservient Congress for the purpose of ridding the nation of its farm problem.

Wisconsin State Farmer was forced to point out that not even Jim Hightower could reverse the direction of farm policy after GATT ratification. In fact it was Hightower publication of a GATT fact sheet that brought the authors of frustration economics up fighting from their chairs. Here, in part and in abstract form are some of the paragraphs the Texas Department of Agriculture circulated shortly before negotiator Carla Hills and then USDA Secretary Clayton Yeutter ran into a European stone wall.

It is a fact that the Reagan administration wanted to use GATT to eliminate farm programs it did not support. U.S. Trade Representative Carla Hills stated this intention clearly in a letter to the government of El Salvador. She assured the Salvadoran government that the current administration was "pursuing the elimination of the U.S. sugar program through the agricultural negotiations in the Uruguay Round."

In October 1989, Hills and Yeutter outlined a U.S. proposal to GATT. The plan covered four areas of agricultural trade: import access, export competition, internal support, and sanitary and phytosanitary measures. The Bush administration proposed . . .

1. *Elimination of import quotas by converting quotas to tariffs, which would then be gradually reduced to zero or near-zero.* All quantity based import control measures, such as Section 22 of the farm bill and Senator Lloyd Bentsen's Meat Import Act of 1979, would be lifted. This would mean unlimited imports of beef, veal, mutton, goat meat, dairy products, cotton, peanuts and sugar into the U.S.

2. *Elimination of all export subsidies over a five year phase out period, except for bona fide food aid.* This included the U.S. Export Enhancement Program (EEP), export credit guarantees and marketing loans.

3. *Removal of GATT Article XI 2(a) and 2(c). Article XI 2(a).* This allows nations to restrict food exports in times of local shortage or famine. Restrictions of food exports in times of shortage or crisis are more important than ever for developing nations. Often today, large portions of their agriculture sectors are controlled by foreign corporations which grow produce exclusively for export. If Article XI 2(a) is removed, a nation in crisis might be unable to direct these companies to alter their farming practices, or their sales to meet the nation's domestic needs, even on a short-term basis. Article XI 2(c) permits each country to impose import quotas on agricultural products as long as a domestic supply management program is in place. Also, the U.S. proposal would ban export taxes on raw materials. These taxes have generated funds which have allowed many developing nations, Brazil and Argentina, for instance, to construct processing industries.

4. *Reduction or elimination of all domestic price-support policies.* This would include CCC loans, deficiency payments, input subsidies (federally subsidized irrigation water; advantageous federal grazing fees; seed, fuel and fertilizer subsidies, electric power, some market-promotion programs, inter-

national marketing assistance and credit subsidies such as reduced interest FmHA loans. The proposal would "cap" spending levels for conservation programs, disaster assistance, domestic food aid, some marketing programs, research and extension, resource retirement programs and some food reserve programs.

5. *Global harmonization of food safety and health standards on food imports.* Authority for setting standards in such areas as pesticide residues, veterinary drug residues, and environmental contaminants in imported food would be delegated to an international scientific body called the Codex Alimentarius Commission, a subsidiary organization of the UN's Food and Agriculture Organization (FAO) and World Health Organization (WHO). Imported foods would have to meet Codex standards instead of stiffer FDA or EPA standards. Any health and safety regulations holding imported foods to stricter standards than those set by the Codex could be challenged as trade barriers.

Any farm bill would have to comply with the GATT agreements. All Commodity Credit Corporation price support programs (including the no cost programs for peanuts and sugar and marketing loans for cotton and rice) would be eliminated. Deficiency payments for wheat, feed grains, rice, cotton and wool would be annihilated. The only income support that would be allowed under the Hills proposal would be direct welfare-type payments to farmers "decoupled" from production. Decoupled payments would be gradually phased out over either a five or ten year period. Given current budget constraints, such welfare-type payments would almost certainly fall to the budget cutter's axe sooner rather than later. The decoupling proposal was clearly rejected by farmers and congressional agriculture committees when it was first proposed in 1986.

The USDA projects that while higher prices will result in greater cash receipts for farmers from actual sales in the marketplace, the increase in prices will not be sufficient to offset the loss of income from support payments.

USDA economists have calculated the "domestic price

changes" resulting from the implementation of world multi-lateral trade liberalization. What they refer to as "price changes" are actually a comparison of U.S. prices after "liberalization" to the prices plus subsidies prior to "liberalization." In short, they compare a farmer's gross receipts before and after "liberalization" for each bushel or pound of production:

Beef, veal, lamb	+7%
Pork, poultry	+2%
Dairy products	-15%
Wheat	-44%
Feed grains	-33%
Rice	-59%
Oilseeds and products	-7%
Sugar	-69%
All farm products	-13%

The "price changes" for meat products compare the change in gross prices. With increases in the cost of feed, net returns on meat products would decline, and lower incomes at the feed-lot would be passed along in the form of lower prices paid to cow-calf operators.

Given these income losses, there would be another "shake-out" of family farmers. Small and moderate sized farms would be the hardest hit. According to USDA, farmers in the $40,000 to $99,999 gross sales category would lose 103% of their net farm income, and be wiped out. Farmers with gross sales of $100,000 to $249,999 would lose 56% of their net farm income. The resulting shakeout would accelerate the concentration of land and assets into fewer and larger farms.

While free trade might mean greater U.S. access to export markets, the removal of import quotas also would mean multi-national trading companies would have unlimited access to U.S. markets, and all other overseas markets. For example, many developing nations are pressured to export raw agricultural products in order to earn foreign exchange to meet debt payments to U.S. banks, the International Monetary Fund or the World Bank. In many cases, developing countries have undercut the world price to boost their export sales because of their desperate need for foreign earnings. Production of food and other raw materials for export has taken priority over the environment, domestic hunger relief and development needs. There is significant pressure to open U.S. markets for the purpose of solving the Third World debt crisis.

Ironically, the reverse may be true. The removal of U.S. import quotas (in the case of sugar, for example) means developing nations which currently enjoy access to the U.S. market would have to compete with Australia (the lowest cost producer of sugar) for that U.S. market. The U.S. sugar import quota currently provides guaranteed access to the U.S. market for Argentina, Peru, Haiti, Mexico, the Philippines and several other developing countries including El Salvador. And, under the U.S. sugar import quota system, these countries are paid a substantially higher price for their sugar in the U.S. than they get on the world market.

Hightower's staffers posed a necessary question. Won't some U.S. farmers clean up in a free market? Some will do okay. But for producers of the biggest crops—corn, wheat, soybeans, cotton, rice—and livestock products, namely beef, pork, dairy, wool, it's not that simple. No matter how efficient or innovative U.S. farmers are, they are saddled with higher production costs which put many of them at a disadvantage in the global marketplace.

Chemicals prohibited in the U.S. for environmental and food safety reasons are available to foreign producers, and U.S. farmers participating in commodity price support programs comply with federal environmental regulations and soil and water conservation requirements unheard of in most other nations. Land costs in the U.S., while not as high as in Japan and some other nations, are much higher than for most of our chief agricultural export competitors.

Farm labor, while at the low end of the wage scale in our country, costs substantially more in the U.S. than in Third World nations. In addition, many farmers in the U.S. are required to carry liability and/or workers' compensation insurance—and comply with state and federal health and safety standards not demanded of farmers in many competitor nations.

U.S. farmers, in an often futile effort to maintain even a moderate standard of living, have increased their gross incomes by farming more land. To do this, they've had to purchase—in addition to land—more and larger tractors, combines and other farm implements. The cost of this equipment has increased five and six-fold over the past two decades. Also, the cost of living in America is higher than in most of our competitor nations. U.S. farmers must pay U.S. prices for their groceries, clothing, housing and medicine. They feel as entitled as other Americans to enjoy decent cars, TVs and labor-saving appliances, and like other Americans, they want enough to provide for their children's educations and for their own retirements.

If our innovative and efficient U.S. farmers were willing to accept a Third World standard of living, they could no doubt undercut the prices of farmers in other nations, even with the higher price of land in the U.S. If global agriculture is indeed liberalized, as the U.S. negotiators are demanding, U.S. farmers are not only going to lose some export sales, they're going to lose some domestic sales as well. For while global trade—particularly the removal of import restrictions—may mean that some U.S. producers would have greater access to foreign markets, it would also mean that other nations will have greater access to our market. One option is to encourage our family farmers to find other lines of work while U.S. consumers look to Third World nations for more and more of U.S. food supply.

And that's the crux of the ideological debate over agricultural trade. The negotiators—preaching the sanctity of the market and the gospel of comparative advantage—maintain that each nation should get its food from the least expensive source, even if it means bankrupting its own producers and becoming more dependent on foreign suppliers.

Under the harmonization proposal, American consumers would see some food safety standards lowered, since in many cases U.S. standards are more stringent than the standards established by the Codex Alimentarius Commission. For example, the Codex allows much higher levels of U.S.-banned pesticides like DDT, heptachlor and aldrin than does the EPA. Imported bananas and peaches could have fifty times the amount of DDT allowed under U.S. law, and our federal Food and Drug Administration (FDA) would be unable to stop their importation without violating GATT guidelines. In effect Codex standards, not our own U.S. standards, would be applied at our border. And if the U.S. becomes reliant on the least cost producer, more and more of our food will be imported and therefore subject to the standards of the Codex rather than the FDA.

Since Codex standards would apply only to imports, the U.S. could continue to impose its own standards on U.S. farmers. However, this would put U.S. farmers at a competitive disadvantage with foreign producers who farm by less strict standards, and it would almost certainly generate political pressure to ease safety standards on products grown in the U.S. The GATT harmonization proposal could preempt decision-making by state governments, as well. State efforts to ban specific pesticides, like Alar, would be rendered ineffective because a treaty is the highest law in the land.

The big international grain trading companies would be the big winners under the GATT system. They could operate for the first time with not even minimal concern for national borders, import quotas and tariffs, export restrictions or variations in international health and safety standards. They would be able to buy commodities cheap from countries that need the foreign exchange to cover their debts. With the elimination of GATT's Article XI, which currently allows countries to restrict exports, the big traders would be able to buy and export commodities even from nations with starving people. They'd sell the commodities at a profit to industrialized and oil rich countries which have the cash to pay. And if they sell at below the cost of production of the farmers in the importing nation, those farmers will be out of luck.

As U.S. commodity programs (officially termed "price

stabilization" programs) are dismantled and the markets become more volatile, the commodity futures traders at the Chicago Board of Trade and the Chicago Mercantile Exchange would have greater opportunity to "buy low, sell high" and in general manipulate the markets even more than they have in the past. Global trading via satellite would soon command the world scene in even more commodities.

If agreement is reached among GATT countries, the Bush administration will write enabling legislation which will amend existing law or create new legislation to bring U.S. law into compliance with the GATT agreement. The legislation will be placed on a fast track, meaning Congress will have a sixty day deadline to vote on the legislation, with a limit of twenty hours of debate. No amendments will be allowed. Congress will be required to make either a *yes* or *no* vote. Congress authorizes this fast track, up or down approach to provide the administration full authority to negotiate. The assumption is that our negotiators need the authority to make some potentially controversial concessions in the interest of reaching an agreement which is beneficial to the U.S. overall. In the current round of talks, however, U.S. negotiators are serving a radical ideology representing the view of a handful of giant corporations and are pursuing a course detrimental to U.S. farmers, consumers and the environment.

Such is the GATT picture. It stands stark naked in terms of economics. Farmers of the high plains know they cannot take a 44% cut in wheat prices, not while they are barely surviving on a 33% of parity price level. The more astute of the farmers know that 33% of parity means a shortfall in the generation of national income via wheat production times price, and total annihilation of income generating activity via the multiplier when whole grains are shipped out of the country.

Shipping into cheap markets and importing into a cheap market defies the arithmetic of prosperity for the many. The elite know this. But from the vantage point of Olympus, farmers probably appear to be only so many peasants up to their armpits in mud.

In the final analysis, farmers divested of their earning power by public policy start consuming their capital. The mechanism is debt, and debt has delivered the last cloud of darkness to the farmers of the Great Plains.

—*Charles Walters Jr.*
Publisher, *Acres U.S.A.*

NARRATIVE

6

ALFALFA COUNTY,
A CASE REPORT

I have tried to get statistical information from the federal land bank system and from the FmHA. The federal land bank system stated that it is private and needs not respond, and FmHA takes the position that the Privacy Act prevents disclosure. I could force this through the Freedom of Information Act, but elect not to do so because I want to complete this study within a few years and I do not want the nastiness that often goes with forced disclosure. Also I have learned not to pay too much attention to information from the FmHA. It is often inaccurate. For example it stated that only four farmers in Oklahoma have been foreclosed upon during this economic crisis. Actually they foreclosed thirty in Alfalfa County, Oklahoma alone. They once stated that fewer than 5% of their borrowers were in default. Actually it was over 35%. One should beware of FmHA propaganda. To say the least, I have learned to be skeptical of any statistical information put out by the USDA. There is a better way to get the information.

Title to land is governed by state governments. The federal

government does not prescribe how title to land is to be secured or how it is to be mortgaged or foreclosed upon. It does not make many recommendations about land titles. However it should be noted that the federal government is concerned that land titles not be used to discriminate against minorities and due process questions must be resolved according to the U.S. Constitution. But in general, it is state government that decides land title questions. The six states in the Great Plains have delegated much of the day-to-day administration of the state land title laws to county governments. Thus the county courthouse is the first and final depository of what is going on in land titles. The federal courthouse has only a few federal cases and bankruptcies that affect land titles.

To trace the problems of farmers today, one should visit the county courthouses in the Great Plains. Since the federal government does not want me to have this information, I will get it in the county courthouses. The county courthouses in Oklahoma City, Wichita, Omaha and Houston are so large that it would take months and years for an outsider to see what is going on. Also these four counties have few farmers and their mortgages are commingled with the securities of other people and businesses. You could work for years in one of them and not really come to grips with the farm problems. So I will select small thinly populated counties and investigate them in depth to see what the problems are.

I selected Noble County, Oklahoma as the control county to investigate in depth. This was the home county of the father of the Farm Credit Act of 1971, Senator Henry L. Bellmon. However, I found that this county photocopies all land titles and the indexes are of poor quality. It is easy to make a mistake with them. So I turned to Alfalfa County, Oklahoma. This county has an accurate system of legible land indexes and the county clerk maintains a fine office. Also, I have knowledge of what is going on there, and of the value and use of its land.

A few minutes' examination of the land and court records yielded an immense amount of information about the follies of the federal land bank system and the FmHA. The long term mortgages are as follows.

	FLB	FmHA	PRUDENTIAL	JOHN HANCOCK
1960	18	11	8	4
1961	24	10	16	8
1962	20	16	14	6
1963	43	21	13	11
1964	27	12	10	9
1965	22	7	4	8
1966	21	13	11	3
1967	30	24	11	2
1968	25	10	4	3
1969	27	10	0	1
1970	29	31	2	0
1971	23	27	2	0
1972	54	31	2	0
1973	39	40	0	0
1974	67	19	0	0
1975	63	24	1	0
1976	70	16	0	0
1977	79	21	1	0
1978	59	33	0	0
1979	79	29	0	0
1980	94	26	0	0
1981	129	42	0	1
1982	71	17	0	0
1983	35	18	0	0
1984	24	14	0	0
1985	9	17	0	0
1986	20	22	0	0
1987	20	4	0	0
1988	24	7	0	0

From my investigation, I found that the farmers enjoyed a mixed economic system between 1916 and 1971, and the passage of the Farm Credit Act of that year. Prior to then the largest long-term lender to farmers was the Prudential Insurance Company of America, which held about 35% of the long term debts of farmers. In 1971 Prudential made a decision to abandon the county and let the federal land bank have all of the business of the entire county. In 1985 the company sold all of its mortgages and it does not now have a single dollar invested with farmers in Alfalfa County, Oklahoma. At one time this company was the largest lender and now it is gone. The basic cause of this is the fact that the company did not want to compete with the federal land bank system in driving up the appraisals of land values, and it did not want its mortgages destroyed by FmHA squirting credit all over the scene. So it left. The statistics in the county courthouse clearly bear this out. I have listed the number of mortgages since 1960 that were held by the federal land bank, FmHA, Prudential Insurance Company of America and the John Hancock Mutual Life Insurance Company. These two insurance companies were once the largest lenders to farmers all over the Great Plains. They left after the Farm Credit Act of 1971. The mortgage statistics tell the story.

These statistics show that in 1966, when the Vietnam War was building up, the Lyndon Johnson administration restricted credit. The federal land banks did not want to do this, but they decided to do so when President Johnson made it clear that they were part of the federal government and would be required to follow orders. The FmHA did the same thing. The two insurance companies also followed suit. So credit was restricted as the inflationary impact of the war grew. This is Keynesian economics in operation. When Nixon took office in 1969, the restrictions on the FmHA were brushed aside and the number of farm mortgages by that institution increased some 300%. There was no economic justification for this because the Vietnam War was still on, and inflation was running rampant.

As soon as the Farm Credit Act of 1971 went on the books, the federal land bank system vastly expanded its credit activities. First it could loan over $200,000 per farmer, which meant that rich farmers could get credit there in vast amounts. In 1960, the federal land bank made eighteen mortgages in the county. In 1971, it made twenty-three mortgages. In 1981, it made 129. These data represent a vast increase in mortgage activity, actually an increase of over 650%.

The federal land bank helped get rid of the insurance companies, keeping the long-term credit of farmers pretty much to itself. But as vast as the increased number of mortgages became, the amounts became even more staggering. In 1961, federal land bank was loaning less than $40,000 per wheat farm. By 1976 it had gone up to $60,000. In 1981 it was up to $300,000. Even rampant inflation could not explain those increases. These are increases based on a federal land bank takeover of long-term credit and a manipulated pricing mechanism used to inflate prices of the land. In other words, the system became socialized starting in 1971.

The figures of FmHA reveals the same thing. In 1961 the government gave ten loans to farmers. In 1971 it loaned to twenty-seven. And in 1981 it loaned to forty-two. This increase got rid of the insurance companies and helped the federal land bank secure the dominant and only other position of credit to farmers in the long-term field.

Notice that in 1971 and thereafter, John Hancock Life Insurance Company made only one loan, and that was to an old customer who needed additional financing. The same is true of Prudential. It rescheduled two loans in about fifteen years to help old trusted customers. But no new credit was extended to farmers since 1971 and the passage of the Farm Credit Act of that year. The U.S. government has dominated the field since 1971. At no time did Congress discuss this during debates on this Act.

The Congress has never authorized the socialization of the long-term credit system for farmers. But that is what has happened. Old retired employees of the two insurance companies have been interviewed and they state that these companies left the field because the FmHA squirted credit behind their mortgages to make farmers insolvent. The insurance companies would then have to fight in court to protect their investments. They quickly learned to not fight with the government. So they pulled their money out of Alfalfa County, Oklahoma and out of the rest of the Great Plains, and put it in shopping centers in distant cities and in stock brokerage firms. They are now making more money than ever. It is the federal government that is underwriting all of the losses in Alfalfa County.

Had the federal government maintained a proper credit system for farmers after its agencies took over the field, no one could seriously complain. Surely the farmers would not. Neither would I. But the government did not do this. When Reagan destroyed the price floor under wheat in April 1981— when he removed the Carter embargo—he destroyed the economics of the Great Plains, and a depression was off and running. The government then started to restrict credit in the Great Plains. Notice that in 1981 the federal land bank loaned money to 129 farmers, yet in 1985 they loaned to only nine. The FmHA made forty-two loans in the county in 1981 and then went to only four in 1987. This shows the complete collapse in the long-term credit system for farmers in this county. The government did not stand by farmers during crisis as did the insurance companies in past decades. It should also be noted that the federal land bank—after 1984—did not extend much new credit to farmers. Instead it sold off farms taken in foreclosure, and took mortgages back on them as they were transferred. That is what the figures say after 1984.

In 1988, twenty-four mortgages were filed by the federal land bank. Ten were made to the same farmer on ten separate tracts of land. Three were made to another farmer on three tracts of land, and two were to a single farmer on two tracts of land. In other words the federal land bank inflated the number of mortgages to try to make the statistics look like they were providing credit to farmers. Actually they served only twelve farmers in 1988, not twenty-four as the figures would seem to suggest. There has been a sharp drop in the amount of each mortgage. In 1981 the amounts were often over $300,000 per farm, but this dropped to around $60,000 per farm in 1988, which is about all the debt a wheat farm will carry.

The bottom line is damning in its finality. The federal government has done a miserable job of providing long-term credit to farmers. When I get to making recommendations, I will recommend that the government set up a lending agency in the Treasury and abolish both the federal land bank system and the FmHA.

Let's go to the court clerk's office in the county courthouse.

I find that there were no farm foreclosures between 1960 and 1983, at which point federal land bank filed one. This represents a twenty-three year period when farmers were not bothered by foreclosures. When it comes to dealing out economic hardship to farmers, the foreclosure procedure is in a class all its own. First when the land is taken from the farmer he is hurt beyond repair for the rest of his life. He is left with many skills that he learned in farming, but these are of little use in earning a living in a depression. Most of the jobs he can do have evaporated with the ongoing economic collapse.

In every case of suicide I have investigated, the federal land bank has been involved. FmHA has been involved in about 75% of the farm suicides. The insurance companies do not have a single such case on their record. Suicide alone is a cruel index of the hardship the federal government is causing the Great Plains.

So let's look at the foreclosure rates. John Hancock Insurance Company filed one suit. It was triggered by FmHA foreclosing first. Prudential Insurance Company of American filed three suits and dismissed two when the firm came to terms with the two customers involved. The federal land bank filed sixty-seven foreclosures and the FmHA filed thirty. When you put this on a chart it is even more revealing.

Name of Plaintiff	Number of suits	percentage of suits
John Hancock	1	none
Prudential	3	3%
Federal Land Bank	67	67%
FmHA	30	30%

The federal government thus has filed 97% of the foreclosure suits. You can see that most of the economic grief is being handed out by the U.S. government. The suit filed by John Hancock was an effect, not a cause, for which reason I am not giving it a designation. FmHA declared a mortgage in foreclosure and cross-suited John Hancock, which forced the insurance company to foreclose. Prudential filed three suits and dismissed two, which gives that firm a dismissal rate of 67%.

The federal land bank dismissed sixteen cases, which gives that lender a dismissal rate of 24%. FmHA did not dismissed any cases, and this gives the agency a dismissal percentage of zero. Thus the two insurance companies have a much better suit rate and a much better dismissal rate than the two agencies of the government. FmHA sued thirty farmers. The federal land bank sued sixty-seven individuals. So it is easy to see that the two agencies of the government filed practically all of the legal foreclosure suits against farmers. By 1980 the government had socialized the long-term credit field, and a deep economic depression had settled in on the Great Plains.

Let's analyze each of these foreclosure cases and see some of the bad practices of the U.S. government. Each court case has a number. The first is C-83-8. The C means it is civil rather than criminal, the 83 means that the case was filed in the year of 1983, and the 8 means this was the 8th civil case filed that year. I will not list the name of the farmer because I believe he has suffered enough. If a reader has occasion to pull one of these court files, remember the farmer has suffered terribly. Please do not add to his woes.

Case No. C-83-8. On January 23, 1983, the federal land bank filed a lawsuit against a farmer and the FmHA. It said that it held a mortgage against the farmer for the original amount of $70,000 which represented a loan made in 1976 on 240 acres. The suit said the federal land bank was owed $88,784.81 on January 28, 1983. FmHA cross-sued the farmer and foreclosed on its second mortgage in the amount of $51,082.31. On July 7, 1983 the court entered a judgment that said the federal land bank's mortgage was now $95,082.31, and this represented an increase of over $6,200 in only six months. Here we see the beginning of a pattern wherein the land bank gets, via court judgment, more than it sued for. As the cases unfold, one can see unethical courses of action the federal land bank practiced against farmers.

This property was sold at sheriff's sale for $159,000, and the federal land bank received the full amount of its mortgage plus costs, interest and an attorney fee of $9,508.23. This attorney fee was excessive in every way. I had two attorneys look at this file and suggest that a proper fee for the work done in an *uncontested* case would be about $1,000. In other words, it became common practice for the federal land bank to pile on attorney fees not justified by work done in the case. There was no deficiency judgment.

In the act of 1916 that set up the federal land bank system Congress mandated that the farmer-borrower buy 5% of loan value as stock in the system in order to build up the cash reserves of the system. In this case the farmer bought $3,500 in stock. His land was sold and the bank received the full amount of the mortgage, but this farmer received nothing for his stock. In another circle this would be considered outright theft.

In 1987 Congress mandated that banks give credit by repurchasing the stock, but this law came too late for the farmer in this case. He was given nothing. This was probably a safe loan when made by the federal land bank, but after the FmHA started loaning money behind the bank mortgage, the farmer became insolvent. This caused both government agencies to go to court to recoup the losses caused by FmHA. This case is troublesome in another way. After the land was sold the federal land bank filed a motion to disburse the funds the sheriff got for the sale. The motion asked, and the bank got, $103,052.20. This was considerably more than the amount of the judgment, which was $95,082.31, and more than the $88,764.81 which the bank said it was due when the case was filed, and much more than the $70,000 which was the amount of the original mortgage.

The only case to go to judgment involving the insurance companies was one brought by Prudential Insurance Company of America. Prudential sued a farmer and the FmHA. FmHA then had the case removed to federal court in Oklahoma City on grounds that there was federal money involved, and this made it a substantial federal question. This is the only time the FmHA has done this. It is thought by some that the government did this to make it as hard as possible for the insurance companies to recover. It is noteworthy that the FmHA was never involved in such a legal stunt when the federal land bank was involved. After arriving in federal court, FmHA cross-sued the farmer and then brought in the John Hancock Mutual Life Insurance Company as a third-party defendant. This forced John Hancock to foreclose against the farmer. The two insurance companies got a judgment for $98,839.40, which included principal, interest and attorney fees. Two farms were involved. They sold for $289,000, which gave the insurance companies full return on their loans.

FmHA made loans to this farmer as cafeteria type credit, and $385,649.84 was owed to it with unpaid interest of $73,815.58. FmHA received $190,160.60 on its debt. This left a loan loss for the taxpayers to pay in the amount of $195,489.24. This is the largest recovery that I could find on any FmHA loan in the Great Plains. The two insurance companies loaned less than $60,000 per farm. This shows that when loans are properly made, they can be serviced without losses. In this 1979 case, FmHA demanded that all of the income of the farmer be brought to the county offices of the agency so the officer could decide who got what and when. He decided in 1979 that the two insurance companies would not receive anything and from 1979 to 1985, they never received anything. John Hancock was willing to go along with this situation for a little more time, but Prudential was not. When things like this happen, the companies are required to post additional reserves with the state insurance commissioner. Neither company was willing to do so.

This case also shows the arrogance of the FmHA in refusing to allow anyone to receive money from the farmer except FmHA, thus the foreclosures. Had these companies and the FmHA been willing to divide the money that the farmer came up with, foreclosure might have been prevented, but the government refused to save the farm.

Many people, and some agencies of state government, have presented the idea that moratoriums, counseling and debt management are the best way to handle the economic problems of the farmer. I disagree. I am not against debt counseling, debt management, moratoriums, debt reconciliation and mediation. They have their place in our legal and financial system. But a well-managed lending system is what our society needs. I would not overdose the farmer or anyone else with too much credit. Credit should be strictly rationed. FmHA enjoyed too much power, and this power became badly abused. The loan officer in the county offices decided on the interest rate the farmer would pay, how much money he got, what he did with his income, what he could plant, the technology he would use, and so on. At no time was the farmer given much freedom.

Many farmers do not sell their wheat in the year that it is harvested. They carry it forward to the next year in the hope of getting a better price. A farmer such as the one in this case is not given this option by the loan officer in the county offices of FmHA. In fact, he is told what to do, and if he does not want to do it, criminal charges are filed. In this case the farmer followed the dictates of the FmHA, which in turn abused the two insurance companies, and they had to go to court to stop the financial carnage. It should be noted that both of the insurance companies had prior and first mortgages, and the FmHA had inferior mortgages, but the government still ruled the roost.

The farmer who refuses to have anything to do with the federal land banks and the FmHA will clearly survive the present economic collapse. Trusting souls who go to these amoral lenders will be forced out of farming. It is highly ironic that two government agencies set up to help the farmer—more particularly to help small, poor and tenant farmers—have been prostituted into helping only the gullible, namely people stupid enough to borrow from the government. It is even more ironic that the taxpayers must pay $195,489.24 plus lost interest to the tune of $73,815.58 solely to force insurance companies out of the long-term lending field. Under federal law these insurance companies were operating properly and lawfully, but they were forced out anyway.

Case No. C-84-88. Federal land bank sued a farmer and the FmHA. FmHA then cross-sued the farmer. FmHA loans were

February 11, 1977	$47,980
December 22, 1977	42,480
January 24, 1979	62,400
January 24, 1979	304,600
December 14, 1981	8,880

for a loan total of $466,340, close to half a million dollars. When Nixon swept aside President Johnson's restrictions, he set the stage for a loan of almost half a million dollars in this one case. This farmer made a few payments. In the cross-suit, FmHA asked for judgment of $419,029.25 with interest of $112,927.34 added for a total of $531,966.59. The loss to the U.S. Treasury was $419,029.25. Also, there was a loss of $112,937.34 in earned interest that was never collected. The attorney fees for the federal land bank attorney was $6,000. It should be noted also that here the FmHA bought one of these tracts of land for $96,000, which has to be paid for by the taxpayers of the country. In short, this money flows from the U.S. Treasury to the federal land bank and then is spent for riotous business overhead including excessive attorney fees, expensive office buildings, and a smaller amount to the bondholders of the system. The judgment was for $211,120.54, but the final payout was kited to $245,245.12. There is no explanation for this huge increase and I can think of none.

Case No. C-84-100. It was brought by the federal land bank against a farmer and the FmHA. The federal land bank held two mortgages, one for $123,000 and another for $850,000. FmHA then cross-sued the farmer for $400,000. This case was bitterly contested. The federal land bank had its attorney file a series of interrogatories. An interrogatory is a written question asked by one of the parties to the lawsuit directed to the other party. The second party must then answer that question in writing. The object is to reduce the contested issues before trial of the case. In Interrogatory No. 3 the federal land bank asked whether the farmer received the proceeds of the loan *"less 5% for purchase of stock in the federal land bank association of Enid?"* The farmer answered the question that he'd gotten the money from the loan *"less 5% for purchase of stock in the federal land bank of Enid."*

The Act of 1916 that up the federal land bank required stock to be paid for in cash by the farmer. Here the federal land bank admitted it was selling the stock on credit. And the farmer is admitting that he did not pay cash, that they took it out of the proceeds of the loan. The object of the legal requirement that all stock is to be paid for in cash was to build the reserves of the bank.

In the Farm Credit Act of 1971, Congress again mandated that this stock was to be paid for in cash. In every foreclosure case filed in Alfalfa County, Oklahoma, the law was flaunted. In other words, the federal land bank follows the laws of Congress only if it wants to. Yet the attorney for the federal land bank is under an ethical obligation to see to it that his client complies with the law. And yet this attorney actually participated in flaunting the law.

A lawyer is to warn his client of approaching danger. This lawyer participates in the approaching danger.

When the federal land bank got in trouble in 1984, there were insufficient cash reserves to carry the system through an economic collapse. So it went back to Congress for more money. Someone has to stop this. Too many of our national financial assets are being wasted in illegal procedures.

The federal land bank hires attorneys from the private sector. FmHA also hires attorneys from the private sector to handle all details of loans up to foreclosure. From then on the agency is represented by the federal district attorney. In the many hundreds of court cases I have read all over the Great Plains, I have observed a high professional competence in the work of federal district attorneys. They never charge a fee, never charge excessive interest and never kite the amount of the judgment. I have never noted one single penny difference in what they sued for and what the judgment was. At no time have they stooped to do the things common for private attorneys of the federal land bank.

The farmer in this case filed bankruptcy. This ended collection on his debt by both the federal land bank and FmHA.

The court at Cherokee, Oklahoma granted judgment *in rem*, that is against the land, not the farmer, in favor of the federal land bank for $1,352,129.06 with attorney fees of $15,000. There is no economic justification for such an attorney fee. My informants says $3,000 was all what this attorney was worth. What this fee does is to put this attorney ahead of the U.S. Treasury in recovery on an FmHA judgment which the court set at $398,716.93. The federal land bank wanted to hold the sale away from the courthouse, which is against Oklahoma state law. The court refused to follow this request and the sale was held at the courthouse.

The land sold for $499,502, which means that the federal land bank lost $852,627.06 and FmHA lost everything, the total of which was $398,716.93 with an additional amount for earned interest not paid in the amount of $198,593.82. The cost to the government by this one farmer was $1,251,343.99. I can't think of a single reason why the Congress should punish the taxpayer by making him pay these losses. If a helpless widow needs an additional $10 a month to buy both food and medicine, everyone comes unglued, yet the government has lost over $1.2 million dollars in one case on one farmer. Incidentally the attorney for the federal land bank in this case returned to court and asked an additional $35,000 for his attorney fee, making the attorney's fee in this case $50,000. A sum of $3,000 would have amply rewarded the attorney for what little he did in this case.

At no time did the federal land bank have a safe loan. It abusively extended credit in an extremely large amount, and FmHA repeated the error.

> *Case No. C-84-101.* The federal land bank sued a brother of the farmer in the preceding case and FmHA, and FmHA then cross-sued the farmer. The federal land bank got a judgment for $376,452.50 on its mortgage covering 240 acres. This represented $1,568.55 per acre on wheat land. Remember, an insurance company limited the farmer to not over $60,000 per 160 acres, which is $375 per acre. I cannot find a case in which an insurance company lost a single dollar on a farmer, yet the federal land bank lost millions.

When the insurance companies left the field, the federal land bank went wild making high risk loans. There is not one farm in Alfalfa County, Oklahoma that can carry a loan of $1568.55 per acre. With an interest rate of 8%, the interest tab to the federal land bank was $125.48 per acre each year. The county historical average on the production of wheat is thirty-one bushels per acre. Where the government got this figure is a mystery. I believe the average is not over twenty-five bushels per year. But at thirty-one bushels and at $4 per bushel, this farmer would only have an income of $124 per acre, yet his interest bill would be $125.48 per acre per year. His interest per acre exceeded his crop income. Proper banking rules would dictate this loan never be made. In this case the farmer would get a government subsidy payment of about $20 per acre. This is all he would have to pay for the rest of the expenses of his operation and to live on. There is absolutely no way that this farmer could pay. Yet the flim-flam artists in both government offices could not understand the economic situation.

In 1984, when the federal land bank got into financial trouble, it raised the interest rates on all of its customers from 8% to 13.75%. At this rate the farmer's interest bill went from $30,116.20 to $51,762.15 per year. The interest rate used to be $125.48 per acre, but after this rate increase it jumped to $215.67 per acre. At the same time, the price of wheat dropped from $4 a bushel to $3 a bushel, giving the farmer a crop income of $93.50 plus a $20 per acre government subsidy. This factors into being a cash income of only $113.50 per acre to meet an interest bill of $215.67 per acre. The variable or changeable interest rate did much to undermine the farmer's solvency and his mental health.

The judgment for the federal land bank was $376,452.50. In turn, and the land sold for $179,301 leaving a loss to the federal land bank of $197,151.50. This, then, became the figure the federal land bank wanted the taxpayer to pay. FmHA obtained a judgment against the farmer for $398,716.93 plus an additional amount for delinquent interest to the tune of $198,593.82, both figures being a total and complete loss to the U.S. Treasury. No matter how much taxes are cut by the federal government, we are still stuck.

Case No. C-84-186. The federal land bank sued a farmer and the FmHA. FmHA then cross-sued the farmer and got a judgment for $298,338.19, which was a total loss to the U.S. Treasury. The federal land bank got a judgment for $441,909.40 plus an attorney fee of $8,000. The land sold for $228,500, leaving a loss to the federal land bank of $213,409.40. This loan should never have been made. It violated every rule of money lending. Since the farmer filed bankruptcy, there is no way any of this can be recovered.

Case No. C-84-201. This is another case in which the federal land bank sued a farmer and FmHA. The federal land bank received a judgment for $298,928.50 on a 160 acre farm. This means that this land was mortgaged for $1,868.30 per acre. Interest was 8% per year, but in 1984 the federal land bank raised it to 13.75%, making an interest bill of $256.89 per acre. It is impossible for the land to support such a payment. With wheat selling at $3 a bushel and a historical yield of thirty-one bushels per acre, the farmer would get $93 per acre income. With a government subsidy payment of about $20 per acre, the farmer would have $113 per acre income to meet an interest payment of $256.89 per acre per annum. Since the land could not crop and cash flow that much money, the farmer filed for bankruptcy, thereby ending any collection activity against him.

The land in this case sold for $136,000. Remember the statement made by an agent of the federal land bank that I would not live long enough to see wheat land go below $1,000 per acre? Well, I have lived that long. This 160 acre farm sold for $136,000, which is $850 per acre. So this agent knew very little. The land is now destined to go much lower. The loss to the federal land bank in this case was $162,928.50 and the loss to the FmHA was $111,793.27. FmHA then reported a further loss of $31,126.77 in earned interest. In this case the attorney for the federal land bank got a fee of $5,000 when a fee of $1,500 would have been ample. A motion for a deficiency judgment was filed by the attorney for the federal land bank saying that the fair market value of the land was actually only $114,500. The court did not buy this argument. With the farmer in bankruptcy, it was a silly argument to start with. Why the attorney would "churn" the case with this canard may become apparent later on.

Case No. C-84-125. The federal land bank sued a farmer and the FmHA. The petition was filed on July 25, 1984, and asked for $95,800. A judgment was entered by the court on January 3, 1985, less than six months later. In the judgment the amount owed to the federal land bank increased from $95,800, to $142,099.87, representing an increase of $46,299.87. With an interest rate of 16%, this mortgage could not have earned over $7,764 in a six month period. In other words, the federal land bank would sue for one figure and then just a few months later get a judgment for a great deal more with no rational explanation for what went on. I will leave that as it is. Maybe an explanation will come to light later. In fact, I promise you it will. FmHA cross-sued this farmer. The agency had set him up on cafeteria credit basis so that he could take what he wanted and leave the rest. Unfortunately he took all he could. The following amounts were loaned in this case:

October 26, 1976	$16,240
October 25, 1978	40,000
May 23, 1979	98,200
January 7, 1981	27,170
January 7, 1981	17,840
January 7, 1981	26,990
August 17, 1981	50,000

The total FmHA loan was $276,440. In other words the U.S. Treasury loaned this farmer over a quarter of a million dollars. The land was sold for $50,000 in this case and the inflated figures of the federal land bank indicated that it lost $95,099.87. FmHA in turn had a total loss of $275,065.52, plus an additional amount of $78,883.48 in unpaid but earned interest. A proceeding after judgment by garnishment collected $1,350.89. This reduced the losses of the federal land bank to $90,748.98. However in the deficiency judgment the bank got $123,270.66. The bank only loaned $55,800.

This completes the lawsuits filed by the federal land bank in Alfalfa County, Oklahoma during the year of 1984.

In late 1984 the Federal District Court at Bismarck, North Dakota, entered an order restraining FmHA from foreclosing on farmers because that agency of government had not complied with the due process requirements of the 5th Amendment to the Constitution. I should note that most due process requirements involve state governments or instrumentalities identified under the due process clause of the 14th Amendment. The 14th Amendment is clearly directed at the state governments. To involve the federal government in a due process case, one must invoke the protection found in the 5th Amendment. This was done by a farmer named Coleman in North Dakota. Judge Dale Van Sickle of the federal district court agreed with him. The Department of Justice was ordered to stop all foreclosure actions until FmHA could reorganize its collection procedures to comply with the 5th Amendment.

Due process of law has been widely debated among lawyers and courts. I believe that it means the government must act fairly when dealing with a citizen. One of the first requirements of due process is that the concerned citizen be notified when a decision is to be made. Such notice must give the time and place where the meeting is to be held. This is done in court procedures by summons that have the appropriate information listed on them. The person is then allowed to be present when the decision is made and is given an opportunity to present his side of the case. He can have an attorney present if he desires. The FmHA has fallen into the bad practice of discriminating against farmers represented by an attorney. This causes a "chilling effect" on the position of the farmer, bureau billingsgate had it. Under procedures of FmHA, a farmer could be declared in default on his mortgage payments, ordered off his land and in general be put out of business, and be the last person in the county who knew about it. There was no procedure for notifying him of any change in his status with the government. Judge Van Sickle ruled that this procedure was unconstitutional and the 5th Amendment clearly applied to FmHA.

It must be noticed that many errors are made in and out of courthouses by people who think the Constitution has a Bill of Rights. Actually it does not. It has a Bill of Prohibitions. The first ten amendments prohibit the government from doing certain things. I am not guaranteed freedom of the press by the Constitution. The Congress is *prohibited* from passing a law that prohibits freedom of the press. The government is thus prohibited from violating due process of law when acting through FmHA. Bills of rights are found in such dictatorial governments as Cuba and Russia.

In other words, the court ruled that FmHA must obey the due process clause of the 5th Amendment. It took about sixteen months for FmHA to draw up guidelines and procedures to guarantee due process protection. When this business was completed, Judge Van Sickle released FmHA from his court order.

This did not help farmers as much as many people think. Many writers, including press reporters, felt that this order immediately favored the farmers. Actually it did not. Of all the cases filed in Alfalfa County, Oklahoma prior to the Coleman case, all were filed by the federal land bank system, and then the FmHA was made a defendant in the case and counter-sued the farmer. After this court order the FmHA continued to do the same thing. It did not actually file suit against a farmer while the order was in effect. The *modus operandi* of FmHA was to let the federal land bank start the suit, and then FmHA joined in. Thus the court order in North Dakota was of little use to the farmer, but it did clean up some of the bad office practices of FmHA. The *Coleman vs. Block* case as decided by Judge Van Sickle illustrates how hard it is to control a bureaucracy when it is against a change. This agency of government earlier appeared in the federal court in North Dakota and asked that exceptions be made to the ruling of no foreclosures. One exception was that the FmHA could sue the farmer if someone else started the suit. Judge Van Sickle allowed this. When Judge Van Sickle agreed to the exception, he effectively lost control of the case.

> *Case No. C-85-18.* This suit was filed by the federal land bank against a farming partnership and the FmHA. Judgment was rendered on October 17, 1986 in favor of the federal land bank for $775,437.67. FmHA cross-sued the farmer for $445,000 plus an additional amount for earned but unpaid interest of $27,336.91. Notice that FmHA sued the farmer even though there was a court order in North Dakota not to sue. This case was appealed to the Supreme Court of Oklahoma and dismissed by that court on April 1, 1988. The case has not been acted on further. No sale of land has been made.

This case raised a defense of *forbearance.* The farmer involved felt that he had not been given an opportunity to restructure his loan as provided for by the Farm Credit Act of 1971. The federal land bank filed a brief in which it stated that this law did not apply to it since it was a private corporation. Notice how the bank has switched sides, and now said it is private. This incredible declaration came after several federal courts clearly ruled that it was an agency of the government. Basically, this bank simply ignored any law that it did not want to comply with. The court held a scheduling conference and did not require the bank to comply with forbearance. The problem here was that a state judge in a state court sat with two federal agencies before it, one of which was determined not to comply with federal law and did not do so. Later, under a different judge, this very same court reached the opposite conclusion in an identical case. Judges judge, and they can reach opposite conclusions on the same law or on the same set of facts. A judgment was entered for the federal land bank for $775,437.67. Another was entered in favor of FmHA for $150,000 on its first mortgage and $295,000 on its second mortgage. An additional $27,336.91 was entered for earned but unpaid interest. This case was appealed to the Oklahoma Supreme Court. My informants believe that federal land bank will lose over $300,000 in this case. The loss to the federal treasury will be $445,000 plus the unpaid interest of $27,336.91.

Case No. C-85-30. The federal land bank sued a farmer and the FmHA. FmHA then cross-sued the farmer for a basic $54,363.80, and for $20,612.02 in earned interest on the mortgage. The federal land bank held a mortgage for $174,000, but its attorney stated at the pretrial conference that the amount owed was actually $217,193.37. When judgment was rendered on August 11, 1986, the judgment for the federal land bank had jumped to $256,734.97 plus an attorney's fee of $2,122.52. No man born of woman can rationally explain this large increase in the amount the bank claimed was owed. The property was sold to the federal land bank for $97,500, or for considerably less than $1,000 an acre for this 160 acre wheat farm. The loan officer in the federal land bank once said that I would never see wheat land sell for less than $1,000. Yet this land sold for $606.25 per acre. The amount of the bank loan on a 160 acre farm was $174,000. Then the FmHA loaned $54,363.80 for a total debt of $228,363.80 or $1427.27 per acre. Assuming that this land was all in wheat, which it was not, and assuming further that it would make the government county average of thirty-one bushels an acre, which it couldn't, assuming further that the wheat would sell for $4 a bushel, which it wouldn't, gross income would be as follows: 160 acres times thirty-one bushels equals 4,960 bushels at $4 per bushel gives crop income of $19,840. Add $4,000 government subsidies and you would have a gross farm income of $23,840. Interest at federal land bank was now 15.75% and on what they claim is due, namely $256,734.97, the rate would generate an annual interest bill of $40,435.61 to the federal land bank. At 11% at FmHA, a loan of $54,363.80 generates an annual interest bill of $5,980.02. The juxtaposes a total interest bill of $46,415.63 against a farmer's total gross income of not over $23,840. How could a farmer make up the difference? This one didn't. He went broke. The farmer also has many bills to meet. He has fuel and lubrication for his equipment, repairs, seed, feed, supplies, taxes to local government, fertilizers, etc. He also has to have money to live. Neither of these two loans should have been made.

This case led to a deficiency judgment against the farmer in favor of the federal land bank for $185,123.68 and loss to the federal government of $54,363.80 plus the earned but unpaid interest, $20,612.02.

After sale of the property, the federal land bank garnished an insurance settlement due the farmer and got an additional $4,053. Later there was a sale of minor mineral interest that the farmer owned elsewhere. There was a legal contest with a commercial bank in Kansas that held a judgment against this farmer. The sale of this mineral interest was appealed to the Supreme Court of Oklahoma. I will close my coverage of this case without an answer on the mineral issue. If the federal land bank gets the proceeds, about $16,866 plus an insurance settlement, the total will be $20,919. This would leave the federal land bank with an overall loss of $164,204.68. If the Supreme Court of Oklahoma hands this money to the federal land bank, the bank will still have a loss of over $1,000 per acre.

Case No. C-85-54. In this case, the federal land bank sued a farmer who had a business on the side. The mortgage to the bank was for $452,200. The judgment was for $695,939.94. An attorney's fee set by the court came to $8,000. The farmer asked questions in this case, and the senior vice-president of the federal land bank association at Enid, Oklahoma filed a sworn answer. The farmer got the loan "less 5% of said amount reserved to purchase federal land bank association stock in the name of the farmer," the Land Bank officer said.

Is the federal land bank now complying with the law? Apparently not. Records reveal that land bank has violated the law in every single loan transaction examined, and continues to do so.

In this case it can be seen for the first time what magically increases what the farmer owes to the bank. The farmer asked pointed questions and the court insisted on answers. The federal land bank finally filed settlement papers showing how they arrived at what it claimed was owed. The farmer owed the mortgage. Then they added everything that they could think of, including the slop bucket, pond dam, fire box, attorney fees and unnecessary insurance. On the settlement sheets there was a charge against the farmer for binder insurance in the amount of $1,565. Binder insurance covers the title to property, not the property itself. It is used when one is closing a loan with title insurance, but full documents have not been completed. Binder insurance covers the time until the loan is completed. Binder insurance bought by the federal land bank is a total waste of money and is an unnecessary expense to the farmer. Then there are on the attorney fees. For example the settlement sheet showed charges by the bank's attorney follows:

DATE	AMOUNT OF FLB ATTORNEY FEE
Mar. 4, 1984	$21.75
Oct. 3, 1984	87.45
Nov. 9, 1984	55.98
Dec. 9, 1984	252.86
Feb. 6, 1985	17.00
Apr.9, 1985	175.00
May 7, 1985	184.87
Jun. 6, 1985	80.06
Jul. 3, 1985	68.63
Aug. 7, 1985	17.82
Sep. 9, 1985	211.22
Oct. 9, 1985	179.39
Nov. 11, 1985	351.59
Jan. 9, 1986	618.95
Total attorney fees	$2322.57

The attorney for the federal land bank system in this county sent a bill each month for fees in this and other cases. The bank added these fees to the amount that it claims was owed by the farmer, and then the bank computed interest since the last charge. In other words the bank added interest at a compound rate, not a straight rate, which is all that is allowed under Oklahoma law. The bank's attorney billed for $2,322.57 attorney's fees. This was added to the amount the farmer owed plus compound interest. This meant the amount owed by the farmer was not $452,000—which the original amount of the mortgage—but $695,939.94, which included attorney's fees of $2,322.57, and binder insurance of $1,565. In another case the federal land bank added the cost of fertilizers that it did not buy. In still another case, it added on taxes that it did not pay. The padded list can be almost endless.

In this case the attorney for the federal land bank appeared before the judge on judgment day, asked for and received an attorney's fee of $8,000 which the farmer had to pay. No mention was made of the fact that the farmer already paid $2,322.57, as noted on the settlement sheets of the bank. In other words, this attorney was double paid. The attorney also represented that his fees should be $8,000, yet his own time charts revealed that fees should not be over $2,322.53. Under Oklahoma and federal law, interest on attorney fees is not allowed. The attorney is to wait until the case is over, at which time the judge sets fees on the basis of work done, and this amount is then added as court costs. Attorney's fees never earn interest, and charges to this effect are fraudulent.

This land was sold for $695,000 which paid the judgment except for $939.94 and for the additional attorney's fees of $8,000—a total of $8,939.94. It will be recalled that when this suit was filed, the federal land bank sued for $452,200, the amount the bank said was due. Yet the judgment a few months later was for $695,939.94. This represents a difference of $243,739.94. There is no rational or honest way to explain this difference except to say that the farmer was systematically robbed. But the robbery did not stop there. This farmer had stock credits in the system for $22,610 and the federal land bank then issued a release of judgment and canceled the stock, giving the farmer nothing for the difference between the face value of the stock of $22,610 and what it said was due, namely $8,000—this for an excessive attorney fee which was already partially paid, and $939.94 which is what the federal land bank said was still due. This farmer was robbed of his stock exactly the way the old ex-slave was robbed of his cotton crop each year. Even by the false figures the federal land bank maintained, this farmer was entitled to $13,670.06 cash refund on his stock in the system. Chronic cheating of the farmer out of his stock has caused great concern in Congress. In 1987 Congress mandated that the farmer receive the face value back. This mandate is to last for only five years and expires in 1992. Presumably the land banks can resume cheating at that time. In the case mentioned here, the farmer never got his money because the federal land bank took the position that stock was not worth 100 cents on the dollar. This may be true. Since the federal land bank is insolvent, stock could not remotely be worth 100 cents on the dollar. It made no difference to this farmer, because he was not going to get anything anyway.

The best solution to this mendacity is to abolish the system. The federal land bank has abused farmers in an unconscionable way, and is much too corrupt to survive. Congress should abolish it.

In this case, the farmer asked for punitive damages against the federal land bank. The court refused punitive damages and cited the bank's brief in the case as controlling. The bank's brief said that it was a federally chartered instrumentality of the U.S. government and as such was subject to the sovereign immunity of the U.S. government for which reason punitive damages could not be awarded against it. Again the bank switched its argument and for the purpose of this case was no longer private, but is an agency of the government. I must admit that it is part of the government. Thus it cannot be corrected by suits or attacked by suits for punitive damages. If this bank were truly a private business, punitive damages would clearly be in order for the corrupt, crooked, unethical, and illegal way that it settled with this farmer. Even though Congress has acted and demanded that the bank take corrective action, this farmer has never received anything. The bank simply defied the Congress.

Case No. C-85-55. Here the federal land bank sued a farmer and the FmHA. The FmHA counter-sued the farmer and received a judgment for $148,503.13 plus earned interest of $10,976.10. The federal land bank sued for $129,209.60 plus attorney's fees of $2,500. Later it got a judgment for $148,503.13. This enormous jump in what the federal land bank finally received is not explained in the court files. It is only when the bank files a settlement sheet in the court files that one can see the duplicity. The land was sold to a private buyer for $101,500, and the federal land bank lost $47,003.13. FmHA and the taxpayer lost $148,503.13. The farmer filed for bankruptcy, and his affairs were liquidated in bankruptcy court. Consequently there is no possibility of either agency collecting anything more.

Case No. C-85-56. The federal land bank sued a farmer and the FmHA. Then FmHA cross-sued the farmer. The defense in this case was that the federal land bank would not participate in the policy of forbearance with the farmer. Under forbearance, the creditor is required to help the farmer work his way out of debt without the bank having to go to the extreme of foreclosing and setting him out in the road. The bank simply refused to participate in this case. It would have taken only about 15 minutes to do this. Court officials did not know and could not remember what went on in the case. One surmised that this was the way the federal land bank treated all of its customers. The court did not press the issue. Judgment was rendered in favor of both the bank and the FmHA.

The property had not been sold at the time I examined the case, so there is no way I can report on losses. This case is enlightening nevertheless. Congress has twice mandated that the stock in the bank be sold for cash only. The attorney for the federal land bank filed a brief in this case and he said: "Generally the association lends the funds to purchase the stock required." This statement is false. The federal land bank, not the association, lends the money. In a brief filed in an adjoining county, the same attorney for the federal land bank said he never participated in a loan where the farmer used cash to buy the stock. The utter inconsistency of the federal land bank also came to the fore in this case. In a brief, the attorney for the federal land bank said that, "The federal land bank is not a government agency." Later in the brief the attorney said, "The federal land bank of Wichita is a federally chartered instrumentality and as such is an agency of the U.S. government and consequently subject to sovereign immunity." In a response brief in the same case the same attorney said, "The federal land bank of Wichita is a private corporation chartered by the U.S. and is not a governmental entity."

Here we have the breath-taking absurdity of an attorney changing his mind in the same brief and in the same case on the same point of law as the need to be private or public changed. I do not believe that Congress should let the banks get by with this. More to the point—why are attorney's fees charged to the farmer when intellectual mediocrity seems to be the only product.

If these banks are private, they fall under state law. If federal land banks are an agency of the U.S., then they fall under federal law. But no land bank should be allowed to twist the situation with impunity. Such arrogance has not been seen in the banking community since the Second U.S. Bank went out of existence in 1836.

The property in this case had not been sold at press time, but my informants believe that the federal land bank will lose about $150,000 and the taxpayers will have to pick up a loss of about $152,112.10 on loans made by FmHA. There was also $39,637.80 unpaid interest on the FmHA loan.

> *Case No. C-85-95.* Here the federal land bank sued a farmer and then quickly dismissed the case. There is nothing in the files to indicate why this was done.

> *Case No. C-85-107.* It was brought by the federal land bank against a farmer. The suit was for $145,253.60 on a 160 acre farm. The judgment the bank got was for $145,253.60. The property sold for $50,000. The loss to the federal land bank was $95,549.14. A total of $1,328 was received on a garnishment and this reduced the loss of the bank to $94,221.14.

This farm finally sold for $50,000, or for $312.50 per acre. Again I am forced to recall the statement made by the a loan officer, that I would never live to see land go below $1,000. The problem here is that these bureaucrats could not conceptualize anything going down in price, thus exhibiting complete ignorance of basic economics. This feeling that prices would never go down became an essential characteristic of the real estate "bust" in 1926-1927 which preceded the stock market collapse of 1929.

> *Case No. C-85-110.* The federal land bank sued a farmer and FmHA and the latter cross-sued the farmer. The bank got a judgment for $486,025.48 and FmHA got a judgment for $200,600 plus earned but

unpaid interest in the amount of $10,484.93. The land sold for $133,500, leaving the losses to the federal land bank in the amount of $352,525.48, or more than a third of a million dollars. The U.S. Treasury lost $200,600 on the loan by FmHA plus earned but unpaid interest, $10,484.93. The farmer filed bankruptcy.

Case No.C-85-199. The federal land bank sued a farmer and then dismissed the case.

Case No. C-85-200. The federal land bank sued a farmer and FmHA. In this case the federal land bank also sued the tenant who farmed the land. The tenant had to hire an attorney and he filed a pleading in the case. The federal land bank then filed a response and said that the mortgage makes it clear that the lender gets the tenant's crop. This case illustrates the hard life of a tenant farmer on the Great Plains. A tenant does not own the land and is not involved in the mortgage to the bank. The tenant works the land and gets a percentage of the crop, or he pays cash rent. A percentage of the crop goes to the landlord. In this case the federal land bank tried to get the entire crop. Under Oklahoma law, the bank can't do it because there has to be a financial statement or chattel mortgage filed each crop year. The bank had not followed this law. The bank argued that it was an agency of the U.S. government and did not need to comply with state law.

After a long struggle, the tenant got his crop. Unanswered was the question, *why should the federal land bank abuse tenant farmers?* Tenant farmers are the poorest farmers, and they are least able to withstand the loss of a crop. Moreover, this tactic represented nothing more than attempted theft by the federal land bank. It revealed the utter lawlessness of the bank in its relations with people, particularly poor tenant farmers.

In an adjoining county this same bank's officers appear in court to say that the tenant was a trespasser on the land and did not have a valid lease. The officers lied repeatedly. Fortunately, the tenant computer printouts from the land bank showed that he did have a lease. The jury took eleven minutes to give the wheat crop back to the tenant.

I cannot find a single case in the Great Plains where the federal land bank system did not abuse every single tenant farmer it could.

When the federal land banks had financial problems, they ran to Congress for—money, newer and cheaper laws and more loan guarantees and tax exemptions on bonds. But Congress does not even try to protect the tenant and poor farmer from the financial ravages of the banks. It is any wonder that hatred of the government is on the rise in the Great Plains? The Congress should show a little bit of mercy and compassion for the poorest of farmers—the tenants. So should the federal land banks. Farmers have a saying that illustrates the problems. "When a crop is lost, a landlord suffers, but the tenant starves."

In this case the federal land bank received a judgment for $85,384.07 and attorney's fee of $4,000. FmHA received a judgment for $42,841.53 and an additional $11,104.17 for earned but unpaid interest. The land sold for $37,500 and so the losses to the federal land bank came to $47,884.07. The taxpayers picked up the bill—$42,841.53, plus the unpaid interest of $11,104.17 on the FmHA loans. Attorney's fees billed to the tenant exceeded his profit.

> *Case No. C-85-210.* In this case, the federal land bank sued a farmer. The judgment was for $114,166.78 on 320 acres of wheat land that sold for $52,000 leaving losses of $62,166.78 to the federal land bank. In asking for the deficiency judgment, the bank said it was short $68,160.42, a difference of $5,993.64. How the figure of $5,993.64 was added into the judgment was not explained.

This case is noteworthy because it shows the utter collapse of the economy of the area. Here 310 acres sold for $52,000, or for $167.70 per acre.

> *Case No. C-85-218.* The federal land bank sued a farmer and the FmHA. The FmHA cross-sued and received a judgment for $70,691.64. The judgment for the bank was $93,390.79. The land sold for $21,500 leaving losses of $71,890.79 to the federal land bank, with taxpayers scheduled to pick up the tab. Losses to FmHA came to $70,691.64 plus unpaid interest of $15,569.19.

> *Case No. C-85-221.* The federal land bank sued a farmer and the FmHA. The latter counter-sued the farmer for $77,239.09 plus interest in the amount of $7,551.25. The bank got a judgment for $158,455.68. The land finally sold for $149,300, leaving a loss of $9,155.68 to the federal land bank. The loss to the U.S. Treasury on the FmHA loan

was the full amount plus interest as stated above. Notice that in every one of these cases, FmHA was under a North Dakota court injunction not to foreclose on a farmer, yet it sued anyway. That Van Sickle court order was really rather meaningless.

Case No. C-85-233. The federal land bank sued a farmer for $469,750.62 on 275 acres of land. The farmer responded that the federal land bank was not following the policies of Congress on granting forbearance to the farmer. Forbearance requires the answer to four questions and they are:
1. Is the borrower doing his honest best and is he cooperative.
2. Is the borrower putting income on his debts and not wasting it.
3. Is the farmer taking proper care of the property that he mortgaged to the federal land bank.
4. Is the farmer capable of working his way out of the existing debt loan.

If a farmer met all of these four requirements, then the farmer could refinance, extend the payments, reamortize the mortgage, or go into partial or complete liquidation, all as the facts indicated. This is what the Congress wanted done. It wanted the banks to sit down with farmers and work out the situation short of legal foreclosure. The federal land bank of Wichita did as little as possible to comply with these mandates of Congress. However, the federal land bank of St. Paul, Minnesota did its best to be in compliance. The difference between these two banks was the difference in the philosophy of the officers. It was the same law and it was wheat farmers that the law was passed to benefit.

The federal land bank system is governed by a board in the USDA. Obviously it is not working very much. This board is not supervising the system very well and it is not aware of what is really going on.

It should be noted that most farmers probably cannot meet requirement No. 4 of forbearance, that is, showing a capability of working out of debt. The federal land bank and the FmHA threw money out in such huge amounts that I don't believe most borrowers could ever repay. Further, when Reagan destroyed the price floor under wheat by setting aside the Carter embargo, this made it nearly impossible for wheat farms to be profitable. I have talked to income tax preparers all over the Great Plains. They tell me that fewer than 5% of the wheat farmers are in a profitable operation. Fully 95% are losing money constantly. Such a situation makes forbearance impossible.

Why can't the federal land bank of Wichita sit down with these farmers and their attorneys, and spend fifteen minutes explaining the situation? The federal land bank at St. Paul has done this. In the case that I am now reviewing, the question came up whether the 1985 forbearance act of Congress would apply to a loan that was made before that time. The bank's attorney filed a lengthy brief attempting to prove that forbearance could not be a defense for loans made prior to 1985. That question overlooks the fact that forbearance was a part of the Farm Credit Act of 1971, and Congress was only making clear what it did in 1971 when it repeated itself in 1985. Forbearance applies to all loans made since 1971. Every loan in default in Alfalfa County, Oklahoma was made after 1971. The loans made before 1971 were made by responsible loan officers and were not in default. This case has not been completed by the court at the time of this writing.

Let's pause for a moment and try to answer the question on why these farmers took out all of these bad loans. Why would a farmer do such a thing?

Let me answer these questions by telling you a personal experience I had several years ago. I was sitting in the waiting room of one of our judges. He was late that morning because he had to take his son to the emergency room at the hospital. While I was sitting there, an elderly woman came in, leaning heavily on her cane. She sat down and then asked the secretary to call her attorney and tell him she was there. The secretary did so and told both the attorney and the woman that the judge would be late. The woman said she would wait since she did not want to drive back home. She surveyed the room and started talking as if addressing a large crowd. This is her story.

Her husband died a year ago after spending over sixty years as a bank officer in a small community. Their son had contracted spinal cancer a few months ago, and now at the age of eighty-seven she was the managing officer of the family bank. All of her property was tied up in that bank. The bank had to be profitable. Four generations of her family were dependent on income from the bank. She was managing the bank solely on what she picked up living with a bank officer for more than sixty years. She criticized the government for getting the economy into the mess it was in. She deplored the fall in the price of wheat. The farmers were having a tough time and they were the chief customers of the bank. Nearly all of the farmers were losing money. They were badly in debt. Their huge debts made to the federal land banks and the FmHA made it nearly impossible for the bank to carry them through. She was doing the best she could. She surveyed the room and then she asked: "Who made these bad loans?" Everyone including myself was totally absorbed in what she was saying. I was experiencing a bit of banking Americana that no college of business teaches.

She then asked the question again: "Who made these bad loans? Did the farmer make these bad loans? No!" she shouted, "The farmer does not make loans. Bad loan officers make bad loans. ALL BAD LOANS ARE MADE BY BAD LOAN OFFICERS," she said. Indeed, that is who made these bad loans shown in these court cases. The wheat farmer did not make these bad loans. Bad loans were made by the bad loan officers, the managers and shysters, in the offices of the federal land banks and the loan shills in the FmHA. Farmers just got in line.

But most farmers did not get in line. Over 50% of the farmers have no debts at all. About 25% have some debts, but not in an excessive amount. Long time farmers were skeptical of these *narodnik* types, and that skepticism saved them from economic ruin.

Case No. C-85-235. This case involved the federal land bank suing a farmer. The judgment was for $75,023.30 and the property sold for $18,400, leaving a loss to the bank of $56,623.30. The bank filed and got a deficiency judgment of $63,764.68. There was no explanation in the file of how this kiting of the amount took place.

Case No. C-85-248. The federal land bank sued a farmer and the FmHA. FmHA then cross-sued the farmer and got a judgment for $254,801.29 plus an additional $43,085.24 for interest. The farmer argued that he had not been given an opportunity for forbearance. The court did not extend credence to this argument, and overruled the farmer before proceeding to judgment. The Farm Credit Act of 1985 makes it clear that a federal land bank is to give notice to the farmer prior to filing any foreclosure. This notice is to spell out the benefits of forbearance, and the conditions for availability. In general the banks have not done this.

Here is another case wherein the federal land bank of Wichita defied the Congress and got by with it. The judgment for the federal land bank was for $209,782.77. My informant believes that this property will not sell for over $80,000. Losses to the federal land bank will be around $129,782.77 and the cost to the taxpayers for the FmHA end of the transaction will be $254,801.29 plus earned but unpaid interest in the amount of $43,085.24.

Case No. C-85-252. Here the federal land bank sued a farmer but quickly dismissed the action.

Case C-85-253. The federal land bank sued a homeowner in a small town in the county. The property sold for $18,700 and the loss to the federal land bank was penciled in at $26,588.71. This case shows that the federal land bank has no more expertise in lending to people in town than it has in lending to farmers in the country.

Case No. C-85-281. The federal land bank sued a farmer and then shortly thereafter dismissed the case.

Case No. C-86-15. The federal land bank sued a farmer and FmHA. FmHA then cross-sued the farmer. FmHA got a judgment for $131,853.26 plus earned but unpaid interest of $45,113.75. The bank got a judgment for $140,729.96 and attorney's fees of $7,000. The farmer filed bankruptcy, which ended collection activities against him. The land was then sold for $102,300 and the losses of the bank were nailed down at $38,429.96. Taxpayers harvested FmHA's loss, which came to $131,853,26 plus interest of $45,113.75.

Case No. C-86-28. The federal land bank sued a man and the FmHA. FmHa then cross-sued the debtor and got a judgment for $24,413.31 plus $7,045.59 unpaid interest. This debtor lived in another part of the state and was not a resident on the land. Federal land bank got a judgment for $88,736.81. Its attorney wanted a fee of $5,000 but the court cut this to $2,500, which was still excessive since nothing was used in this case but computer-generated forms, and the case was not contested. The land sold for $20,000. The loss to the federal land bank was $68,736.81. The loss to the U.S. Treasury on the FmHA end of the transaction was $24,413.31 plus an interest of $7,045.59.

Case No. C-86-29. The federal land bank sued a party for foreclosure on a house in a small village, but this case was dismissed.

Case No. C-86-31. The federal land bank sued a farmer. The farmer answered that the forbearance statutes had not been complied with. The federal land bank dismissed this case rather than answer the farmer's complaint.

Case No. C-86-35. The federal land bank sued a farmer. The farmer answered into court that the bank had not granted forbearance, and the farmer insisted that he met all of the four requirements. The bank finally responded that they had indeed held a meeting, but that no conclusions were reached. This is the first case I have found in which the federal land bank admitted that the farmer was entitled to a forbearance hearing, and was given one. The bank then suddenly dismissed the case without comment.

One of the reasons that this case may have been dismissed might be that it was slowly dawning on the bank that a big mistake was being made in refusing to even consider forbearance. Federal land bank policy and attitude were forcing farmers to write Senators and Congressmen. Lawmakers were beginning to question what the bank was doing. New bankruptcy codes were being considered in Congress, and the federal land bank might not fare so well. Forbearance pleas were getting into federal courts in various parts of the country. Oddly, federal courts of appeal ruled that the forbearance statute represented permissive legislation, and the federal land bank could comply with it if the banks wanted to, but they need not comply if the banks did not want to. These decisions were never appealed to the Supreme Court of the U.S., and many people have wondered what that court would have done.

But these court decisions were of little value to the federal land bank because the farmers just put political pressure on Congress and Congress amended the bankruptcy code and set up a new bankruptcy chapter. This chapter allowed any farmer with fewer debts than $1.5 million to file in bankruptcy for reorganization and a scale-down in debts. No creditor had more hot air in its portfolio of loans than did the federal land bank and these banks were hurt the worst by this new legislation. One farmer in an adjoining county owed the federal land bank over $400,000 on a sand hill farm. The bankruptcy court scaled this down to $60,000 leaving the land bank with a loss of $340,000. This is perhaps the worst scale-down I have encountered.

There can be few arguments against laws passed by Congress in bankruptcy, because bankruptcy is a power that is specifically enumerated in Article 1, Section 8 of the U.S. Constitution. It is believed by many lawyers that federal judges are stiffer and tougher than state judges. One should always beware of making such generalizations. In Alfalfa County and in other counties across the Great Plains, state judges would overrule the farmer on forbearance and hold for the federal land bank. Many of these farmers and their lawyers believed that the state judges were giving in to the attorneys of the federal land bank. I can see where this may not be true, but this is the feeling of most of the attorneys I have interviewed. But make no mistake about it, the judges in the U.S. Bankruptcy Courts have taken no sass or back-talk from the federal land banks. Bankruptcy judges have let it be known that when Congress passes an act, it will be enforced in their courts. Accordingly, federal land banks have not profited from obstruction in bankruptcy courts. And they have actually paid a high price for not granting forbearance in state courts.

Case No. C-86-39. The bank sued a farmer and the FmHA. FmHA then cross-sued the farmer. Perhaps the reader will notice that when the FmHA is a party defendant in a case, there is no hope for economic rehabilitation of the farmer. In this case, federal land bank got a judgment for $302,483.68 and the FmHA got a judgment for $356,059.66 plus $146,171.85 interest. The property sold for $109,550, delivering a loss of $192,933.68 to the federal land bank. The loss to the U.S. Treasury on the FmHA end of the deal was the full amount or $356,320 plus $146,171.85 interest. In this case the loss was $549,253.68 on one farmer.

Case No. C-86-50. The federal land bank sued a farmer and the FmHA. FmHA then cross-sued the farmer. In this case the federal land bank got a judgment for $139,505.14 plus an attorney's fee of $2,500. Halfway into the decade, federal land bank was no longer getting the attorney's fees it used to get. In 1983 it got $9,508.23 on a case no larger than this one, and certainly no more complicated. A new and different judge seemed to be on the bench. This judge did not believe that $5,000 had been earned in an uncontested case based solely on computer-generated forms. So he refused outrageously large attorney's fees for the federal land bank. FmHA got a judgment for $47,003.49 plus interest of $5,911.21. The land was sold for $39,100. Since only 160 acres were involved, this case reveals land values down, $244 per acre in this case. The loss to the federal land bank is $100,405.14 and the loss to the U.S. Treasury was $47,003.49 together with interest of $5,911.21, which the taxpayers now has to pay.

Case No. C-86-57. The federal land bank sued a farmer. The FmHA was not involved. The bank dismissed the case.

Case No. C-86-74. The federal land bank sued a farmer and the FmHA. Here the federal land bank was owed $94,729.64 on a 160 acre farm. The farmer had trouble repaying this loan. Such land cannot carry a debt of just over $500 per acre. FmHA swung into action with cafeteria credit. The following loans were made:

DATE	AMOUNT LOANED
Aug. 19, 1980	$61,700
Feb. 21, 1980	11,200
Jul. 29, 1981	8,800
May 28, 1982	39,900
Nov. 18, 1983	63,700
Nov. 18, 1983	20,720.71
TOTAL FmHA LOANS	$206,020.71

The farmer collapsed into insolvency. Judgment was entered by the court and the farmer filed for bankruptcy. The land was then sold for $39,100 with the federal land bank suffering a loss of $55,629.64. The loss to the taxpayers was total on the FmHA end of the deal, or $87,938.48 plus $11,454.88 interest. In this case the farmer was having a hard time repaying the bank. He got information from an employee of the federal land bank that the U.S. government would loan him the money he needed. The bank sent him to the FmHA, which in turn set him up with cafeteria credit. In the years 1980, 1981, 1982 and 1983, this farmer got a new loan each year from FmHA. This money went largely to repay the federal land bank which in turn spent its earnings on riotous office overhead expenses, enormous attorney fees, imported limousines and finally spent a token amount on bondholders.

Case No. C-86-80. The federal land bank sued a homeowner in one of the small villages in the county. A 1971 Act of Congress allowed the bank to loan money to people in cities and towns of less than 7,500. This allowed everyone in Alfalfa County, Oklahoma, to qualify for bank loans since there are only about 6,000 people living in the entire county. The judgment for the bank was for $62,061.22 and the property sold for $19,400. Losses to the federal land bank were $42,661.22.

Case No. C-86-86. The federal land bank sued a dentist who had never been a farmer. He lived in a distant city. The judgment was for $132,716.88 and the property sold for $46,300, causing a loss to the federal land bank of $86,416.88.

I can show you cases in other counties and other states where the federal land bank loaned money to doctors, lawyers, rich people of all types, pool halls, bowling alleys, and in one case, a massage parlor.

During the debates on the Transportation Act in 1940, an obscure Senator from Missouri said that when Congress passes an act it takes from twenty to forty years before rich people develop a liking for that law and prostitute it so that they can rake off of it. That Senator was Harry S Truman. That is what has happened to the federal land banks. It was a good idea when Congress passed it in 1916, but it has now been twisted and prostituted so badly that it needs to be abolished. There is no justification for making a loan to dentists and massage parlors. And let me hasten to add that lawyers and tax accountants have been involved in signing up for land bank loans. One lawyer in Oklahoma cost the land bank more than a million dollars. Another lawyer cost the bank a loss of over $800,000. A state district judge in Kansas cost the government the loss of $239,700 with unpaid interest of $29,907.28 added.

Case No. C-86-91. The federal land bank sued a farmer. The FmHA was not involved. This case has not gone to judgment at the time of this writing. In fact, it seems as if the bank and the farmer may work out their differences.

Case No. C-86-186. The federal land bank sued a farmer and the FmHA. The farmer asked for dismissal on grounds that the Oklahoma Legislature had passed a new law in which the federal land bank was not to foreclose for one year. This law was designed to force the bank to take farmers through a forbearance procedure. The Attorney General of Oklahoma was notified that the bank made a claim of the unconstitutionality. The Attorney General filed a full brief. He carefully argued the case for the act. A year passed before the Supreme Court of Oklahoma could rule in a case in another county. Many trial judges across Oklahoma asked the bank to wait out the year. The bank refused. The case was decided by the Supreme Court of Oklahoma quite a while after the expiration date of the law. The Court felt that the law presented a question that needed to be answered, and it ruled that a moratorium on debt in Oklahoma was not constitutional. The high court voided the act even though it had expired.

Case No. C-86-191. The federal land bank sued a farmer and then dismissed the case.

Case No. C-86-192. The federal land bank sued a homeowner over a small tract of land. Judgment was for the bank for $32,960.16. An attorney's fee of $500 was allowed. Notice how the attorneys fees have been falling. The judge was closely watching what was going on. The property was sold for $19,700 and the losses to the federal land bank were $13,260.16.

This completes the legal activity of the federal land bank in Alfalfa County, Oklahoma, during the year of 1986.

Case No C-87-1. This was the first civil case to be filed by the federal land bank in 1987. It sued a farmer and the FmHA. The FmHA then cross-sued the farmer and got a judgment for $120,000. The federal land bank got a judgment for $220,627.53. The land was sold for $76,000 and the federal land bank suffered a loss of $144,627.53. The U.S. Treasury suffered a loss of $120,000 plus interest of $25,764.65.

Case No. C-87-2. The second 1987 case filed in the county was filed by the federal land bank when it sued a farmer. In this case the farmer counter-sued federal land bank, charging that the land bank had raised its interest rate to 13.75%, an unreasonable rate. He asked for a jury trial on this and other questions.

The case was fully briefed by both sides. The farmer had asked for the protection of the forbearance statute, and the federal land bank very reluctantly granted a hearing on this, but then refused to release its findings. Under the forbearance statutes, there is a right of appeal. This farmer was denied this right of appeal.

By the time the case was being briefed, four federal cases had been decided to the effect that forbearance was voluntarily, and federal land bank could grant forbearance or deny it. In this instance, federal courts are saying that an act of Congress is meaningless. This is a dangerous conclusion. When the first forbearance statute was passed in 1971 as part of the Farm Credit Act, the Board of Governors in the USDA were asked if they were going to issue regulations on forbearance, and they answered that they would not since the law was so clear and so proper, regulations would not be needed. Since then the federal courts have answered that it was not something that a farmer should ask for or even expect. The Supreme Court of the U.S. has never ruled on this. The Act of 1985, however, is clear on one thing. The bank is not even to file a foreclosure case until it has granted the benefits of forbearance to the farmer. This act of Congress is written in simple, plain English and its meaning is understandable to laymen and professionals alike.

The question must be asked, *Why would Congress pass the statute at all if it was only permissive?* The insurance companies have practiced a policy of forbearance for a hundred years. To end any question about what Congress intended, Congress passed a new law in 1988 ruling that courts could not foreclose any farm mortgage until the federal land bank granted a hearing to the farmer on forbearance. Congress also passed the Agriculture Credit Act of 1987, which was signed into law by President Reagan on January 6, 1988, and one of the section reads as follows:

> No qualified lender may foreclose or continue any foreclosure proceedings with respect to any distressed loan before the lenders has completed any pending consideration of the loan for restructuring under this section.

Here the Congress is affecting the docket and the rules of the courts. The courts are to stop all foreclosure proceedings until the lender grants forbearance. This is what the Congress is saying and doing. The federal land bank of St. Paul has always done this. It has not been affected adversely. The federal land bank at Wichita has never granted forbearance. It is doing so now. Because of this development, the number of foreclosure cases will drop sharply.

When the Congress or a state legislature passes a law, lawyers should not scheme to avoid it. We should all make a continuous effort to not only apply the law, but also to obey the law. The federal land bank did not do this, and they will suffer more than any other lender, because they are now the largest lender to farmers. FmHA has granted forbearance in some cases. The private insurance companies have had their collection departments work with borrowers for more than a century. The tyranny of the federal land bank is what the Congress tried to curb here, and the federal land bank is the only creditor that will be adversely affected by the new law.

In general it is best when one can file a lawsuit and have it fairly and promptly heard by the courts. In general I do not want the jurisdiction of our courts affected by decrees from Congress or state legislatures. But I also do not want the courts to rule that acts of Congress are permissive and meaningless when they are clearly mandatory.

It seems to me that this question of jurisdiction is one that affects the very essence of this nation as a nation. In general, bar associations and attorneys do not want the court system stripped of its ability and duty to grant judicial review. However, this continuous defiance of the will of the Congress got out of hand on the question of forbearance.

Why the federal land bank of Wichita has absolutely refused forbearance is a mystery. Perhaps its officers enjoy seeing farmers in financial trouble. Some may argue that forbearance is a weak thing for Congress to do. Four federal courts have agreed with that position. But that overlooks the fact the Congress has many demands made upon it. If the farmer is forced off of the land, he may very well wind up on food stamps. Congress has to finance food stamps. So by keeping the farmer on the land, Congress does not have to deal with food stamps for him. Therefore it is not an unreasonable request that every effort be made to keep the farmer on the land. Other voices in other rooms may decree comparative advantage in world food production, but vantage point ground level says farmers must do the farming. Old George Norris, when he was a state judge in Nebraska, was opting to keep farmers on the land a hundred years ago. His idea is not impossible to apply.

But the arrogance of the federal land bank system in general is totally hostile to these clearly mandated laws of Congress. For example, in the case that I am now discussing in the courthouse at Cherokee, Oklahoma, the federal land bank of Wichita filed a law brief and in it I find the following bit of arrogance:

There is simply no duty on the part of the Federal Land Bank to forbear or grant restructuring to any borrower in default.

These words were underlined in the brief of the federal land bank. There you have it. The federal land bank of Wichita is simply not going to abide by the law. The federal land bank dismissed this case on September 11, 1989 rather than comply with forbearance. This farmer had been a good customer of the bank for over twenty years. No explanation was given.

Case No. C-87-6. The federal land bank sued a farmer and got a judgment of $152,504.51. Attorney fees were set at $1,300. The judge was closely watching attorney fees—he thinks! The land sold for $103,500. The loss to the federal land bank was $49,004.51, but the bank jerked this up to a deficiency judgment of $52,760.47, without any explanation for this creative bookkeeping. One new item emerged from this file. In cases and years past, the federal land bank refused to settle with its farmer-owners on the stock they had been required to buy from the system. Here the bank filed a partial release of judgment for the sum of $6,005. This was not cash to the farmer, but was a credit on the judgment. Oklahoma and federal law require that all offsets be made at the start of a case. If one is owed $1,000, but also owes the other party $500, then the maximum that can be obtained by judgment is $500. The federal land bank at Wichita will not follow these laws on the premise that they are a federal agency. It is interesting to note that the federal land bank of St. Paul, Minnesota, gives an offset to all farmers for their stock at the start of any suit. If the farmer owes the bank $100,000 and there is $5,000 in stock, the bank at St. Paul puts this in its original suit petition asking for $95,000.

Case No. C-87-10. The federal land bank sued a farmer and FmHA. The FmHA had given cafeteria credit as follows:

Mar. 6, 1978	$14,000
Mar. 6, 1978	3,340
Mar. 6, 1978	10,310
Mar. 6, 1978	11,850
Oct. 29, 1979	66,150
May 7, 1981	172,000
Mar. 1, 1982	41,810
Mar. 1, 1982	6,490
TOTAL FmHA LOANS	$325,950

In the judgment that followed, the federal land bank got $204,174.58 and the FmHA got one that was $448,268.65. These data suggest that there is another loan in another county, not covered here, or interest is involved in the loans. This is the only discrepancy that I have found on FmHA figures in Great Plains cases.

This property has not been sold at the time of this writing, but my two informants believe that the federal land bank will lose $100,000. The loss to the U.S. Treasury will be total. Taxpayers will get to pick up the tabs for $448,268.65 plus $60,762.93 in interest.

Case No. C-87-34. The federal land bank association at Woodward, Oklahoma sued a farmer. The case was settled and dismissed.

Case No. C-87-37. The federal land bank sued a farmer. In this case the farmer questioned whether the federal land bank sold his mortgage to the Capital Corporation which was set up by Congress to bail out the system. If the mortgage been sold, then the proper party to sue would be that corporation and not the land bank, the farmer argued. He believed that the federal land bank may have done this to get around Oklahoma law. Suddenly this case was dismissed by the federal land bank. The foul play suggested in this case can only be seen if and when the bank opens its files.

Case No. C-87-38. The federal land bank sued a farmer for $452,548.30. The farmer filed for bankruptcy and asked for reorganization under the new Chapter 12 of the Bankruptcy Act. This chapter was signed into law by President Reagan just before the Congressional elections of 1986. There has been a question in the minds of many farmers, lawyers and bank officials, as well as federal judges, whether Congress should interfere with the right to contract by forbearance. That question has now been resolved. Congress can clearly act in bankruptcy and reorganization in bankruptcy is now a new ball game for farmers. In this case the bankruptcy court will put a valuation on the value of the land, and will not follow the faked appraisals of the federal land bank. The bankruptcy court will take testimony from real estate agents, attorneys and others on what the real value of the land is. Since the federal land bank always inflated appraisals, it will be hurt more than any other lenders. It seems highly ironic that the biggest abuser of the appraisal system, the biggest abuser of the farmers, should now be the biggest loser. The reason I hate such justice is that it has a habit of cutting in all directions, and that is what has happened here. Had these land bank officials stayed in their plush offices and granted forbearance, this law may never have been passed. This case has not been completed. Bank losses can be expected to $352,550.

Case No. C-87-51. Here the federal land bank sued a farmer for $546,430.05 and received a judgment for that amount. The federal land bank probably will lose $250,000.

Case No. C-87-55. The federal land bank sued a farmer for $104,436.63. The case was uncontested. The judgment for the bank came to $114,464.89. No explanation was given for the increase. The land was sold for $62,001 and the bank suffered a loss of $52,463.89.

Case No. C-87-86. This case was soon dismissed. Land in several counties and in two different states was involved.

Case No. C-87-87. The federal land bank sued a farmer but soon dismissed the case. One of the reasons for this dismissal was the failure of the bank to comply with forbearance.

Case No. C-87-88. Federal land bank sued a farmer and the FmHA. The latter cross-sued the farmer. The bank sued for $221,061.66. This is a case of cafeteria credit run amok. Here are the take-out amounts.

Dec. 20, 1978	$316,000.
Dec. 20, 1978	83,000.
Nov. 6, 1980	212,800.
Jun. 24, 1981	50,000.
Nov. 30, 1981	69,780.
Nov. 30, 1981	72,480.
May 4, 1984	142,427.04
May 4, 1984	50,000.
May 4, 1984	130,000.
May 4, 1984	90,000.
TOTAL FmHA LOANS	$1,216,487.04

In this case the federal land bank loaned $221,061.66, which represents an overdosing of credit. FmHA loaned $1,216,487.04. The total debt came to $1,437,548.70 on 560 acres of the sorriest land in the county. Each acre had to support a debt load of $3,567.05. In this case the federal land bank finally lowered itself to consider forbearance, but then violated the statute on appeals. It refused the farmer the right to appeal its decision as guaranteed by Congress. This case is not complete.

I don't believe that I can get it across to the average reader how easy it was to get FmHA to loan money to farmers. This farmer got $1,216,487.04.

I have documented one case in Oklahoma that is a moral tragedy. This man was so stupid when he was in high school, his teachers begged him to quit school because he was such an intellectual problem. Fellow students said they did want to learn but could not when he was in the classroom. This fellow was so stupid that the school board asked him to quit school because they were tired of his capers. His parents begged him to quit school because they were on the verge of despair. They even agreed to buy him a car if he would give it up. So he quit school and got the car. Would you believe that he clipped the U.S. government for over $600,000 via cafeteria credit furnished by FmHA.

Case No. C-87-97. Federal land bank sued a farmer. This case was dismissed.

Case No. C-87-121. the federal land bank sued a farmer and got a judgment for $119,954.53. The property sold for $45,500, leaving the bank with a loss of $74,454.53.

Case No. C-87-131. Federal land bank sued a farmer and the case was dismissed.

Case No. C-87-132. Federal land bank sued a farmer and the judgment was for $137,173. The land sold for $42,100, leaving a deficiency of $106,406.79 as a loss to the bank. The actual difference between these two figures is $95,073, but the bank's attorney's added in his attorney fee of $1,500. There was a partial release of judgment on the stock, which yielded a new deficiency judgment and loss to the bank of $106,406.79. Adding an attorney's fee into the judgment where it can earn interest is unethical, of course.

Case No. C-87-134. Federal land bank sued a farmer and FmHA. In this case extensive negotiations took place as they should in all legal actions. This represents the first case in the county in which federal land bank made an effort to settle. The farmer filed bankruptcy and asked for reorganization or a scale-down in debts. Federal land bank agreed to take title to the land at fair market value, not the usual excessive appraisal figure.The bank agreed to give a credit $120,000 for the land. What the bank did here was to repudiate its own corrupt appraisal system. The farmer signed the deed to the property giving title to the federal land bank, and the bankruptcy case was dismissed. The federal land bank did not file the deed but kept it in its offices. They tried to rent out the land. In general they made a bad mess of the situation. In the end the federal land bank refused to file the deed and asked the court to issue judgment for the full amount of the mortgage. The farmer then re-entered the case and started to defend himself. He asked interrogatories of the federal land bank. One of his questions was about the rate of interest being charged. Another question was whether the bank was favoring some farmers over others on interest rates. The bank did not want to answer this one, but the court ordered an answer, which is very revealing. The bank, in fact, charged different customers different interest rates. The court files in this case overflowed four very large folders and provide a gold mine of information on corruption in the federal land bank system.

For example, an oil well was involved. Royalty checks went directly to the federal land bank to be applied to the loan balance. This well was not a major producer, yet it yielded a check to the bank every month for a number of years. The federal land bank finally admitted that it had not kept an accounting record of these receipts, and the farmer not been given credit for them. Finally the bank was forced to file an accounting, which came to some fifty pages. Depositions were forced upon the bank. The senior vice-president of the federal land bank association admitted the bank had not given the farmer credit for the oil payments. His secretary swore under oath that they had continuous problems with their financial records. A certified public accountant examined the records in this case and testified that the federal land bank padded its claim by more than $100,000. The modern farmer, upon examination, was really no better off than the old black ex-slave standing in the plantation store while the ex-slave owner figured up the bills. Here a wheat farmer was being fleeced by the federal land bank, and its officers admitted under oath that is what was going on. Yet federal courts have refused to let punitive damages be lodged against the bank and its officers. If a private insurance company was involved, that company would be disciplined by the court, and their officers know that.

The officers of the bank admitted under oath that they claimed fertilizer bills were paid, but no fertilizer was used. The bank's attorney asked for continuous fees, and these were added to the bill and interest compounded. In this case the attorney for the federal land bank sent his time charts to the bank each month and was given a fee at that time. This fee was added to what the farmer owed, and interest was computed and added in. The next month the attorney fees were again computed and added to the total due and interest then computed and added in. Fees were demanded for seventy-five separate items of work between 1983 and 1988, with a total of $15,660.23.

DATE	FLB ATTORNEY FEES	DATE	FLB ATTORNEY FEES
Sep. 9, 83	$34.19	May 29, 86	$367.46
Oct. 5, 83	52.00	Jun. 4, 86	20.00
Nov. 9, 83	32.00	Jun. 25, 86	26.25
Dec. 7, 83	36.00	Jul. 10, 86	41.25
Jan. 9, 84	24.23	Aug. 4, 86	195.00
Feb. 8, 84	66.18	Aug. 8, 86	98.89
Apr. 4, 84	204.10	Sep. 11, 86	5.00
May 15, 84	5.38	Sep. 30, 86	401.56
Jun. 22, 84	42.50	Oct. 24, 86	291.25
Jul. 9, 84	12.75	Dec. 12, 86	1,156.65
Aug. 6, 84	17.00	Dec. 30, 86	36.95
Sep. 13, 84	55.26	Feb. 4, 87	85.39
Oct. 3, 84	281.71	Jun. 18, 87	2,115.07
Nov. 8, 84	179.00	Feb. 9, 87	134.01
Dec. 3, 84	42.82	Feb. 13, 87	100.06
Jan. 23, 85	4.25	Apr. 7, 87	769.61
Feb. 13, 85	123.50	Apr. 10, 87	65.00
Feb. 25, 85	12.75	May 7, 87	675.94
Mar. 12, 85	62.15	Jun. 11, 87	21.81
Apr. 9, 85	20.00	Jul. 8, 87	22.81
May 7, 85	105.00	Jul. 20, 87	56.74
Jul. 3, 85	41.12	Aug. 3, 87	14.99
Aug. 7, 85	70.00	Aug. 7, 87	247.90
Aug. 22, 85	398.00	Aug. 24, 87	958.41
Oct. 2, 85	773.30	Sep. 3, 87	8.21
Oct. 9, 85	395.63	Sep. 21, 87	64.73
Oct. 25, 85	752.63	Oct. 8, 87	418.52
Nov. 25, 85	1,573.92	Oct. 28, 87	13.75
Dec. 19, 85	75.00	Nov. 9, 87	169.57
Jan. 9, 86	15.00	Dec. 16, 87	11.00
Jan. 21, 86	197.23	Jan. 12, 88	125.77
Feb. 26, 86	93.41	Feb. 4, 88	174.73
Mar. 4, 86	10.00	Mar. 9, 88	46.78
Mar. 28, 86	92.50	Apr. 8, 88	115.38
Apr. 4, 86	3.13	Jul. 29, 88	105.17
Apr. 28, 86	184.60	May 9, 88	90.13
May 7, 86	30.00	Jun. 6, 88	220.00
		Jul. 7, 88	70.25

Attorney fees on a different loan but in the same court case were charged for seventy-five items, totaling $15,427.68.

DATE	FLB ATTORNEY FEES	DATE	FLB ATTORNEY FEES
Sep. 9, 83	$34.20	May 29, 86	67.46
Oct. 5, 83	52.00	Jun. 4, 86	20.00
Nov. 3, 83	32.00	Jun. 25, 86	26.25
Dec. 7, 83	36.00	Jul. 10, 86	41.25
Jan. 9, 84	24.22	Aug. 4, 86	195.00
Feb. 8, 84	66.17	Aug. 8, 86	98.88
Apr. 4, 84	204.10	Sep. 11, 86	5.00
May 15, 84	5.39	Oct. 24, 86	291.25
Jun. 22, 84	42.50	Dec. 12, 86	1,156.65
Jul. 9, 84	12.75	Dec. 30, 86	36.94
Aug. 6, 84	17.00	Feb. 4, 87	85.39
Sep. 13, 84	55.25	Feb. 9, 87	134.01
Oct. 3, 84	281.70	Feb. 13, 87	100.06
Nov. 8, 84	179.00	Apr. 7, 87	769.60
Dec. 3, 84	42.83	Apr. 10, 87	65.00
Jan. 23, 85	4.25	May 7, 87	675.94
Feb. 5, 85	12.75	May 11, 87	227.22
Feb. 13, 85	123.50	Jun. 11, 87	21.81
Mar. 12, 85	62.16	Jun. 18, 87	2,115.06
Apr. 9, 85	20.00	Jul. 8, 87	22.80
May 7, 85	105.00	Jul. 20, 87	56.73
Jul. 3, 85	41.13	Aug. 3, 87	15.00
Aug. 7, 85	70.00	Aug. 7, 87	247.89
Aug. 22, 85	398.01	Aug. 24, 87	958.40
Oct. 2, 85	773.30	Aug. 3, 87	8.22
Oct. 9, 85	395.62	Aug. 21, 87	64.73
Oct. 25, 85	694.50	Oct. 8, 87	418.52
Nov. 15, 85	1,573.91	Oct. 28, 87	13.75
Dec. 19, 85	75.00	Nov. 9, 87	169.57
Jan. 9, 86	15.00	Feb. 16, 87	11.00
Jan. 21, 86	197.23	Jan. 12, 88	125.80
Feb. 26, 86	93.40	Feb. 4, 88	174.72
Mar. 4, 86	10.00	Mar. 9, 88	46.77
Mar. 28, 86	92.50	Apr. 8, 88	115.37
Apr. 4, 86	3.12	May 9, 88	90.13
Apr. 28, 86	184.60	Jun. 6, 88	220.00
May 7, 86	30.00	Jul. 7, 88	70.25
		Jul. 29, 88	105.17

TOTAL FEES TO DATE $31,087.91

Here the attorney for the federal land bank has added the sum of $31,087.91 to the amount that the farmer owes. In this case the federal land bank also added two abstracting bills—when one is all that is needed until final judgment—seven bills for insurance that did not insure, one for advertising that had nothing to do with this case or the collection problem of the case, and a bill for $212.50 for miscellaneous items not identified. Then there was a bill for taxes not paid and fertilizer not used. That is how these amounts in these cases grew as if by magic.

This case also reveals that the federal land bank refused to produce documents several times, even though ordered to do so. In a companion bankruptcy case, the federal land bank admitted that it submitted a false 1099 form to Internal Revenue Service. This form is used to report forgiveness of debt. When this was pointed out to the federal land bank, it corrected the form 1099—however, the correction was wrong. In any case, Congress has exempted forgiveness of debt for farmers on such loan transactions, and such 1099 forms are not even needed. What the federal land bank is doing here is stirring up IRS when it has a collection problem with the farmer. The farmer left off the $120,000 because it was exempted by Congress and it was wrong in this case anyway because he never got it.

All of the above facts were admitted to by the federal land bank under oath and are in the files in the two courts.

Case No. C-87-145. It involved a question on a deed given from a debtor to a third party. Oklahoma law voids transfers that are made to avoid paying debts. The federal land bank invoked this state law since it is a private company and not part of the U.S. government. The case was uncontested and the federal land bank was given punitive damages of $50,000 plus expenses of $11,028.33 which were not itemized, and an attorney's fee of $465. This is the only honest attorney's fee I have seen in this county.

Case No. C-87-105. Federal land bank sued in a dispute over possession of land, and the court agreed that it was entitled to possession of the tract involved.

Case No. C-87-174. Here the federal land bank sued a farmer. The judgment was for $96,072.55. The property sold for $27,000, leaving a deficiency of $69,072.55. However the bank said the deficiency was actually $72,979.79. This case shows a substantial loss to the federal land bank but I cannot verify their figures to show the same loss they show.

Case No. C-87-180. Federal land bank sued a home owner in Cherokee, Oklahoma. It got a judgment for $31,407.95 and the property sold for $14,600, leaving a loss to the bank of $16,807.95. Here the bank kited this up to a deficiency of $20,049.70 with no clue whatsoever to indicate how this marvelous stunt was pulled off. After the judgment was handed down, the property owner bought the deficiency judgment for $10,000 and the bank issued a full judgment release in the case. The bank suffered a loss of $6,887.95 or a loss of $10,049.70, depending upon one's viewpoint of whether "kiting" should or could be a legal procedure. It is not under Oklahoma law and I believe the loss to the bank was $6,887.95 which is the figure I will use in my summary sheet. However, lawyers love to argue, debate and discuss, and so this could be argued for the larger figure.

Case No. C-87-193. Federal land bank sued a farmer and this case was dismissed. The act of Congress stopping all foreclosure until forbearance was used to support dismissal.

Case No. C-88-46. Federal land bank sued a farmer for $391,518.04. The bank admitted that the land was not worth over $15,500. This case was then dismissed and filed in an adjoining county.

Case No. C-88-78. In this instance, federal land bank sued a farmer and the FmHA. The latter cross-sued the farmer. Federal land bank obtained an initial judgment for $85,429.97 but it was increased to $94,710.64. I could not arrive at the higher figures used by the bank. This case was unusual because FmHA got paid the sum of $45,940.35 and suffered a loss of only $25,839.65. This is only the third time FmHA got anything in this county.

Case No. C-88-79. This one rates attention as a travesty on justice. The federal land bank sued a farmer and then cross-sued the Equitable Life Assurance Society of the U.S. Apparently the farmer and the federal land bank agreed on what the farmer should pay, and the farmer borrowed from the Equitable Life Assurance Society and to pay the federal land bank in full, taking a mortgage release, which was duly filed in the courthouse. Under oath the federal land bank admitted that it had no just claim against Equitable Life Assurance Society whatsoever. Apparently the insurance firm was brought into the case for purposes of intimidation to keep this lender out of the county. Over the years, Equitable loaned money to a few farmers and then quit the field, much as other insurance companies did after 1971. It came back to help a farmer, and federal land bank saw this as an opening to abuse Equitable. Undoubtedly the federal land bank will get by with this judicial travesty because it lays claim to being part of the federal government. In this case the federal land bank was ordered to produce documents which would show whether its claim was valid, and the bank refused to produce the documents. The court then ordered the federal land bank—in writing—to produce the documents. It refused.

All of the above facts have been admitted by the federal land bank in open court. Under both federal and Oklahoma law, a party in a civil lawsuit cannot refuse to produce relevant documents. It is only in criminal cases that the production of documents can be refused on the grounds that they might be incriminating.

> *Case No. C-88-108.* In this case Farm Credit Bank of Wichita filed a lawsuit against a farmer. In 1988 the bank changed its name from the federal land bank designation to the Farm Credit Bank of Wichita. This change was allowed by congressional act. One of the objects of the change was to get away from all of the bad public relation problems the federal land bank caused. In short, the bank had gotten a bad reputation by walking all over farmers. Farmers who could, paid off their mortgages and walked out of the system. A sharp decline in the lending activity of the bank followed. If this pattern could not be reversed, the bank eventually would have to be liquidated even though Congress made money available. Two years have come and gone, and customers continue to vote with their feet. In this case, the land was sold for $61,000. Loss to the bank was $58,557.89.

This takes me to the end of 1988.

At this point I believe a summary of cases is in order. FmHA brought 30 foreclosure cases. All were cross-petitions after the federal land bank had started an action. Judge Van Sickle's injunction in North Dakota prohibited foreclosures, but it did not in any way stop or slow down collection activities through the court in this county. Of 30 cases filed, all but five went to judgment. A total of $6,480,322.75 was actually at risk in loan balances taken to court with these suits. This factors out as an average loan of $216,000 per farmer. FmHA collected back only $292,511.90. There are few or no possibilities for further collections. Three cases were not completed in court at the time of my summary, however the cases are far enough along so a fairly accurate estimation of what is going to happen can be made. I believe the U.S. Treasury will lose $1,916,288.33 in these three cases. When this sum is added to the above losses, $6,364,805.08

will be lost in this one county. Two cases were are not far enough along to permit an estimate. They are not included in these figures.

FmHA always included interest that the loans earned but was not collected. This component came to $1,248,563.73. When added to the basic loss, the actual loss was $7,613,368.81 for twenty-eight cases in one county. Had this money been saved and placed on deposit at 6%—which is what Series EE U.S. bonds are earning—the annual income would be $456,802.08, or enough money to wipe out all poverty in Alfalfa County, Oklahoma, possibly forever. In a few years such surplus earnings could up-grade all dwellings, eliminating substandard housing. Within a few years this surplus would have been sufficient to gold-plate the football stadiums of area rural high schools. Yet the USDA lost all of this money on only twenty-eight people. Several were not even farmers.

There are two cases not in judgment at this writing. FmHA had a number of delinquent loans on which nothing had been done at the time of my summary. A few had been rescheduled and the amount of the principal reduced. These losses were apparently quite high. Although the figures were denied to me, I know enough about what is going on in the county to conservatively estimate that the losses exceeded $3,000,000. There are also cases in which the property was abandoned and nothing was done. In seven cases FmHA took title to farms. I suggest the government will lose as much as a million dollars on these farms. The government is a poor farmer and a poor manager and an impossible steward of farmland. The land is growing up in weeds. Many of these weeds are perennials. Once established, they increase and multiply. Chemical herbicides have some effect, but often merely pollute the eco-system. Adverse effects can last for decades.

One of the farms has been owned by the government for more than five years. The government pays no taxes on this farmland, and this hurts county government and schools dependent on land taxes as a source of income.

Land titles in Alfalfa County clearly reveal that FmHA

operated in the county from 1946 to 1983 and never suffered a loss nor filed a foreclosure action. Loan officers forced out of office by the Nixon administration, could and did operate properly a lending service that was of great benefit to farmers and no loss to taxpayers.

It is ironic that while these college trained come-lately people in FmHA were compiling a disgraceful record, public servants within Oklahoma, hired by the state, were operating a farm lending service in Alfalfa County and were not losing a penny. These public servants are employees of the Commissioners of the Land Office at Oklahoma City. Their job is to loan out money received when the state sold some school land obtained during early statehood days. At that time Congress reserved two sections of land out of each thirty-six sections in a township in the west, and dedicated this land for the support of common schools. When Oklahoma became a state in 1907, title to this land passed to the state. Over the years the state has sold part of this land. When a city is expanding, school land is often an obstruction to development. In such a situation, the state usually sells and the city builds on such land. Money received is held in a perpetual trust fund. Interest earned is used for schools. This money has been loaned to wheat farmers in the main, and is an important item of income to every school district in the state.

Loan officers of the Land Office are not college trained, but they do take a basic civil service test. Almost all are hired at the request of—and are a part of—the political patronage list of some state senator or representative. They are sometimes called political hacks, which is often unjust. They certainly can manage and lend money competently.

But the operators in the USDA lose money hand over fist. Those who believe—as I have for over forty years—that education is a solution to most social and economic ills, might ponder this disgraceful record turned in by the USDA and its college-trained hacks.

Attention should be called to a news report issued by FmHA on September 22, 1989. It stated that losses in Oklahoma exceeded $88,083,109 in write-downs alone. One large and rich farmer in Oklahoma was given a debt forgiveness ticket of $5,600,000 on one debt alone. Had this amount—$88,083,109—been properly lent to farmers, this loss would never have occurred. Had this amount been put out on interest at the rate of 6%, it would have earned annually $5,284,986, a sum large enough to wipe out all human poverty in the following Oklahoma counties: Alfalfa, Harper, Cimarron, Beaver, Roger Mills, Ellis, Dewey, Major, Blaine, Beckham, Caddo, Washita, Harmon, Lincoln, Jefferson, Greer, Kiowa, Tillman, Cotton, Grady, Pushmataha, Kingfisher, Choctaw, Ottawa, Washington, Nowata and Adair. In other words, the annual income on the losses sustained in one afternoon by FmHA in Oklahoma would have been sufficient to wipe out all human poverty in twenty-seven of the seventy-seven counties of Oklahoma.

Let's turn to the federal land bank in Alfalfa County. Federal land bank filed sixty-seven cases. Of these, sixty cases give us a trail as wide as a forest fire. And yet the figures I ought to rely on are suspect. Often the bank has misinformed the court. In a few cases the bank made unpardonable errors. In one case the bank was obviously committing fraud, and in another the attorney's fees were added with taxes, fertilizers, insurance and other items—all improper procedures. The duplicity uncovered and cited in the several case reports represent a long tale of woe, and need not be reiterated here. Bottom line figures reveal that the bank loaned $8,991,881.03 and collected back through court action the sum of $4,081,691.31 and lost $4,910,189.72. Federal land bank lost approximately 55% of the amount of money it said it loaned. FmHA lost approximately 95% of the money it loaned out. Prudential Insurance and John Hancock lost nothing. Equitable Life will lose only its cost of defending a baseless and groundless suit filed by federal land bank. The insurance companies and private banks cannot absorb over 2 to 3% in loan losses without getting into trouble. I don't know what percentage of losses federal land bank and FmHA have on their total portfolio because of their secrecy. It has to be horrendous.

Who pays for the losses of the federal land bank? The bank would like Congress to assume all loan losses. So would the farmers. But Congress has indicated that this cannot be done. The Congress has made available some tax exempt bonds and has made possible loans from the Capital Corporation. This Corporation has sold bonds, largely to the Japanese, and in turn infused this money into the banks. But at no time is there an indication that the federal government is going to assume these loan losses.

This means that loan losses will be paid for by the farmers who borrowed money from the bank. Earlier, I called attention to the fact that when a farmer signs loan closing papers, he pledges his property to repay the debts of himself and other borrowers from the system. This is the reason the banks raised their interest rates from 8% to 13.75% in certain instances. They were trying to cover their loan losses and pay for extravagances in the system.

This has caused an exodus from the system. When highly solvent and thrifty farmers leave the system, only farmers who have high leverage debts with little or no equity remain. This has brought a new term to the fore—negative net worth.

Exodus from the system has become enormous. In 1987, 13,000 people per month left the system. In some counties of the Great Plains, the exodus has been almost totally debilitating. In just a few years the bank will have few or no customers, yet the bank will be fully socialized and the most expensive farm credit system in the history of the world. Such is the agony of the Nixon and Bellmon experiment in socialism.

The constant outflow of farmers or exodus out of the system should cause concern in Washington, but apparently it has not. It has in these banks. They are starting to advertise in magazines and newspapers that circulate widely. These advertisements stress that if the borrower would come to the friendly office of the federal land banks, they would find friendly help and a desire to loan money. The ads stress the many options that the banks give to their borrowers. In general these advertisements are slanted at anyone who is not a farmer. They now loan a great deal on nonfarm assets. At no time do these advertisements explain to the potential borrower that he will be subjecting himself to underwriting the horrible loan losses the system has rolled up.

Farmers in general have learned to stay away from these two agencies of government and this is the first hopeful sign that some recovery is beginning in the Great Plains. Still the activities of these two agencies have caused a dark night to fall across the farms of the Great Plains.

7

THE FARM CREDIT SYSTEM
IN KANSAS

I have seen many bad practices of over-extending credit, kiting appraisals, horrible losses and utter lack of managerial control over the bank and its employees and activities in Alfalfa County, Oklahoma. It made me wonder whether this was going on everywhere in the Great Plains. Bank employees have told me Alfalfa County was an isolated phenomenon. Is this true? Did the government lender drive the insurance companies out of business in only Alfalfa County, Oklahoma, or have they done it all over the country? I have asked for statistics from the bank and from the state offices of FmHA, and have been refused. Indeed, to ask an officer for information brings an explosive answer. I decided to go to Kansas to see if the same conditions existed there.

I wanted merely to see whether the same basic trends of Alfalfa County were being played out all over the Great Plains. I selected Clark County, Kansas. Ashland is the county seat.

I drove to Ashland, Kansas to see what was really going on. My first stop was the Register of Deeds office. Kansas has continued its historical separation of this office from all other offices. Oklahoma has combined Register of Deeds with the administrative part of the county clerk's office. After seeing Kansas in operation, I believe their system is best by far.

Kansas had a bad experience several months ago. Insurance agents reviewed the records in an office in another part of the state and then used the information to hustle the people concerned. The Kansas legislature over-reacted and passed a new law requiring a sign-in sheet for anyone desiring to see the official documents. Unfortunately, hiding documents will bring on far more evils than a few salesmen on the hunt for business. In some few counties in Kansas, this new law is ignored, but not at Ashland. I zipped on my best poker face and signed in. Of course the law will be of some benefit. If something turns up missing, Kansas officials will know who to look for, provided of course the thief uses his correct name.

The basic figures are set out below.

ASHLAND, CLARK COUNTY, KANSAS

	FLB	FmHA	PRUDENTIAL	JOHN HANCOCK
1960	3	0	4	1
1961	7	1	2	2
1962	3	0	4	2
1963	19	1	1	3
1964	7	6	2	5
1965	10	3	4	1
1966	13	4	1	0
1967	7	6	0	9
1968	13	4	2	0
1969	9	6	0	0
1970	4	6	0	0
1971	6	11	0	0
1972	2	8	0	0
1973	0	0	0	0
1974	0	0	0	0
1975	0	0	0	0
1976	0	0	0	0
1977	15	16	0	0
1978	17	17	0	0
1979	11	3	0	0
1980	19	0	0	0

	FLB	FmHA	PRUDENTIAL	JOHN HANCOCK
1981	39	0	0	0
1982	13	0	0	0
1983	7	1	1	0
1984	6	0	0	0
1985	5	0	0	0
1986	2	0	0	0
1987	1	0	0	0
1988	6	0	0	0

These data suggest the Alfalfa County, Oklahoma syndrome. The Johnson administration order for a slow-down in credit while the Vietnam War was building up is evident. The loans of the federal land bank dropped from nineteen in 1963 to seven in 1967. The insurance companies slowed down their lending and never really got started again. While the Farm Credit Act of 1971 was being debated in Congress, they abandoned the county. Prudential Insurance has made one loans in twenty-four years and John Hancock has not made any loans in twenty years. In 1981 the federal land bank made thirty-nine loans, a far cry from the two made in 1972 when they did not have a full grasp of the long-term credit system in farmers. Yet they fell to only one loan in 1987, a year in which there were none by FmHA. Look at the complete collapse of the long-term credit system in the county in 1987. Only one loan was made in the whole county. This certainly did not represent overdosing farmers with credit. Thus the basic economic problem of the Great Plains today: there is no credit for farmers.

I question the figures for the years from 1973 to 1976. There was a change in the personnel in this office each of these years. The indexes are in very poor shape for that time frame. But this is what they show. I believe that these data are in error, but they will not change any conclusion in this book.

Case No. 85-C-34. There were no farm foreclosures from 1960 to 1985, at which time the federal land bank sued the estate of a farmer. Kansas uses a slightly different system in numbering its court cases. The 85 means the year of 1985 and the C means that it is a civil case and the 34 means that it was the 34th civil case filed in 1985.

Case No. 85-C-34. The federal land bank sued the estate of a deceased farmer who died suddenly and unexpectedly. The loan involved was for $600,000. It was made in 1974. This represented an overdose of credit. The suit was for $777,670.73 and the final judgment was for $791,364.07. The land sold for $777,995.40. These data suggest a small loss. The bank filed a partial release of judgment showing stock of $30,000. However this was done after compound interest was computed on the deceased farmer. This is an issue for the state of Kansas to decide, but I cannot see how this bank can charge compound interest on stock that it has in its custody and can cancel at will. This gouging of the farmer is what disturbs me.

Another thing I find disturbing is the fact that this stock was sold on credit, not cash as the Congress has twice mandated. Such transactions do not deserve the protection of our courts.

Case No. C-86-18. The bank sued a farmer and got a judgment for $269,362.38. The land was sold for $116,801. This indicates a loss of $152,561.38. This was an overdose of credit.

Case No. 87-C-40. The bank sued a farmer. The bank said it was owed $355,931.92 and the judgment rendered by the court was for $423,626.58. This property was sold to the federal land bank for $425,914.09, which suggests the farmer was due a small rebate. The bank filed a partial release of judgment for the stock and this should have been in the neighborhood of $17,796.55, but I could not find that the farmer ever received credit for this. There may be something that was not filed. In this case the farmer requested a jury trial, request denied.

Case No. 87-C-6. The federal land bank sued a farmer for $53,740.47. Bankruptcy was filed. The land was sold for $89,700, providing sufficient cash to pay the bank. I found no record of where the difference went.

Case No. 86-C-10. A farmer was sued by the bank. It was said that he owed $33,192.21 on a 120 acres. My local informants said that this case did not represent an over-dose of credit. The judgment for the bank was for $35,526.16. The property sold for $34,853.48 leaving only a small loss. The bank cancelled the stock and the file is not clear, but apparently the farmer was not left owing much money.

The difference between this county and Alfalfa County, Oklahoma can be seen in the FmHA. FmHA did not have a resident loan officer constantly running up and down the roads talking farmers into making large loans. The agent who served Clark County, Kansas came into the county only about one-half day a month. He only had time to see farmers who wanted to see him, and he did not have time to drum up unprofitable business for the government. This county leads me to the conclusion that abolishing the FmHA is not only a good idea, it is a necessity.

8

RED WILLOW COUNTY, NEBRASKA

I selected Red Willow County, Nebraska for review because it is in the western end of the state. I knew that I would work in the eastern part of the two Dakotas, therefore Nebraska represented a fair balance. McCook is the county seat of Red Willow County. It was the home of the late Senator George Norris, the fighting liberal. Senator Norris would be quite an oddity today. He was once a judge in the state court system of Nebraska. He came up with the idea of a judicial moratorium on sales of farms during times of financial distress. He explained this in his autobiography, *Fighting Liberal*. Essentially the plan was to let the farmer stay on the land if he was doing a good job of farming and trying in good faith to meet his farm debt payments. The foreclosure court case would proceed, and the farm would be sold. Then the moratorium would take effect and remain in place as long as the farmer would do his best to meet his payments. If the farmer did not do a good job, the court would sustain the sale and the farmer would be ordered off the land.

This idea is now a part of the statutory law of Nebraska. It gives the farmer an opportunity to work out a payment plan before, during and after the foreclosure suit. Court files would occasionally reveal that this helped a farmer.

Also, it must be noted, a lot of farmers in Nebraska have incorporated their operations. There is little or no evidence that this has any beneficial effect. A lot of farmers in western Nebraska have taken bankruptcy in order to reorganize. This has led to a scaling down of their debts, but I did not find a single case which has been completed. Many have a ten year payout. Thus there has not been sufficient time to complete a program.

Red Willow County has about 12,500 people. Over 8,500 of them live in the city of McCook. The farm area of the country is thinly populated. Farmers generally grow wheat, soybeans and corn. Almost all are more diversified than farmers in Kansas and Oklahoma.

Nebraska has maintained the old historical division in its court system. The probate section handles the cases and problems of deceased people. It has a separate clerking system and is housed in its own room. There is also a court which handles a lot of the larger cases. This court has a separate clerking section in a separate office on a different floor. All this does is cause one to wander from floor to floor, office to office and official to official, attempting to make the proper connection.

Financial and land title records are neatly maintained in this courthouse. I have set down basic data on the long term credit system for farmers. Red Willow County records exhibited the general pattern of economics I have reported before. The restrictive credit policy of the Johnson administration was instituted in 1966, and both land bank and FmHA obeyed it. As soon as Nixon took office credit was poured into the area. While the Farm Credit Act of 1971 was being debated in Congress, the insurance companies left the scene, and the credit system was fully socialized.

Here are the pertinent data.

MCCOOK, RED WILLOW COUNTY, NEBRASKA

	FLB	FmHA	PRUDENTIAL	METROPOLITAN LIFE	JOHN HANCOCK
1960	8	0	1	18	0
1961	6	0	10	18	0
1962	17	1	47	4	0
1963	15	1	31	12	0
1964	14	1	10	39	0
1965	19	0	2	39	0
1966	9	2	3	26	3
1967	13	0	1	0	0
1968	5	4	0	1	0
1969	13	6	1	1	0
1970	5	4	0	0	0
1971	5	3	1	0	0
1972	19	10	0	0	1
1973	13	11	0	1	0
1974	16	28	0	0	0
1975	14	61	0	0	0
1976	22	47	0	0	0
1977	21	66	0	0	0
1978	22	70	0	1	0
1979	22	71	0	0	0
1980	44	49	0	0	0
1981	31	35	0	0	0
1982	16	37	0	1	0
1983	11	25	0	0	0
1984	13	17	0	0	0
1985	44	22	0	0	0
1986	3	8	0	0	0

I have ended with 1986 because the title book for later data was not available.

In 1981 the farm economy collapsed. By 1986 only eleven long term farm credit loans were made, a tiny fraction of the eighty-seven made in 1977. By the mid-1980s, there was no adequate credit available for farmers. From 1960 to 1984 there were no farm foreclosures.

The land records also indicate that in 1965 farm loans were between $12,000 and $25,000 per farm. The average grew to about $600,000 by 1980. This inflated value of farmland became the "boom," which is now a "bust."

Case No. 12,441. Here the federal land bank sued River Canyon, Inc., a farm corporation, for $710,106.99. The court granted the Norris stay, giving nine months for a work-out on the loans. In the meantime this corporation filed bankruptcy and a scale-down was asked.

Case No. 12,918. Federal land bank sued a farmer and the FmHA. The latter cross-sued the farmer. The federal land bank got a judgment for $235,119.54 and the FmHA got one for $41,700. The court granted a 13 month stay of execution. Bankruptcy was filed.

Case No. 13,048. Federal land bank sued a farmer for $300,000, and bankruptcy was filed.

Case No. 13,006. Federal land bank sued on a business mortgage. No farm land was involved. A thirteen month stay was granted by the court. The business was sold and the bank suffered a loss of about $3,000.

Case No. 13,049. Federal land bank sued a farmer for $600,000, and bankruptcy was filed.

Case No. 13,100. Federal land bank sued a farmer and FmHA. The latter cross-sued the farmer. Cafeteria credit spawned the problem. FmHA on April 10, 1979 loaned the farmer $85,000 and $67,000 and $17,400, and on June 18, 1979, another loan of $15,000 was made. On May 8, 1985, a loan of $67,000 was made. These loans represented a total indebtedness of $252,000. Bankruptcy was filed. All indications suggest that the government will lose all of this money.

Case No. 13,105. Federal land bank sued a farmer and FmHA. The latter cross-sued the farmer in this cafeteria credit scenario. Federal land bank took a mortgage on 400 acres for $63,600 in 1977, which was a safe loan at the time. In 1978 FmHA started to loan money to this farmer. Over a period of three years the agency loaned $202,670. The farm operation then collapsed into insolvency. My informant says the land is worth about $250 per acre. FmHA will lose the entire loan.

There were many other cases, all confirming the pattern reported so far. The diversified farmer of Red Willow County is doing fairly well. The Norris stay or moratorium is at work, but I would hesitate to say that it is of real value to farmers. Both Nebraska and North Dakota have such a Norris system. Oklahoma does not. It may be that Nebraska and North

Dakota do not rush to judgment, as is so apparent in the Oklahoma cases. However, delay of a case can exacerbate financial losses.

9

MINER COUNTY,
SOUTH DAKOTA

I wanted to review Kingsbury County in eastern South Dakota, the childhood home of Laura Ingalls Wilder. Laura Wilder wrote nine books, six of which have a setting in the town of DeSmet. I wanted to examine records in this county so that her six books could focus the changes in farming and financial problems over a period of 100 years. Upon arrival at DeSmet, I found that the Register of Deeds microfilmed all of the land records, and these microfilms were so poor in quality they were essentially unreadable. The microfilm machine was also of poor quality. This was the worst land title record system that I have ever encountered in the Great Plains. Old historical records had been packed away in other buildings and were scattered and unavailable. Also, this Register of Deeds insisted on charging $5 each time a question was posed.

Because of this I moved my investigation to Miner County and Howard, the county seat. This county has a population of about 3,700 people. About 1,200 live in the county seat.

Below you will find the long term loans made since 1960 in this county.

HOWARD, MINER COUNTY, SOUTH DAKOTA

	FLB	FmHA	METROPOLITAN LIFE	JOHN HANCOCK
1960	18	1	1	4
1961	20	2	1	5
1962	27	7	3	4
1963	22	7	2	2
1964	29	9	2	5
1965	32	7	3	6
1966	11	17	0	3
1967	27	8	0	3
1968	13	12	0	0
1969	13	13	0	0
1970	15	20	0	0
1971	8	12	0	0
1972	15	20	0	0
1973	19	11	0	0
1974	22	19	0	0
1975	8	28	1	0
1976	17	27	0	0
1977	18	91	0	0
1978	12	34	0	0
1979	21	24	0	0
1980	19	25	0	0
1981	13	117	0	0
1982	10	49	0	0
1983	9	9	0	0
1984	6	9	0	0
1985	4	15	0	0
1986	1	4	0	0
1987	4	1	0	0
1988	1	3	0	0

These data suggest a two tier system of long-term credit to farmers in Miner County prior to 1969. When Lyndon Johnson put the nation on restrictive credit in 1966, the insurance companies cut back on their loans, as did FmHA and the federal land bank system. After 1971, the insurance companies abandoned the credit field. Since 1969—a period of over twenty years—they made only one loan was made by an insurance lender, this to an old customer. Prudential was never active in the county, thus the appearance of Metropolitan Life in the third column.

In 1981 the system started to collapse, and in 1986 there were only five loans made by both of the government agencies. In 1988 there were only four loans. Ten years earlier there had been 109, more than twenty-seven times more. In 1981 there were 130 loans. There is no credit available at present.

The Federal Reserve System was charged by Congress with the task of keeping a steady flow of credit available to the nation. During the stock market decline in October 1987, the Fed did this in New York City by flooding the banks with cash. No such consideration was extended to the farmers of Miner County, South Dakota. Here the economy and its credit system had collapsed and the Federal Reserve did nothing.

> *Case No. C-86-35.* A review of the records in the court clerk's office revealed that the basic problem in Miner County was the same as it was elsewhere in the Great Plains. In this case the federal land bank sued a farmer and the FmHA, who in turn cross-sued the farmer. It was a classic case of cafeteria credit. On July 14, 1977, FmHA loaned $35,000 and on the same date advanced $65,000 more. On April 20, 1982 another $43,050 was loaned, and on the same day the sum of $28,950 was advanced as a take-out loan. On April 11, 1985 an additional $74,341.71 was handed over to the farmer. The total of $246,341.71 was lost. The farm was sold to the federal land bank for $170,395.10, which represented full payment to them. Had the loss of FmHA in this one case been put out at interest, the earnings would have wiped out poverty in the county in perpetuity, given the present population.

The worst human tragedy that I learned about in this court-house had to do with a legal fight that had developed among various Bruderhofs among the Hutterites. A Bruderhof is the local agency or church of the Hutterites. Several lawsuits were filed. The Hutterites generally refuse to sue.

This group of people came from Russia in the early 1870s and settled in eastern South Dakota. Only about 2,000 came, but their number has now increased to about 200,000. The sect has Bruderhofs in both Dakotas, and also in Idaho, Montana, and Canada. All property is held in common. Families eat in communal kitchens. Almost all marriages produce huge families. Fifteen children born to one couple is not at all uncommon. The children are kept in day nurseries so that both parents can work. Men work in the field and women in the kitchen, nursery, gardens, etc. They all eat the same food and wear very similar clothing. They are allowed to have TVs and radios, and electricity is evident everywhere in the Bruderhofs. Religious services are held every night and on Sunday. Services and everyday talk is in German. English is a language used only when talking to an outsider. Communion is once a year and baptism is at about twenty years of age. The Hutterites do not practice child baptism. They marry at about age twenty. A convert into the Bruderhof is a rarity and an oddity. In over 100 years, there have been only two divorces. Hutterites are generally counted as Protestants.

The Hutterites work very hard. They raise as much of their food as possible and they are fairly self-sufficient. Unfortunately, the government overdosed several of the Bruderhofs with credit, and they went broke. Other Bruderhofs tried to help them out, and now those that borrowed in the first place are unable to return the help.

I visited several of the Bruderhofs that were suing each other. I found the people to be well-dressed and well-nourished. There was a pinch of poverty about their buildings. One Bruderhof had sold all of its livestock and equipment in an effort to pay its bills. The men work in town. One Bruderhof northwest of Yankton, South Dakota moved its lodging into one of the small towns and is now a town-operated Bruderhof. This is an odd situation for Hutterites.

10

EMMONS COUNTY, NORTH DAKOTA

Insurance companies have not invested in North Dakota. Excessive taxation of profits and an anti-insurance bias toward out-of-state companies is generally cited as the reason. Basically these policies have merely kept insurance companies from loaning to North Dakota wheat farmers. Long-term credit thus became the property of the government, and this is not likely to change in the near future. North Dakota is often known as a populist state and its people believe that the state is continuously drained of money and credit by outsiders, particularly large cities such as Minneapolis. I have not found a single life insurance company operation in the long-term credit field covering the last 50 years.

The following data were gathered at Linton, North Dakota, which is the county seat of Emmons County.

YEAR	FLB	FmHA	PRUDENTIAL	JOHN HANCOCK
1960	14	9	0	0
1961	21	13	0	0
1962	23	8	0	0
1963	15	25	0	0
1964	26	25	0	0
1965	24	24	0	0
1966	12	30	0	0
1967	12	34	0	0
1968	18	20	0	0
1969	7	27	0	0
1970	11	18	0	0
1971	9	25	0	0
1972	6	33	0	0
1973	7	33	0	0
1974	12	18	0	0
1975	11	47	0	0
1976	11	21	0	0
1977	26	55	0	0
1978	10	65	0	0
1979	24	50	0	0
1980	27	61	0	0
1981	26	106	0	0
1982	18	39	0	0
1983	23	28	0	0
1984	20	30	0	0
1985	10	19	0	0
1986	4	34	0	0
1987	10	13	0	0
1988	4	6	0	0

Notice how in 1982 a slow down of credit started. In all of 1988, only four loans were made by the federal land bank, six loans by FmHA. Some two-thirds were loans to people who lived in town. There is no adequate credit system available to farmers.

I interviewed a number of people around Linton, North Dakota. Not one recalled having heard of an insurance company that would loan to a farmer. A public official in the courthouse at Linton said that he did not know of such a loan in the past fifty years. The records, of course, agree with this statement. I interviewed in Bismarck, North Dakota, the capitol of the state. I could not find a single person who had heard of an insurance company financing a citizen of their state.

When I pointed out to them that insurance companies traditionally made credit available to farmers in other states until about 1971, they were dumbfounded. They could not believe it.

Only ten long-term loans were made by the government in all of Emmons County during 1988. This cannot be considered adequate by any historical standard. Notice on the chart that in 1980 there were twenty-seven federal land bank loans and sixty-one FmHA loans. In 1981 there were twenty-six federal land bank loans and 106 FmHA loans. Credit was forced into the county during highly inflationary times. There were twenty-three federal land bank loans in 1983 and only four in 1986. This does not represent an increase in credit. Many people expressed the opinion that North Dakota is just an economic colony of the rest of the nation, and is exploited as such. My research in several counties indicates that these complaints have validity.

The economy of Emmons County, North Dakota is constantly being drained of cash and credit. Carl Wilken proved that when farmers receive 100% of parity for crops, cash is always available. During busts or bad times, (which are the consequence of economic mistakes), there should be an increase in cash flow and credit. Thus it seems our government has been going backwards, downhill, at night, blindfolded.

The records in the Register of Deeds office show that there were only thirteen mortgages in 1987 to FmHA. Most of these represented loans to people in town. One courthouse revealed that mortgage releases in 1987 were heavy. This meant a lot of farmers were paying off their mortgages one way or another and leaving the system.

On one sheet in the Register of Deeds office in Emmons County, there are forty-one mortgages by farmers. All were held by the U.S. government. This was the worst situation that

I found in the Great Plains. The very next page had forty-one mortgages by farmers, thirty-nine of which were to the government. Two were to small banks that operated in the county. No other state even came close to this record.

The record in the court clerk's office revealed that from 1960 to 1984, there were no farm foreclosures in Emmons County. After 1984 a new record was rolled up.

Case No. 4514. Federal Land Bank of St. Paul sued a farmer and joined FmHA as a party defendant. Federal land bank took judgment for $16,741.72. FmHA cross-sued the farmer. The land bank gave the farmer credit for $800 for the stock that he purchased in the system. The farmer did not have to fight as farmers do in Kansas and Oklahoma. I believe that the land bank at St. Paul tries to obey the law and the one at Wichita, Kansas does not. One reason for this is that the bank at Wichita refuses to retire stock. The problem in this case was created by the activity of FmHA. That agency had too much money and simply overdosed this farmer with too much credit. On April 6, 1979 FmHA loaned him $22,000. On May 22, 1981, the same agency loaned $20,150. On May 22, 1981, an additional $119,400 was loaned. An additional loan of $161,550 followed. Several payments were made, but on the bottom line this farmer owed FmHA $238,858.56 at the time of judgment. The farmer's total debt in this case was . . .

Federal land bank	$16,367.72
FmHA	238,858.56
TOTAL INDEBTEDNESS	$255,226.28

This was on a 160 acre wheat farm. This figures out to be a debt of $1,595.16 per acre, and no wheat farm can support such a debt. The farm in question could not make over thirty bushels of wheat per acre. In fact the county average is a lot lower. So, 160 acres times thirty bushels is 4,800 bushels of wheat. In August 1985, when the farmer harvested his crop, wheat was selling at the Houston Port for $3.34 per bushel. So 4,800 bushels at $3.34 is $16,032. Government subsidies would add less than $3,000, making a total gross income of $19,032. This is gross income, not profit.

The interest on the federal land bank loan was $2,086.79 and on FmHA package it was $26,274.38, the total interest bill to the two creditors came to $28,361.17, yet the total gross income this farmer could come up with was $19,032, leaving a net loss in interest alone of $9,329.17, and there were many other expenses. There was simply no way this farmer could meet his debts. He went broke. Had the loan people put the pencil to the application, the loan would never have been made. The federal land bank had a good loan that was properly secured, but FmHA came in and larded credit all over the place.

In this case the farm was sold for $16,367.72, which covered the loan of the federal land bank. The federal land bank itself bought the property.

The U.S., of course, has the right to redeem property sold at a sheriff's sale within one year of the sale. The object of this law is to prevent fraud. In this case the government elected to redeem the property for the sum of $18,650.10. This gave the federal land bank a profit on the transaction of $2,282.38. Such money goes to the federal land bank as ordinary income, and is thus available for expensive buildings, excessive overhead, enormous attorney fees, imported cars, etc. The loss to the U.S. Treasury was $208,858.56.

Most citizens would agree that this is a good law. But note how it was administered. Who committed the fraud? It was the U.S. government acting through one of its instrumentalities, the federal land bank at St. Paul, Minnesota. No obstreperous farmer, crooked lawyer or anyone else practiced the fraud. The fraud was practiced on the U.S. government by the U.S. government.

The late Vice President John Nance Garner held that a good law could be made bad by its enforcement. In this case, an essentially good law was turned into a racket in favor of the federal land bank system.

FmHA redeemed the property in 1986 and still owned it in the summer of 1989 when I was there. There is little reason to believe that FmHA can ever get over $20,000 by selling it. The original judgment for FmHA was $238,858.56. This agency redeemed the farm for $20,000, which is all it was worth. This meant that the government lost $238,858.56 on one farmer.

Case No. 4569. Federal land bank sued a farmer and obtained a judgment for $248,514.29. The property was sold at a sheriff's sale for $255,636.91. This was enough to get the farmer out of debt. No deficiency judgment was received. The original mortgage on this 1,910 acre farm was for $245,000. The debt factored out to $128 per acre. This was too much for the farmer to repay, but it was a loan amply secured by collateral, and therefore safe. In this case the farmer and his wife separated and divorced while the suit was in progress. A high divorce rate is not uncommon under financial stress. Also it should be noted that the federal land bank did not ask for and did not receive attorney's fees in the case.

Case No. 4603. Federal land bank sued a farmer. The judgment was for $146,726 on 639 acres of wheat land. This land was indebted for the sum of $229.61 per acre, which should have worked out. But here the land could not carry a debt of $229.61 per acre in a case complicated by human tragedy. The farmer's wife died just before the case was filed, having suffered from a long bout with cancer. The two had shared their lives with five children, none of whom were able to help their father. In this case the farmer asked for forbearance. In 1985 he lost $24,703 on the farm. This complicated forbearance. Since this case in on appeal at the time of this writing, I will not calculate losses to the government, or make further comments. I might note, however, that the bank presented many documents to explain its forbearance policy. This represented the best compliance I have yet seen. The farmer was unhappy, but the court record clearly shows that he was treated fairly.

Case No. 4604. Federal land bank sued a farmer and FmHA. FmHA then cross-sued the farmer. The federal land bank got a judgment for $127,468.13 on 960 acres of wheat land. This was once a safe loan. However FmHA set the farmer up on cafeteria credit, extending the following amounts.

May 31, 1979	$36,000.00
April 3, 1980	$61,000.00
April 9, 1986	$215,945.88

The total debt to FmHA was $312,945,88, which was a total loss to the government. The federal land bank had the land sold and bid it at $141,130.56. With stock credit, the farmer ended up not owing the bank. Here the bank loan was safe until FmHA started ladling credit all over the place. Loss to the federal land bank was nothing in this case. Loss to the U.S. Treasury was $312,945.88.

Case No. 4645. Federal land bank sued a farmer and joined FmHA as a co-defendant. The FmHA then cross-sued the farmer. First the federal land bank got a judgment and it was paid off. Land bank exited the case leaving FmHA as plaintiff. The mortgage of the federal land bank on 1,520 acres was for $60,000—a safe mortgage until FmHA started to spill credit all over the place. No attorney's fees were charged by the bank, which helped the farmer. The projected loss on this case was in excess of $585,600, but this could be true only if $100,000 could be realized for land, a very unlikely development.

The federal land bank did not lose money in Emmons County on any of these cases. In fact, it actually showed a profit of $2,282.38, but this would be true only if one felt that the U.S. government acted properly when it redeemed one of the farms. By no stretch of the imagination do I feel that this was legitimate.

However the government lost $1,346,263 in this county on three loans. One case was not fully decided and any loss there is not a part of the above figure. Had this money been put out on interest at 6%, it would have earned $80,775.78 annually— enough to eliminate all poverty in Emmons County at the present population.

The county courthouse in Linton was built in the early 1930s as a New Deal work project. It is in perfect condition after all of these years. Since the population of the county is declining, this courthouse is fully adequate for all governmental needs in the foreseeable future. In the 1930s Lord Keynes taught that it did not hurt the government to go into debt to build things that would be useful in the future. That is what President Roosevelt did, this courthouse being an example.

My conclusion from a visit to this courthouse is that the federal land bank of St. Paul is a well managed and operated land bank, but FmHA is so corrupt it is beyond repair. Still it must be noted that the bank at St. Paul was in serious financial trouble and insolvent. It was being held in place by the United States Congress.

11

OCHITREE COUNTY, TEXAS

I selected Ochitree County, Texas for my Texas study. This county is in the northern part of the Texas Panhandle, Perryton being the county seat. Ochitree County has a population of 9,588. At least 7,991 live Perryton. The other 1,597 people are spread across the farm area. The farms are huge in size and there is a great deal of oil and gas production. Dryland farming is always a problem, crops can be scant at times and abundant at other times. Irrigation mitigates the poor yields.

The federal land bank for the area is located at Austin, Texas, but an association is headquartered at Perryton. As usual, the association bank building is located in downtown Perryton directly across the street from the county courthouse. This is the busiest street in the Texas Panhandle north of Amarillo. This represents a typical pattern in the Great Plains—bank buildings on a busy street. Cheaper quarters could be had anywhere in any direction.

John Hancock Mutual Life Insurance Company was active in the Oklahoma Panhandle, but not in Texas. So the control life insurance company cited here is Prudential Insurance Company of American. Here are basic economic statistics.

	FLB	FmHA	PRUDENTIAL
1960	17	0	0
1961	24	0	2
1962	36	0	1
1963	30	0	2
1964	21	2	3
1965	24	1	2
1966	27	4	2
1967	33	4	2
1968	10	0	2
1969	46	1	3
1970	19	0	0
1971	15	0	2
1972	21	5	0
1973	16	2	0
1974	56	2	0
1975	25	1	0
1976	38	12	0
1977	22	5	1
1978	34	5	0
1979	25	2	0
1980	39	8	0
1981	26	1	0
1982	17	23	0
1983	18	18	0
1984	35	12	2 (Oil Company)
1985	33	13	3 (Oil Company)
1986	4	22	0
1987	17	8	0
1988	17	14	8 (Oil Company)

Notice how in 1982 the farm credit system started to collapse. Data also reveal that life insurance companies left the field after the passage of the Farm Credit Act of 1971, and have not returned. Prudential made loans in the county in 1984, 1985 and 1988, but these were to oil companies, not to farmers. Insurance companies made no loans to farmers after 1977.

It will be noted that lending activity by the federal land bank and FmHA was much lower than in other states of the Great Plains. One reason is that the bank at Austin is the best managed bank in the Great Plains. It did not let its loan officers act like shyster shills, as became the case in other states.

The bank at Austin is in serious financial trouble, but may survive if it receives massive federal funding. At the time of this writing the funding has not happened. The Reagan and Bush administrations got the bank to buy junk loans from the bank at Jackson, Mississippi, which went into receivership. Parenthetically it must be noted that the Reagan-Bush administration became notorious for pushing bad banking practices in another financial institution, and then letting that one collapse. For example, a small commercial bank failed in Enid, Oklahoma, and the Reagan-Bush administration got a national bank to come in and take over the Enid bank. The national bank then failed. At Fairview, Oklahoma, a small commercial bank failed and the same administration got a national bank in an adjoining county to take over. That bank then failed. In Alfalfa County, Oklahoma, the county that I studied in depth, the local saving and loan association failed. A saving and loan association in an adjoining county was forced to assume the failed unit's business, and this delivered it into serious financial trouble. It is conceivable that none of these problems would have arisen in the several second institutions except for the forced mergers. Whether this scenario will be repeated in the federal land bank at Austin can only be speculated. But I believe that this pattern may repeat itself.

Texas has a legal procedure whereby a financial institution can sell the land for payment of a delinquent debt, and that transaction is final unless the debtor-farmer asks the court to take jurisdiction, at which time it becomes a court procedure. There has been no such request, except in the case of foreclosures on homes by savings and loan associations. Oklahoma has such a law, but the attorneys for the federal land bank at Wichita refused to use it. Thus in Perryton, Texas I did not see the legal mess so noticeable in Alfalfa County, Oklahoma. Also, attorney's fees are much lower in Texas. There is no reason to believe that over $31,000 was ever charged in a case that did not even go to trial, as was done in Alfalfa County, Oklahoma.

12

THE FED,
A MODEST PROPOSAL

It is not fair to write a book as critical as this one without making suggestions on what can be done. Moreover, in view of the suffering that is going on in farm communities throughout the Great Plains, the need to do something constructive is overwhelming. The historian often lists what went wrong, and when it went wrong and then lapses into silence. If the historian is not going to advise, does he really have a useful purpose? I think he does, but I suggest that he recommend a course of action. The economist too often has a big plan which has little merit to it, and when things go wrong he does not study the situation but rushes out a new plan which has even less merit, often without reference to the observed facts of the situation. Perhaps the political scientist can do better.

Let me summarize the facts gleaned from trips across the Great Plains, and submit those facts to a concerned nation.

In 1913 Congress charged the Federal Reserve System with four tasks:

1. Keep a steady flow of credit going out to the nation.
2. Help economic growth.
3. Provide for a stable dollar.
4. Keep a balance in the system of overseas payments.

The Federal Reserve has failed to do even one of these things. Overseas payments are out of control. For over sixty years, the dollar has been unstable more than 90% of the time.

There is no economic growth in the Great Plains and in most parts of this nation. Often Washington puts out news blurbs that the nation is prospering, but I fail to find that anywhere. The largest failure of savings and loan associations has occurred in southern California. Florida has a lot of economic problems, and so do the New England states. The lumber industry of Oregon and Washington is in a state of advanced economic decay. So I question whether the Federal Reserve has promoted economic growth.

The first job of the Federal Reserve System is the last one I will discuss. I want to first point out its deficiency as applied specifically to the Great Plains. That job is to keep a steady flow of sound credit going out to the nation. Congress mandated this in 1913 and this was the principal reason Congress set up the system. The Federal Reserve has not done this. There has been a complete collapse in the credit system for farmers. For example, in Clark County, Kansas only one long-term credit loan was made in 1987, only two in 1986. Yet in 1978 there were thirty-four. This does not reflect stability. The Fed has utterly failed its first objective. If a farmer needs to build a machine shop or a dairy barn or buy a farm, there is no credit to make this possible and there are not enough earnings to permit savings. Go to the small towns and you will see the lumber yard boarded up because the lumberman cannot sell anything. No one is building.

In Emmons County, North Dakota, there were 132 long-term loans in 1981, but in 1988 there were only ten. Other considerations aside—this is not sufficient credit under any guidelines, because North Dakota has not had insurance companies to help carry the load as do the other five states of the Great Plains. I could not find a single person in Emmons County who thought that long-term credit was even remotely adequate. Compare that dismal record to the congressional charge that the Federal Reserve keep a steady flow of sound credit flowing out to the nation. The Federal Reserve System has totally failed the wheat farmers of North Dakota.

In Miner County, South Dakota, there were 130 long-term loans to farmers in 1981, but only four in 1988. There is no hope of immediate improvement in the area. Coupled with a great drought and the activity of the *narodniks* I will discuss in the next two chapters, is it any wonder that suicide is the largest cause of violent deaths among farmers?

In Alfalfa County, Oklahoma, there were 171 long-term credit loans in 1981, but only twenty-four in 1988. Remember, in 1988 the federal land bank inflated the actual figures by making ten separate loans to one farmer on ten separate tracts of land, etc. There were only twelve actual loans. There were loans in which the bank was financing farms the bank had taken in foreclosure. How can this represent an adequate flow of credit to a county that is rich in agriculture? This county can produce wheat in such abundance that it can literally feed the whole state. Yet it does not have an adequate system of credit. Ask a farmer what his problem is and he will say, "There is no money available. . . . There is no credit available and I can't get any." While the farmers of the Great Plains were being treated badly by the Federal Reserve, the Fed did not treat stock investors that way. In 1987 there was a major slide in stock prices. The Federal Reserve flooded New York with cash and bank reserves to ward off a collapse. Operatives worked overtime all of one weekend to accomplish this task. In 1989 there was another major downturn in stock prices, and the Federal Reserve stood by to flood the system with cash. But the system has not acted to help the wheat farmers of Emmons County, North Dakota, Miner County, South Dakota or Clark County, Kansas!

One bad feature of the Fed system is that boundary lines do

not follow economic activity, and in fact make no economic sense at all. This warps statistics for planning purposes. There is no real justification for splitting Missouri and Oklahoma and placing a part of each state into different bank districts. Bank boundaries cut across the Great Plains exactly opposite of economic activity. Bank districts are too large. Employees are not spotting economic trends early enough and alerting Washington in time. Maintenance of a nebulous long-term policy comes first. Trauma that requires action is ignored.

District banks are controlled by wealthy bankers from large banks in the larger cities. These wealthy bankers manipulate the banks for their own benefits, and ignore the economic needs of small towns, villages and rural people.

Most banks in the Great Plains, and particularly the small banks in villages, are not even members of the district Federal Reserve Banks, and thus have no voice. Their cash flow and bank reserves are not even subject to control of the Federal Reserve. This scenario describes over 60% of the nation's banks.

The Federal Reserve System often does not know what to do and then does something irrational, usually with great economic pain to the nation. For example, the system lowered interest rates approximately a year before the stock market collapsed in 1929, and this fueled a boom first, then a collapse. In 1979 the system forgot about interest and pumped cash and reserves out of the banks. This fueled the highest interest rates in modern history and led to the biggest recession since 1929. The Federal Reserve was wrong in doing both of these things. In 1979 the Fed responded in exactly the same way as in 1929.

The Fed acts tyrannically. It refuses to follow mandates of Congress. For example, in the Farm Credit Act of 1971, Congress directed the Fed to prevent inflation of land prices. The Fed did nothing. In 1979 President Carter finally stirred himself to do something about the horrible increase in land prices. He sent a letter to the Federal Reserve directing it to carry out the mandate of the Congress. The Federal Reserve did nothing. Under Paul Volcker's management, the Fed engineered some twelve million people into a status of unemployment. Some 66,000 firms entered bankruptcy—and in 1981-82, 4.3 million people entered poverty. In Kentucky the home builder's group printed up a wanted poster, naming the Fed governors "for premeditated and calculated cold-blooded murder of millions of small businesses." They might as well have added "farmers." In 1981, land values collapsed, and this is one of the reasons that night came to the farms of the Great Plains.

The Federal Reserve is a secretive organization. Seven old men meet in a posh room around a small table and discuss what they are going to do to the nation. They either withhold their decisions, or make major announcements for which no preparation has been made. As a consequence, the nation is often faced with sharp economic shifts. The reason for this, they say, is that insiders would find out what is going on and profit by it. Insiders probably know and profit anyway. I am tired of reading of possible shifts by the Federal Reserve in financial papers, and I am tired of news reporters—particularly TV reporters—prophesying what the Federal Reserve might do. If the Fed would open its meetings to the public, the system might work a little better. Secret meetings are incompatible with the ideals of a great democracy in any case. A public official should be a public educator. The officials of the Fed are not. Sometimes the Federal Reserve does not even make a public announcement. For example, after making a mess of the economy after 1979—when they shifted to bank reserves as the controlling lever on economic activity—the Fed switched back to control of interest. No public announcement accompanied this shift. Many people in this country would follow the lead of the Federal Reserve if they just knew what it was.

The Federal Reserve is ponderous, slow acting and inefficient. It takes the Fed forever to change interest rates when to the most casual observer this needs to be done. The Fed will make a slight change in one thing and ignore other economic trends and possibilities. It will try only one economic lever when several could and should be used. For example, in 1951 the system raised interest when the Treasury did not want it to do so. From then until 1979 the chief act of the system was to raise and lower interest as the governors felt this was needed to rally or stall the economy. The Fed never used any of the other levers of economic activity in any significant way. Then suddenly without the slightest public announcement the Fed switched to cash and bank reserves in 1979. And that is how a collapse in land values was triggered.

Using just one economic lever at a time, is totally ineffective in stopping inflation or in rallying a stalled economy. For example, there is an economic slump going on in the Great Plains at the time of this writing. The Federal Reserve has finally lowered interest rates. What effect has that had? Absolutely none. The main problem here is that many bankers do not want to loan in the present economic climate. One banker explained it to me this way. "I can easily loan out $10,000 to a farmer, but he cannot repay it. So I am keeping the money in the bank vaults." A few banks in the Great Plains have a lot of money to loan out, but they don't want to take the risk. For the Federal Reserve governors to meet in secret in Washington and lower interest rates has absolutely no effect out here. If those governors met on the sidewalk and stood on their heads, they would have accomplished at least something—they would have drawn a crowd.

Overall this is a dismal record. For many years the Federal Reserve System has not carried out a single function in a proper manner. It is an independent agency of the government, and thus it can do just about what it wants to do. Sooner or later an independent agency always becomes doctrinaire and tyrannical. An agency of government should be responsible to some official and to the nation. The idea that it can do what it wants whenever it wants is alien to responsible, democratic government.

This evil which Frances Perkins warned against in the 1930s is still present in my government. Many economists have stated that if the Federal Reserve should ever lose its independence, the system would be governed by politics, not common economic sense. One has to chortle when hearing such nonsense. The present Federal Reserve is mired in politics. For example, after Nixon took office in 1969, he appointed Arthur Burns as chairman of the board of governors. Burns flooded the country with cash and bank reserves just in time for Nixon's re-election in 1972. Every presidential election since then has seen the country flooded with cash and bank reserves just in time for the next election. To say the Federal Reserve is non-political is to ignore what is actually happening. The Federal Reserve is part of the government. It will always be at least hip-deep in political slime.

A new approach is badly needed. The Federal Reserve System should be transformed by Congress into a national bank. This new bank would receive cash reserves from all banks in the nation, both state and national banks. A revolutionary idea is a new idea. This is not a new idea. President Herbert Hoover advocated this in his administration, which ended in 1933. So the idea is not new or revolutionary, but one for which the time has got to come. This new national bank would increase and/or decrease the cash and reserves of all banks in the nation at the same time. None of this business of pumping reserves into New York City banks, let the rest of the country hang. This new bank would not be an independent agency of the government. Instead it would report directly to both the secretary of the treasury and the president. It would also take orders within guidelines clearly defined by law. Gone would be the stupid idea that an agency of government can ignore the pleas of the presidents and the public. Presidents Carter, Reagan, and Bush were right in wanting to lower interest, and the Federal Reserve was wrong in not doing so. Political responsibility for one's political acts should be the prime requisite for continuing in office.

There is some concern in Congress about how the Federal Reserve is doing. One suggestion is to make the Secretary of the Treasury a de facto member of the board of governors. This used to be the case from 1913 up to the administration of President Franklin D. Roosevelt, at which time Congress changed it. I can't believe that Congress would seriously consider this old suggestion new. It didn't work then, and I can't believe it would work now. This suggestion is nothing more than a dab of disinfectant when radical surgery is indicated. The secretary of the treasury should command, not act like a timid rabbit hiding in a hole.

This new national bank would have power to raise and cut taxes within broad guidelines, properly "canalized"—as Justice Cardoza used to teach—and Congress and the presidents would retire from this scene. Presidents Reagan and Bush never had a political agenda except to cut taxes, and they used this solely as a means of getting elected. Cutting taxes when the economy is inflating as in 1981 and raising them when the economy is stalled is unwise and actually downright stupid. It is also dangerous. Yet Reagan raised taxes seven times when the economy was stalled and cut them once when inflation was running rampant. This is the exact opposite of what should have been done. The tax cut was totally political. One can look long and hard in the political and economic history before finding similar irresponsibility and political folly on such a vast scale.

U.S. Senator David Boren of Oklahoma had a long political career in the Oklahoma legislature, as Oklahoma governor, and now as U.S. Senator, totally on cutting taxes. He has never exhibited any other political agenda. His lack of judgment while serving on the Oversight Committee on Foreign Intelligence would be an embarrassment if it were better known. But he does want to cut taxes. Senator Sam Nunn from Georgia is often very responsible, and I like him a great deal, but when it comes to taxes, he has only one thought. That is to cut taxes and let the nation go to hell in a handbasket when it comes to financing the deficit. Removing taxes from the political agenda would be a great help in restoring political responsibility to the nation's management. Relying on production and a parity price to reduce the deficit would make even more sense.

The Fed should be the prime lending agency for the government. In the next two chapters I recommend that FmHA and the federal land bank system be abolished. The USDA has repeatedly demonstrated that it can't handle these two agencies. All indications say abolish them and put a lending agency in the Treasury where it was before 1939. When this is done I recommend that this new national bank have a lending agency to cover legitimate loans to farmers. Only small loans in strictly rationed amounts would be made. Gone would be the stupid notion that everyone in Alfalfa County, Oklahoma, is entitled to a government loan. Gone would be the idea that every farmer in North Dakota would be eligible to receive a loan. This new bank would loan only small amounts of money, say, $35,000 in the short-term, no more, and only to a farmer who is indigent. If a farmer wants more, then he should go to the private sector and get it. The farmer and all other borrowers would be expected to repay the money as scheduled. An exception could be made in case of crop failure.

Congressmen and senators should be restrained from beating up on this agency whenever a farmer doesn't want to pay.

In the long-term credit system, this new bank would loan amounts to farmers for legitimate, non-speculative financial reasons, and no more. Not over $200,000 per farmer should be the norm, and that should be properly collateralized according to state real estate standards. Wealthy farmers should be excluded.

This new bank should have rule-making powers and it should professionalize the occupation of loan officers. Gone would be the dismal idea extant in FmHA and in the federal land bank system that a loan officer should merely be a graduate from a college of agriculture. Knowledge about hog pregnancy is not needed to be a good loan officer. The main problem with the present loan officers is their idea that they must throw money at every problem. This is unwise.

These new bank loan officers should not be former employees of the federal land bank system or the FmHA. If these *narodniks* are allowed to go into the new national bank they will take all of their present bad habits with them. *Narodniks* now on the job should be paid their final salaries and sent on their way. That is the way the Congress treated the employees of the Farm Security Administration in 1943. And that should be done again.

The *narodniks* of Russia were really flim-flam men, hustlers who badly abused the farmers they encountered. Their modern counterparts haven't changed. Every *narodnik* that I have met has had one thing in common. All have been mentally narrow. They have had little or no interest in or knowledge of the arts, music, literature, history, economics, current events, governmental sciences, military lore, architecture, or the humanities in general. They have had little or no training in the fields of psychology, sociology, or any of the other people sciences. Loan officers, as well as lawyers, work with people, not pregnant hogs. Composted bull manure may have certain qualities as a soil additive, but I doubt if a loan officer has to know all there is to know about this. But the rules of modern banking should be learned and applied by all loan officers. These rules are not hard to learn. Laura Ingalls Wilder ran a loan office for the federal land bank for over fifteen years and never lost a penny. She had a fourth grade education. The association she worked for was merged into a larger association and now has a college-trained *narodnik* heading it. It is now losing money hand over fist. In fact that federal land bank, which is at St. Louis, Missouri, is insolvent.

The farmers around Jet, Oklahoma, in southern Alfalfa County, Oklahoma ran a loan office for the federal land bank for over fifty years and never lost a penny. Consolidation of the association into Enid, Oklahoma placed management into the hands of college-trained *narodniks* who promptly caused the association to lose tens of millions of dollars. The federal land bank at Wichita, Kansas went broke.

After spending seventy years as a housewife, an eighty-seven year old woman, with advanced medical problems, went into the family bank after the death of her husband and the illness of their only child, and she ran the bank profitably and safely. It is still rated number one by the bank examiners. Why can't these *narodniks* do the same? They are mentally narrow. These three examples show loan officers can be successful without even seeing a college.

This new bank I propose would hire and train people to be loan officers. It would check on them and remove those unable to loan money safely. Many may wonder whether this concept should be applied to commercial banks and savings and loans associations. Frankly, I think it should. I have documented one case report of an Oklahoma loan officer who wrecked three national banks and is now in the process of wrecking another. He slings money out the front door just like the narodniks of FmHA. Why should such a loan officer be turned loose in the mornings?

Attorneys have a great deal to do with some of these situations. I have documented a case in Oklahoma in which one law firm so bled its clients that the charges helped wreck a small loan company, two savings and loans associations, four state banks, three national banks and one insurance company. At no time did even one government regulator ever raise a question. State bar associations are notorious for doing nothing when an attorney turns in such a record.

This new bank I speak of should require strict qualifications of any attorney that works for it. This bank should have offices nationwide and there should be districts small enough so that proper credit work can be done.

This new bank should have no capital stock and that the U.S. government be sole owner. The idea of trying to show private ownership, such as is the case with federal land banks and the Federal Reserve System, is an evil that should not be tolerated. This nation once had two national banks. One was chartered by the Washington administration and one by the Madison administration. The federal government bought one-fifth of the stock in each bank. The rest was held by private investors. During the early days of the first bank, the government sold its stock. Virtually all of the stock in both banks came to be owned by foreigners, particularly the British. Manipulation of the banks became widespread and led to abuses. The new national bank I am advocating would be wholly owned by the U.S. government.

An economic commission should be established in the Treasury Department to levy and collect tariffs on imported goods. This nation cannot continue to pay $150 billion or more a year in foreign exchange debts. One of the reasons for a credit deficit for farmers is the fact that savings are going overseas to finance U.S. international debts. The national deficit is also a culprit here. The nation has savings of about $275 to $300 billion a year. How this is used will greatly affect our prosperity. Substituting debt for earnings has been discussed in *Unforgiven*. Suffice it to say that this innocent ploy became addictive by the time Reagan took office. Reagan increased the nation's public debt by almost 300%. The deficit in 1986 alone was over $225 billion. Subtracted from a total national annual savings of only $275 billion, this means that there is very little money left for private enterprise, farmers included. As a consequence, the U.S. borrowed from abroad to meet the differences. The U.S. people will pay dearly for generations for this stupidity.

The new bank should study taxes and see that, in general, the nation pays its bills. It should prevent foreign nations from buying up America. We need to live, as a nation, with our bills paid at home and abroad. When the economy is in a slump, or when there is a war, debts must be contracted, but these should be exceptions to the rule, and not the rule. Financial responsibility should be made a national virtue.

This new bank should be active in and responsible for providing both short-term and long-term credit for the nation. The present Federal Reserve works only on short-term credit and short-term interest rates. Its record is unfortunate. It does nothing at all on long-term credit.

Congress and state legislatures should pass laws identifying certain crimes. It should be a crime for loan officers to overdose borrowers with credit. This act should have felony status, and ten years would be an appropriate term of imprisonment. If a lending institution—including agencies of the government—overdoses a borrower with too much credit, that lender should forfeit the loan. This would put a premium on proper banking conduct. At the present time there is no such crime and it is probably not even a civil or private tort or injury to overdose. For example, a group of investors at Dallas, Texas, led by the Hunt brothers, tried to corner the silver market several years ago. One of the reasons they could try this was because banks were constantly throwing money at them. When the silver market collapsed, the Hunt brothers went into bankruptcy. In a companion civil case, they have been sued on some of their silver market operations. They have defended on the grounds that some of these creditors deserved what they got because they were overdosing them with credit. The court overruled the Hunts—and perhaps this is a correct decision with the present state of legal affairs. However, Congress and the state legislatures should act to make it a crime to overdose the borrower, and the lending institution should lose its entire investment in the loan if reckless overdosing is involved.

Bankruptcy judges say that because of the excessive and abusive extension of vast amounts of credit, the nation has a high bankruptcy rate. Sometimes these judges are interviewed by the press which report such statements. Yet no one in our society pays any attention to them.

I have documented a situation in the Great Plains wherein small finance companies would madly compete with each other for loans to low-wage workers. As many as five or six loans would be made by these companies on the household furniture of one worker. Bankruptcies soared. The loan officers finally woke up and agreed that not over one loan would be made to such a worker. Bankruptcies amongst low-waged workers promptly fell by 75%.

13

FmHA,
A RADICAL PROPOSAL

FmHA was established by Congress in 1946 to work with and to finance small, impoverished farmers who absolutely could not get credit elsewhere. Loans could be made to tenant farmers, also. The agency would work in both the short-term credit and long-term credit fields. Five years is the time separation factor here. This allowed duplication between the federal land banks which loaned on a long-term basis, and the Production Credit Association (PCA) Congress established in 1933 to loan money in the short-term credit field. So FmHA duplicates the work of both agencies even though it was intended to help farmers who could not get credit at either of these government agencies, or from private sources. A farmer who could get credit was supposed to get it at the federal land banks, PCA or private sources.

Gradually, over the years, Congress weakened the rules and allowed more and more farmers to borrow from FmHA. In time that agency came to loan money on housing in the villages and small cities, on recreational facilities, and in other economic areas. Today, nine out of ten loans made by FmHA have nothing to do with the original purpose of the agency. Chiefly, these loans go to wealthy farmers and city people. I have mentioned how the agency loaned money to a doctor to buy a home in the city. It loaned and lost over $1,500,000 on an Oklahoma farmer who owned over seventeen farms. It loaned $7.3 million to an Oklahoma attorney. These loans were made to build up the political power and clout of the agency, and had nothing to do with small farmers or the original intent of Congress.

Many loan officers joined FmHA in 1946 when the agency was formed, and they served almost thirty years without handling a delinquent loan. The near total prostitution of the agency has been amply covered elsewhere in this book. Suffice it to say that the Nixon type loan officers earned the name *narodniks*, with or without italics.

Almost without exception, they encouraged farmers to participate in the Payment In Kind (PIK) program when it was not in their best financial interest to be in such programs. They supported the USDA against all right and reason. They insisted the farmer sell his crops as soon as harvest was over and pay on the government debts when the best thing for the farmer to do was to wait and sell later. They took freedom of choice away from the farmers and ushered them into a new type of peasantry.

The narodniks favored the rich over the poor. They helped federal land banks socialize the long-term credit system. The narodniks in the federal land banks were also college trained. They were related to the narodniks in FmHA by politics, background, well-to-do families, college connections, etc.

The narodniks in FmHA gained control of the farmer's income and refused to let any of it be paid to insurance companies on first, prior and superior mortgages. This made it necessary for the insurance firms to foreclose. And these lenders quickly learned not to fight with FmHA and left the long-term credit field.

All the details furnished in the previous chapters could provide a summary as long as each original presentation, the abuses have been that blatant. Some need to be restated just the same. FmHA has used criminal procedure to collect civil debts. Private enterprise lending companies cannot use such collection tactics. I seriously question throwing a man into the penal system just because he owes a debt. But the narodniks have so crowded the farmer that he is left with absolutely little or no money to pay his other bills. He is left with very little or no money to support his family. The fear I have seen in the eyes of the farmers across the Great Plains will be carried in my mind for the rest of my life. Farmers are scared to death of FmHA. Many are doing odd jobs, getting food from food banks and horns of plenty, always under an atmosphere of terror that the government will find out and the narodniks will want part of it. Their fear is real and disturbing. Violence lies just below this human surface. Under a color of law, these narodniks will threaten farmers with criminal action. They dictate what he grows, how he grows it, when he sells, how little he is going to get to live on, what little he wears, and what his children will suffer. The narodniks have total control over the economic life of the farmer. This is the worst case of economic peonage and slavery on the North American continent today. There may be no strict violation of the criminal laws on peonage, but what FmHA has done still is a violation of human rights. Most of all it is a horrible violation of American values. I have documented cases that are so gross as violations of human rights that I cannot mention them in a book otherwise suitable for the parsonage library.

A narodnik's power extends to all facets of a loan. For example, if a farmer is somewhat disagreeable, the narodnik can raise his interest almost at will. A farmer who fails to keep his hat in hand properly might find his interest going from 6 to 11%. In some cases financial stability is so marginal, this alone is sufficient to bankrupt a grower. Fully 75% of all farm suicides during recent years have been by farmers who owed money to FmHA.

I have mentioned before that FmHA is totally opposed to a

farmer hiring an attorney. Smart-alecks in state offices of the agency have made bragging comments about this in their speeches at seminars. They say that an attorney causes a "chilling effect" on the agency. In other words the agency is doing things that it does not want the light of day to see. Insurance companies and commercial banks would not dream of insulting attorneys representing farmers. The most wicked criminal in our courts is guaranteed the services of an attorney. But a farmer before FmHA is persecuted if he has an attorney.

FmHA does not want hospitals and doctors to be paid. This is undermining the health delivery system in rural areas. FmHA will make loans to a hospital and then refuse to let the farmer pay his hospital bills. As a result, the hospitals are going broke, their ownership passing into the hands of the government. Congress has never authorized or even discussed this.

FmHA literally created the idea of cafeteria credit.

The agency wants the farmer to have expensive machinery, big buildings, registered cattle, whatever. While this makes for nice *Farm Journal* pictures, it would be even nicer if farm income, not debt underwrote these developments. In studying the history of agricultural credit acts of the 1980s, I am moved by the number of congressmen who mentioned that they thought the answer to the farm problem was further and better mechanization. Often these records indicate that employees of FmHA were in the room at the same time. I wonder whether these large loans to buy machinery and cattle were not caused in part by congressmen who did not know of the lack of profits to a wheat farmer.

These financial Neanderthalers, these narodniks constantly go up and down the roads in rural areas to get farmers to borrow even more. In counties where there is no resident narodnik, the financial problems are a little less pronounced. But if a narodnik is there two to three days a week, the problems magnify accordingly. If he is full-time, the problems he creates swamp the system.

Congress has appropriated money for debt counseling, reconciliation, and mediation for farmers. These are often grant-in-aid to the state departments of agriculture. The state governments have also appropriated money for this service. Rural ministers in Nebraska—early in the crisis—suggested this and they raised private money to start the program. Nebraska has the best debt mediation of any state of the Great Plains. Oklahoma probably has the worst. This debt counseling is remarkably unsuccessful. It goes like this. The village blacksmith wants to be paid $400 and the farmer won't pay. Both agree to mediation. The mediator suggests that the blacksmith is not going to get it all at once, and he further suggests that he take $100 now and wait until after the next harvest to get another $100, the rest to be renegotiated. The blacksmith does not like this but agrees because it gives him an immediate payment of $100, which he needs to support his family.

This is no small thing to a village blacksmith. Before the farmer can pay the $100 he has to go to the narodnik in the county office of FmHA who promptly vetoes the payment plan because the farmer still owes the government. The blacksmith gets nothing even though he scaled down his desire in order to try to get a partial payment. But as long as the narodnik controls the cash flow of the farmer, moratoriums, counseling, debt management, debt reconciliations and mediation are not going to work. The village blacksmith then cuts off further credit to the farmer. Then the farmer has to hunt up a new blacksmith and this may be harder than one might think. As long as the narodniks control the cash flow of the farmer, local credit from the private free enterprise system does not work. The narodniks must be controlled first, or there will be no control over anyone and there will be no local credit available.

FmHA engages in nonsense at times. For example, the narodniks of the agency will attend a sale that the sheriff is holding for the federal land bank. The bank will buy the property. Several weeks later FmHA will buy the property—often at a higher price—from the federal land bank. It is allowed to do this under an act of Congress which says a federal agency can take the property within one year if fraud has been or is being practiced on the government. Who is practicing fraud on the government in this case? It is the federal government acting though the federal land banks. Such sales are soaking the taxpayers solely to help the federal land banks.

At times, FmHA will loan money to a farmer to start a new business. Since only about one in five new businesses will survive the first two years, there is a horrible casualty rate. Obviously the government should get out of such loans.

FmHA will also provide recreational loans. Foreclosures have brought pool halls, bowling alleys, golf courses and even a massage parlor into federal ownership. USDA constantly worries about what the farmer does with his spare time. It is constantly trying to get more recreational activities within reach. I asked one farmer if he worried about what to do with his spare time, and he said he did not have any spare time. That is true for most farmers. In the many years that I have lived on a wheat farm, I can never remember being bored. I have never had a wheat farmer tell me that he was bored. But USDA is constantly working on this situation.

Congress also loves to get into the act. In 1987 Congress amended some prior acts and allowed the federal land banks to loan money on recreational facilities. Earlier it could loan on land only. Now it can loan on recreational equipment, batting cages, bowling alleys, whatever.

FmHA used to control attorney's fees. During the Johnson years the average attorney fee for examining title to land and closing a loan was $25 to $50. Today the same service runs from $750 to $1,500. The agency now sends the check to the attorney and he puts it in his trust account at interest. This has caused some attorneys to stall weeks and months before closing a loan. Some farmers have to hire an attorney to force the attorneys for FmHA to close the loan and pay out.

In the spring of 1988, Ronald Reagan decreed to federal agencies that they were not to allow controversial matters to surface until after the November election. Many believed this was a device to help the Republicans. I smelled a rat when I heard the story, but even I did not dream that the diabolical scheme was hatched in FmHA over the summer and early fall of 1988. In the history of the Western Hemisphere, never have I seen such a tasteless situation.

Throughout the spring, summer and early fall I was constantly reminded by the Reagan administration on how well the nation was doing financially. The press picked this up and ballyhooed it mindlessly. Less than one week after the election in November, 1988, FmHA made its move. It publicly announced that it was sending a packet of forms to farmers who were in default. The announcement said FmHA would give attention to restructuring loans and rewriting notes and mortgages of eligible farmers. Approximately 83,000 farmers were selected to receive this bureaucratic joy.

FmHA emphasized that the forms had to be filled out and returned within forty-five days after receipt. There were to be no missed sheets. All were to be filled out. When farmers received the packet of forms, many were absolutely dumbfounded. The so-called packet contained over seventy pages, each one written in bureaucratic language. The package also called for many attachments such as tax returns, etc.

Texas Senator Bentsen, who had been the vice-presidential candidate on the Democratic ticket, was appalled. He was disturbed that FmHA prepared this packet of forms in secrecy, and sprung it just as soon as the election was over.

Various officials of FmHA contradicted Senator Bentsen and stated that they had not willfully waited until the election was over. Indeed, FmHA had used a full year to train workers to administer the program. This announcement should have been released with violin music, it was that brazen a lie. This procedure had been mandated by the Agricultural Credit Act of 1987 and the administration had well over a year to advise farmers about it. They did not need a year to teach personnel how to administer the program. This restructuring of loans was not complicated. The Congress passed a similar procedure in the Bankruptcy Act of 1986, and bankruptcy courts and their personnel across the nation had administered that program immediately.

When this program reached rural America, every farmer involved wondered how to comply. At the time the announcement from FmHA was made, a veritable chorus of "friends of agriculture" started to counsel the farmers that they MUST comply with the program.

Farm Aid was set up by Willie Nelson, the country musician. He had held various telethons to raise money to help out in the farm crisis, and he obviously was briefed in advance on what FmHA was going to do. Nelson allowed a letter to go out over his signature, a copy of which is reproduced on the next page in facsimile form.

What on earth Nelson was doing giving advise to farmers on how to arrange their legal affairs with the FmHA is something that will be a mystery to me forever. He had no expertise in law and certainly not in dealing with a government bureaucracy that was determined to run over farmers. Nelson doesn't even make out his own income tax returns, I am told. Then how would he know of the tax and cash-flow problems of wheat farmers?

Many private organizations also came out of the woodwork. With little or no knowledge of what was involved, they were quick to advise working with the government. One such group was Prairiefire of Des Moines, Iowa. Prairiefire surfaced at the start of the 1980s depression. It specialized in advising farmers to quit, to salvage something, to go on food stamps, to hold hands in a gesture of solidarity. It saw nothing wrong with the government scheme. It advocated that the farmers work closely with FmHA.

Many religious leaders who have long labored in this field came out in favor of filling out the forms and asking the government for restructuring. These religious leaders had the best of motives, I am sure. Unfortunately they were not familiar with the duplicity FmHA had refined into art form. Many farmers listened to them.

Television stations were adamant that farmers had to answer the forms and return them within the prescribed time. One woman television reporter in Oklahoma City—hired because of her beauty—constantly repeated the litany that farmers just

FARM AID
Keep America Growing!

Special Alert
to FmHA Borrowers

Special Alert
to FmHA Borrowers

November, 1988

Dear Friend,

I'm sending you this flyer as part of Farm Aid's efforts to keep family farmers on the land and in their communities and homes. We don't know your situation but we want you to be aware of your rights.

The Agricultural Credit Act of 1987 entitles FmHA borrowers to a chance to restructure their loans. If you haven't already received it, soon FmHA will send you a packet called, "Notice of Availability of Loan Service Programs for Delinquent Farm Borrowers."

This notice is being sent to almost 90,000 borrowers—over 6,500 people in Texas, almost 4,000 in Minnesota, over 3,000 each in South Dakota, Arkansas, Iowa, over 4,800 in Mississippi, and so on. You are not alone!

The FmHA packet comes by certified mail. It has a complicated package of forms for you to fill out and sign. YOU MUST RESPOND BY COMPLETING ALL OF THE FORMS AND RETURNING THEM WITHIN 45 DAYS. Your response is your only chance to prove to FmHA that forcing you out of business would cost them more than working with you to restructure your loan. Restructuring your loan can include reducing the amount of debt that you owe.

If you do not respond to the FmHA notice on time, you will lose all your rights to restructuring and you may lose your farm to FmHA.

CONTACT SOMEONE FOR HELP. The back of this letter lists information that can help you. It includes phone numbers of hotlines for Farmers Legal Action Group (FLAG). You can write to FLAG to get a video and step-by-step manual for dealing with the notices. Or, call any of the groups listed on the enclosed flyer. They will tell you who can work with you in your local area.

I know that farmers are not to blame for the "farm crisis" and those of us at Farm Aid will continue to do everything we can to help.

Sincerely,

Willie Nelson

Willie Nelson

must cooperate and get the forms filled out and back in.

There are about 300 farm publications in the U.S. These range from large monthly magazines to quarterly newsheets. Almost all echoed FmHA's advice in favor of the farmer completing the forms—if they touched the subject at all. Many of the quarterly newsheets could not take a stand because their next publication date was too far away. Only one farm publication came out against completing the forms. This was *Acres U.S.A.* of Kansas City, Missouri. Here the editor analyzed the forms and concluded that the government was asking the farmer to sign away all of his legal and constitutional rights in and out of court in favor of FmHA. A quit claim deed was cleverly hidden in the packet, and this document conveyed title to the farmer's property. Many farmers failed to see the legal significance of this document until it was too late. The *Acres U.S.A.* editor recommended that the farmers not fill out the forms and instead take their chances in and out of court.

This brought FmHA and the groups it had suckered into supporting the agency up fighting from their chairs. *Acres U.S.A.* and its editor were both denounced, many of these denouncements being orchestrated by FmHA and by private groups that should have known better. Farmers' Legal Action Group of St. Paul, Minnesota lashed out at Charles Walters Jr. with a news release circulated to the farm press, radio and TV stations, and metro dailies. It told how "nationally recognized lawyers," meaning Jim Massey and Dale Reesman, had denounced as "false" and "misleading" the advice offered to financially distressed farmers by *Acres U.S.A.* Massey urged farmers to ignore Walters and bring legal action against him based on having followed the journal's advice to their detriment. On the other hand, Family Farmers Foreclosure Legal Assistance Program (FFFLAP) ran a survey of foreclosed farmers. In cases involving lending institutions, large corporations, or the government, fully 98% of the individuals lost. At least 97% of those who engaged legal talent, opined that they had been betrayed by their lawyer and handled unfairly and illegally by the courts.

Some religious leaders were appalled that *Acres U.S.A.* would challenge the government. Some name-calling resulted. Nevertheless, Congressional Research Service revealed that FmHA had packages with the names of some 83,000 farmers on them. The agency had no intention of rewriting more than 16,000 borrowers. This meant that 67,000 farmers were to be administratively foreclosed and put out of business and off of their property. This may be the largest and saddest foreclosure event in the history of the world. And only one farm paper and one editor foresaw and warned against this danger.

Several state attorney generals in Great Plains states have since publicly concluded that working with FmHA was unwise because its offices allowed the government to practice fraud and deceit.

As soon as FmHA made its announcement, various private groups joined the yammering on where farmers could get the forms filled out. The forms were complicated beyond any reason. Over seventy documents were involved. They appear to have been designed to obfuscate the scheme that the government was hatching.

Almost on signal, various boiler rooms opened to help farmers "comply." Many charged as much as $2,500 to fill out the complicated forms. Farmers who were skinned by these shysters were already impoverished due to the collapse of the farm economy. Now they were fleeced out of what little they had in order to "comply" with the government's request.

Some of these boiler operations even staged public signing events, which the press covered like fleas on a dog. Farmers who signed and returned the forms were made out to look like they had twice the mentality of Albert Einstein. In actuality they signed away their farm operations, which could now be foreclosed administratively.

About ninety days after most of the forms were returned, FmHA announced that the government would write down only if the farmers could come up with some money.

Few farmers could come up with cash. One farmer from Lucien, Oklahoma, stated it this way: "The story of my life is that I have no money. With this farm collapse, I have even less. I guess I won't be rewritten." He wasn't, nor were approximately 63,000 other farmers, according to published data.

The Credit Act of 1987 did not provide that the farmers had to come with cash before restructuring could take place. The Bankruptcy Act of 1986, which provided for the same scaledown in debts, did not provide that farmers had to come up with cash. It has been suggested that the Bush administration invoked this device to gouge some money out of farmers in order to keep the national deficit as low as possible.

Quite a number of farmers did not return the paperwork, and didn't ask for restructuring. Probably many of these could not come up with the cash to get the papers filled out. Some tried to fill them out on their own and failed. Many became so emotionally disoriented they lost interest.

What happened to the farmers who refused to participate in this debacle? As far as I know, almost all are still in business and in the business of farming and are still living in their homes. Federal courts are crowded with cases, particularly with narcotic cases, and there is no time or room to file the foreclosures government cases could account for. So FmHA has not filed foreclosure suits against many of the farmers who refused to cooperate.

This situation was never envisioned by the boiler room experts. Many times a result can be reached that is desirable to someone by sheer timing. The best time to plead a defendant guilty is when the penitentiary is full and overflowing and the governor has invoked the "cap" law and is turning prisoners loose. At that time a judge will do everything possible to keep a person out of the penitentiary. This shows that judges do read newspapers. It also shows that it is possible to get good results by striking at the right time.

The federal government gives power to its employees that are not enjoyed by state employees. Federal judges have the right to "administratively close" a case and throw it out of court. State judges do not have this power. That is what FmHA did here. They got farmers to sign over their land and property, waive their rights to trial in court, waive their right to privacy and then they "administratively foreclosed" and put the farmer out of business. Never have American farmers been so poorly served by their government. As far as I am concerned this is the worst bureaucratic scheme ever cooked up on the North American continent.

Another feature of FmHA activity is that the agency is constantly trying to get publicity illustrating how much good it is doing for farmers. TV reports and news articles often relate how a farmer was in a terrible mess. Then he went down to the kindly office of the narodnik in FmHA and guess what, the narodnik got him straightened out. Then the scene shifts to a long line of farm machinery such as wheat farmers are prone to acquire, none of it being affordable to the wheat farmer, all purchased with government money that will never be repaid. The stories go on to the effect that the farmer is so much better off because of the activity of FmHA. The narodnik usually spews out statistics showing how much better the farmer is doing. The yield of wheat is up, time spent in the field is down, on and on.

Those who have spent a lifetime with wheat farmers and their problems know that none of this is true. FmHA is not the source of well-being for the wheat farmer. In fairness to FmHA, there are many other agencies of government trying to claim credit for the increased yield of wheat and the well-being of farmers. In 1940 a yield of ten bushels per acre was considered good. Today it is not. Yields of twenty-nine bushels [of lower protein wheat] is what the government says I should average in my county. I believe that this is too high, but it is the figure often used. The narodniks in the offices of FmHA try to claim credit for this by providing financing for machinery, etc. Others also claim credit. The county agents, county financial experts, county and district entomologists, the colleges of agriculture and farm magazines also try to get into the act and claim credit for those increased yields. I question these outlandish claims. Most of the increased yields of wheat are explainable, and they have nothing to do with the federal government, its agents or narodniks.

Let me give two examples of this. In 1932 a farmer-blacksmith near Hooker, Oklahoma had many problems on his hands. His wife was ill, his crops failed in the field due to the drought of those Dust Bowl years, and his sons—almost grown—had little economic opportunity. He could walk to any window in his house or any door in his blacksmith and repair shop and look out, and there was nothing but a blizzard of blowing dust. One day he saw employees of the county government grading the road in front of his house. The operation was being done by a tractor with a pull grader that had huge chisels or teeth on it that tore up the hard surface and then behind it was a blade that smoothed out the soil, leaving a smooth roadway. The grader got to the section line west of the house and turned. The tractor operator was unable to complete the turn in the intersection, so he turned out into the wheat field. The grader operator did not raise the teeth and blade of the grader. He tore up the field in a large circle and then smoothed it out. The farmer saw this and hoped that they would learn some day to turn graders properly, but still it was nice to have a smooth road. So he said nothing.

When wheat was sowed that fall, he noted that the soil where the grader turned had more moisture than the rest of the field. What little rain had fallen had run into the little ditches that the teeth made and soaked deep into the soil. So the wheat over the ditches was greener and grew better. All during the winter the wheat over the ditches survived better and grew larger. In the spring, when the crop greened up, the wheat over the little ditches was the best in the field. At harvest time this wheat was a foot taller than the rest of the field, and the heads of wheat were much larger and filled better.

The farmer-blacksmith concluded that what was needed was a new plow. The steel moldboard plow that had been made popular by John Deere almost a century earlier was obviously not working well. It left the soil smooth, soft and bare. Rains fell in torrents and washed a lot of the soil downstream. When it was dry the fields blew away. This had to stop. The farmer noted that the teeth of the grader lifted wheat straw from the last crop up out of the soil where the John Deere plow deposited it, and left it on the top of the ground. The soil here did not blow away. He started drawing diagrams of his new plow. He then went into his shop and made a small scale model of the plow. First he put it on rubber tires. Prior to that time, farm implements generally had iron wheels. The basic running design of the plow was made from wrecked cars. The farmer-blacksmith designed and made teeth such as the grader had. These teeth would be about a foot apart and would sink deep into the soil and make little canals or ditches. This allowed what rain there was to sink deep into the soil. He knew that this plow could not kill all weeds. So he designed a system of "sweeps" or V-shaped blades which would cut all crop residue and weeds off at or near the surface of the soil and then deposit that residue on the surface of the soil as an organic mulch. The wind could not blow the soil when there was mulch on the surface.

This plow was first used south of Hooker, Oklahoma in the fall of 1933. This farmer used it on twenty acres of land. Next to this land, twenty acres were plowed with the John Deere moldboard plow. The wheat on the land tilled with the new plow made thirty bushels per acre. The wheat on the land plowed with the moldboard plow made two bushels per acre. Farmers from miles around came by to see the results. Many individual farmers asked whether he would make a plow for them, and the farmer-blacksmith agreed to do so. In a few years he made thousands of these new plows. Wheat farmers lined up in his yard and waited until he had a plow ready, and they bought them on the spot. Advertisement of the new plow was never needed. This new plow literally saved the agriculture of the southern Great Plains. It added seven to ten bushels to the average yield of wheat. In dry years, it increased the production of wheat to close to thirty bushels per acre. In fact, invention of this plow increased the production of wheat more than everything the narodniks, county agents, colleges of agriculture and government experts plugged into the system. This remarkable man was Fred Walter Hoeme of Hooker, Oklahoma. Hoeme had an eighth grade education, all of it in rural and Lutheran parochial schools. He never saw the inside of a college. His plow encircled the globe and is found everywhere. Fully 85% of all wheat land is cultivated with the Hoeme plow. The Hoeme plow is rated by many as the greatest improvement made in the history of cultivation of soil.

Let me give another example of how the culture of wheat has been benefited by the unschooled. A seven year old boy moved from Nebraska to Kingfisher, Oklahoma in 1893 with his parents. At the age of thirteen he read a magazine article about Luther Burbank and plant genetics. This article changed the life of this boy. He spent his life understanding Burbank and his plants. The boy grew to a man and moved to Beckham County, Oklahoma near the Texas line. He never married and had no close friends. His plants were his whole life. He started to cross-pollinate wheat the way Burbank had cross-pollinated cacti, daisies, plums, etc. In one of these generational crosses, this young man noticed a startling difference. A small seedling showed promise and he kept it. This was in 1924. He kept the plant alive for fifteen years carefully watching and culling it. He developed and marketed the first genetically improved wheat in the history of the world when he introduced it to Oklahoma wheat farmers in the summer of 1939. He called the new wheat Early Triumph and it was the best wheat ever pollinated. It added seven to ten bushels to the average yield of wheat. As WWII spread, so did the production of this new hybrid wheat. It vastly increased the production of wheat and fed the armies of the U.S. and its Allies. There was no bread shortage during WWII as there was in WWI.

Who was this remarkable expert? He was not college-trained. Actually he quarreled with the college-trained experts because they did not understand the grammar of the subject. He was a graduate of the Catholic parochial school system and he never got beyond the eighth grade. He had no formal training in genetics, but he made himself the greatest wheat geneticist in the history of the world. He was Joseph Danne of Beckham

County, Oklahoma. Fully 90% of all winter wheat is related to his Early Triumph or is a descendant of his Early Triumph, Danne, etc. This wheat probably increased wheat production in the United States by a billion bushels each year. At $3 a bushel, this increased farm income and wealth by $3 billion a year,— and national income on the multiplier described by Carl Wilken.

I have full confidence that there will be plenty of wheat bread for all because of these two remarkable men.

These two great but humble men have done more for winter wheat farmers than all governments and college-trained experts put together. These two men are truly great benefactors of God's human family. For college-trained narodniks to claim credit for something they never did is the intellectual disease that caused night to come to the farms of the Great Plains.

14

FEDERAL LAND BANK, A DRASTIC PROPOSAL

In my trips across the Great Plains and in my visits to court-houses, I learned many things about the federal land bank system. My interviews with farmers and their families were enlightening and depressing. Unfortunately I learned many bad things and very few good things about the system. The banks have been very heavy-handed with farmers. They have not been an aid to anyone, except their own employees.

The land banks were set up by Congress in 1916 to close a gap in financing that the Federal Reserve was not handling properly. These banks were to be self-supporting and were to build up their cash reserves though the sale of stock equal to 5% of the loan, and such sales were to be for cash only.

Suffice it to recall that these banks financed the largest increase in farm land prices ever seen on the Great Plains. Prices went from $60,000 per farm to well over $300,000 in many cases. There was no economic justification for an increase of 500% in land prices because wheat prices had been globalized at less than 50% of parity.

The land banks in effect changed the appraisal system for land values. They could set up their own system, and they did. They annihilated the concept of fair market value—which is the price a willing buyer will pay, and the price a willing seller will accept, each transaction being an arms-length deal. The banks were so anxious to make loans, they seldom checked credit, cash flow, or profit and loss statements. Loan officers attended auctions solely to get loans, always with the cooperation of the auctioneer and his sidekick.

The loan officers personally participated in the auction system. They "whooped" up the sales price. They fully believed that the price of land would never go down. This belief ruled the stock market just before its collapse in October 1929. It is ironic how history has repeated itself. So corrupt did the system become that in 1987 Congress imposed a civil fine of $500 on anyone in the banks who did something improper. This proved to be a waste of government ink.

At one sale near Jet, Oklahoma, in southern Alfalfa County, the narodnik from the federal land bank association offered a loan to a farmer for over $200,000 and he did not even know the man's name. Under land bank auspices, honest credit work disappeared. An unholy alliance between land bank and FmHA served to undercut farm stability, and never enhance it. This is the basic cause of the land boom in the 1970s. When Reagan destroyed the price floor under wheat in April 1981, the economy collapsed throughout the region and the boom was over. The federal land banks then went on restrictive credit and have refused to grant new credit to farmers. They nevertheless financed a lot of sales that they made on land taken in foreclosure. But basically there is no new credit for the farmers. In 1981, in Alfalfa County, Oklahoma, the bank made 129 loans but only twelve were made in 1988. In Clark County, Kansas, the bank made thirty-nine loans in 1981 but only one in 1987. In Miner County, South Dakota, the bank made twenty-one loans in 1979 but only one in 1986. In Emmons County, North Dakota, the bank made twenty-six loans in 1981 but only four in 1986. This triggered a complete collapse in the long-term credit system of farmers in the Great Plains. At no time did the federal land bank system stand with the farmers as the insurance companies did in 1930s.

There are a total of twelve federal land banks across the nation. All are totally and completely insolvent and financially broke except for three.

The one that covers Texas is in financial difficulties, but might survive if it receives massive federal financial assistance. The one at Baltimore, Maryland could probably survive and would, if it got some help. The only solvent bank in the system is at Springfield, Massachusetts. This one has been well-managed. Its officers have not engaged in the corrupt activities that the narodniks have used in nine of the banks. However when the banks issue bonds, each bank in the system "jointly and severally" guarantees the bonds of all other banks. So when all twelve banks are considered, they are hopelessly insolvent. Only massive federal monies have been able to prop up the system so far. This money has been raised through the sale of bonds partially guaranteed by the federal government. These sales took place when the Reagan budgets had deficits of more than $220 billion a year, and so the bonds did not sell well in the U.S. The largest buyers were the Japanese, who purchased over 25% of the bonds. Thus the American wheat farmer is being financed by the Japanese. This is the first time in the history of the U.S. that wheat farmers have been dependent on foreign money.

The banks have not made the slightest effort to conserve money, lower expenses or in any way reduce the cost of their operation. They built huge building in the 1970s, none of which can be justified. They have plush offices and roomsful of computers and other exotic electronic gear. All of this must be paid for by farmers.

In many ways these banks resemble American farm cooperatives. In a farm co-op, farmers collectively buy and sell the many things that they need. The farmers can do much better this way since they have no individual control over their own economic destiny when acting alone.

The courts have held that a co-op must do its best for the farmer. The co-op is a trustee. The relationship has the earmarks of a legal fiduciary required to protect the person he or she is acting for. In general this is done in the grain elevator system of co-ops. However, it is not that way in the federal land bank system.

Here the banks exploit the farmer. No effort is made to reduce the expense of the system. They just pile it on. Congress in general has not stopped this. At no time have the committees of the House or the Senate suggested that the banks economize. For example, after the banks got what they wanted in the Act of 1971, they reduced the number of federal land bank associations from over 800 to less than 400 within a year or two. These associations then could hire their own local attorneys. Attorneys were selected not because they knew anything about farming, but because they did not know anything about farming and would go along with any corrupt activity the banks wanted done. For example, one bank attorney proudly proclaimed—in a legal brief—that he had never participated in a loan closing where the farmer did not borrow money from the bank to pay for the stock.

All the practices discussed so far lead to a sad bottom line. Farmers actually have no voice in the management or operation of these banks. In many cases officers refuse to meet with or talk to farmers. They refuse to give out information about the operation of the banks and their associations. In one case, at Enid, Oklahoma, a group of farmers had to sue the bank in order to obtain information on what was going on. The local court in Oklahoma ruled that the farmers were entitled to receive this information. The Oklahoma Constitution has a provision that the books of a corporation are to be opened for inspection. This bank is a corporation. But the federal land banks have refused to comply. In the last instance, the bank took the case on appeal to the Supreme Court of Oklahoma, but before that court could decide the issue the bank decided to drop the suit and give the farmers the information that they sought. Then the bank abused every farmer involved. It called the mortgage on every farmer and demanded full payment and sued to foreclose the loans on their farmland. At no time did the bank act in the spirit of long established constitutional principles.

In Nebraska, a group of farmers had to go to their congressmen and senators to force a production credit association to meet a request for information on how the association was doing. The Farm Credit Bank at Omaha, which is the old federal land bank, refused to give out such information. Yet these farmers are, in legal theory, the owners of the banks and the credit associations.

Private corporations do not conduct themselves in this fashion. The sole reason to refuse the request of the farmer/owner for information is so that insiders who control the banks can profit from it by keeping the money flowing to themselves. In less polite circles this is called "keeping the graft coming." The banks do this under the guise of protecting the privacy of the farmers, but the real reason is to "keep the graft flowing." The bank at Wichita requires that all directors sign an undated resignation when they take office. If a director gives the insiders the slightest trouble, the insiders date the resignation and put it in force.

Through audits and data presented earlier, the distortions and violations have become a catalog of abuses, and they have been the trigger mechanism in keeping the exodus from the land alive. The banks have helped a few farmers tie up the land of the Great Plains and hold it outside the traditional channels of commerce. The farmers thus have huge indebtedness and if foreclosure takes place there is no way to get back but a small part of the loan. I have given the summary before. In Alfalfa County, Oklahoma, the bank got back less than 50% of what it said was loaned. In 1987 Congress directed the banks to grant debt forgiveness to such farmers. This is a type of bankruptcy outside of the bankruptcy courts. The federal land banks promptly prostituted this simple Act of Congress. One lady I interviewed at her request told me about how she and her husband borrowed $40,000 from the bank. They repaid about

$20,000 before he died. She was left with a $20,000 debt. The bank refused to grant debt forgiveness because her land was worth more than $20,000. But the object of the 1987 act was to reduce the high mortgages narodniks had put on the land to a price the bank would get if it foreclosed. Since the bank would get more than $20,000 for this woman's land, probably the bank acted properly. The woman understood this, but she objected to the high cost of operating the bank and the fact that she had to pay high interest to offset debt forgiveness of high bidding farmers. In America, we no longer comfort the widow—instead, the land bank shafts her to help the high-rollers. In fact, the bank keeps it very quiet as to who gets debt forgiveness. Even so, a few facts have leaked out. After all, secretaries and clerks quit the system and vote with their tongues. I have documented a case in the Great Plains where a prominent politician who also farms got debt forgiveness to the tune of $600,000. In another case I know about, the attorney for this federal land bank hated a local state senator. While the bank attorney was looking over the debt forgiveness documents of a man, he suggested that forgiveness could get it doubled if this farmer would run against the state senator in the next election. The farmer agreed to do so, and oddly enough won the election. His debt forgiveness was doubled from $200,000 to $400,000.

What happened to the widow who wanted debt forgiveness? She is now sixty-seven years of age, drives into town each day and works at a minimum wage job and lives on virtually nothing. She is using all of the rent from the farm, and what she can save out on her minimum wage job, and pays it on the bank loan. Her daughter, who lives in a distant state, is sending $250 per month to help pay off the loan. She got nothing, but the rich politician got $600,000 in debt forgiveness. He spends his time running up and down the Great Plains preaching the gospel of free enterprise. In effect, the widow pays, and the politician gets his enterprise free.

At the time the above widow was treated so badly, the land bank carefully guarded the amount of forgiveness it was giving to large farmers. Apparently the triggering device to set off an atomic bomb is less closely guarded than larger debt forgiveness.

Several years ago the federal government and many state governments, such as Oklahoma, provided that the welfare rolls must be opened for inspection by any citizen. The widow who needs $10 a month so that she can get both her food and her medicine is subjected to public scrutiny and scorn. But the political hack who gets $600,000 debt forgiveness is carefully guarded. His privacy is almost total.

Withal, the federal land banks are totally out of touch with the people they purport to serve. They are totally bureaucratic. They are cumbersome, heavy-handed, burdensome and irrational. Their employees and attorneys are solely concerned with themselves and their economic privileges. They are the worst enemy wheat farmers have ever faced. In almost every farmer suicide I have investigated, heavy-handed activity of the federal land bank was there.

The four federal land banks in the Great Plains are consistent on one thing. They will abuse any tenant farmer they find. I have not encountered a single case in which land bank did not attempt to seize the tenant's crops. The worst case I've seen involved an Oklahoma landlord who was having difficulty making the regular mortgage payment to the bank. She went to her tenant and asked for cash rent in advance. The tenant borrowed $6,000 from his village banker and paid the rent by check. The landlord took the rent check to the federal land bank association properly endorsed. The land bank then tried to steal the tenant's wheat crop.

In another case, the tenant farmed the land for many years. The lease was not in writing as is often the case with farm tenancy. When the harvest was over, the tenant continued to farm as in past years. In the meantime, the federal land bank gained title to the land via foreclosure. Once the new crop was planted, the bank charged that the tenant was a trespasser. The bank gave a two-day notice to get off for failure to pay the rent. Oklahoma law said that notice must be ninety days in advance. The bank then said Oklahoma law does not have a crop year termination. It does. After a long legal battle, the tenant got his crop. Not their crop, but his. But his legal expense exceeded his income.

The federal land bank system files more foreclosures against the farmers than all other creditors combined. The small village bankers work on short-term credit. Federal land banks are totally unresponsive to the help that these small commercial banks could give. Land banks absolutely refuse to work with other creditors of the farmers.

For example, I was sitting in my office late one afternoon when I received a call from the president of one of the small village banks. He asked that I wait in the office until he could come to see me. He had just been to the federal land bank. I could tell that he was highly agitated and so I kept the office open late until he got there. After he finally arrived, he spent two hours cursing the federal land bank and its system of obstructing farmers. He had been trying to work out financial details for one of his customers who was having a hard time. This banker was willing to extend credit. About 90% of the payment to the federal land bank could be accounted for, but not all. The farmer also owed a huge payment to a farm machinery company. This farmer unwisely listened to the ACRS fast depreciation story. Too late, he discovered that cash pays the bills, and not ACRS depreciation. If this farmer could have been granted some consideration for two years, he would have been out of the woods. The village banker was willing to help. The federal land bank refused. Consequently the farmer took bankruptcy and the federal land bank lost over $300,000. Had they cooperated with this village banker, they would have gotten paid in full.

Congress granted the federal land banks the right to write off only 5% of their losses in any one year. The rest are hidden in the balance sheet. This is called "creative accounting." It is actually illegal, a distortion of the accounting process, and I believe it should be routed out because it is unethical. These hidden losses must be paid by future borrowers of the system.

There are a number of federal and state laws that protect the consumer. But these laws do not apply to the federal government.

All over the Great Plains, farmers are now voting with their feet. They are doing as the old black man did in the plantation store on settlement day—he left and moved on. The farmer is doing the same thing today. There is a great exodus from the system. In North Dakota I noticed that the exodus was going on in several counties even though there has been a great drought and crop failures were evident. My investigation showed that in one case, a farmer cashed in an insurance policy that he had held for over twenty-five years to get money to pay off a loan. In another case, a farmer borrowed from his mother-in-law, paid his debt and left the system. In a case in Oklahoma, a farmer sold all of his cattle and his wheat crop, borrowed from the village bank and a relative, and paid off the federal land bank. He owed the bank about $100,000 secured by a mortgage on six farms, and was therefore a well-secured loan. But the federal land bank "jacked" his interest from 8% to 13.75%. When the farmer's payment check was delayed by the post office for two days, the federal land bank then "jacked" his interest rate from 13.75% to 15.75% on grounds that he was a poor credit risk. It had taken the post office five days to deliver the check a mile and a half. It is interesting to note that all other federal agencies now give a ten day grace period to letters that are delivered late by the post office, but the federal land banks will not follow this principle.

In one case in Oklahoma a woman inherited about $90,000 from an aunt she had watched over for more than thirty years. The woman wanted this money for her declining years since she was more than seventy years old. Unfortunately her only child, a son, got involved with the local federal land bank association and the bank became so unreasonable that the woman gave the $90,000 to her son and then co-signed a note at the village bank for another $40,000, which freed her son from the clutches of the federal land bank. All of these loans were safe loans and were well-secured. But because of the collection pressure of the narodniks of the federal land bank, the farmer paid off and left the system.

The rural counties of Kansas have stuck to the old system of keeping land titles. All are written out in hand and fortunately—thank God—computers are not used. One can go into the office of the Register of deeds and ask to see the releases of mortgages. These are kept in a separate book. In a few moments, one can see activity that is highly revealing. Indeed, there is a great exodus from the federal land bank system. For example, in Clark County, Kansas, of which Ashland is the county seat, the federal land bank made two loans in 1986. But fourteen other farmers paid off and left the system. In 1987 the bank made one loan and twenty-eight farmers paid off and left the system. In 1988 the bank made six loans and twenty-seven farmers paid off and left the system. This means that in three years the bank made nine loans but sixty-nine farmers left the system. There are only 2,599 people living in this county and 1,096 live in Ashland. About 1,200 live in other villages leaving only 303 people living on farms. While some farmers do live in the villages, most do not. You can thus see that there are very few farmers left to have anything to do with the bank. This may seem to be an isolated event, but borrower's flight is not.

It dooms what little Congress has done in trying to prop up the system.

The banks admitted that in 1987 they lost 13,000 more borrowers per month than they acquired. This means federal land bank in 1987 lost 156,000 more borrowers than it acquired.

Congress should face the facts and liquidate this whole system. The long catalog of abuses that the banks have practiced is not only to be lamented, it should be stopped. The banks should be liquidated in federal courts and the local federal district attorneys should be the attorneys of record on the liquidation.

Those who helped trigger the final episode that caused night to come to the farmers of the Great Plains should be plunged into darkness themselves.

EPILOGUE

After the funeral of Henry, Minerva returned to the farm with the children and found the county sheriff there. He had tears in his eyes. The attorney for the federal land bank had gotten out a writ of assistance in the local courts and this writ directed the sheriff to set her and the children out into the road. He told her that he hated like poison to do that, but he had no alternative. She told him that she and the children would be out at sunrise, but that she could not leave now as the old pickup truck that she was allowed to keep did not have lights and so could not be driven at night. The sheriff said that he understood and told her that he had brought camping equipment and would camp out at the river rather than return to the courthouse in the county seat. Thus the attorney for the federal land bank would not know that he had not executed the writ.

So the next morning Minerva loaded the children and their few remaining belongings into the old pickup and started down the driveway. The oldest son cried out that they were leaving Scamp the dog behind and he did not want to leave without him. So Minerva stopped the truck and the dog bounced into it and they were off. She drove by the cemetery where Henry was buried but *she did not look as she needed both eyes to drive. They made their way to the highway and then into the distant city. She found a small economy apartment that would allow dogs in the backyard. She got a job as hall monitor at the local school. This allowed her to be at home with the children. It paid $400 per month. They are drawing Social Security of $890, food stamps at $270 per month and this gives them an income of $1,560 which is more than they ever had on the farm. The children are all in school and doing well.*

AFTERWORD

WHEN IN 1972 A USDA LEAK flashed the *Young Executives Report* across the media landscape, blips on the political screen gave both sides of an equation that would one day result in night coming to the farms of the Great Plains. The first premise was represented by a code word first turned into current coin during the Wilson administration—SURPLUS! The farm producer was perceived to be producing such a surplus, the American population couldn't make use of it if they stayed up all night eating and otherwise moving farm commodities into trade channels. Because of these surpluses, the experts determined that there were too many farmers, and that the human component in farming was the real surplus.

Accordingly, *Young Executives Report* called for elimination of 2,000,000 farmers and the formation 500,000 super corporate farms to take over the role of food production on the American continent. It was a thesis Committee for Economic Development had dusted off in 1962, a decade earlier. *Unforgiven* detailed the incestuous origin of CED essentially as follows.

As testimony before the House Committee on Agriculture

was to reveal, CED's *An Adaptive Program for Agriculture* had been hatching since 1959. Backup papers had been commissioned, and steps had been taken to lock together the nation's educators of distinction with business leaders of distinction through the medium of foundation funds. Intentions were honest, Theodore O. Yntema, Vice President and Chairman of the Finance Committee, Ford Motor Company, defended. ". . . we do not regard ourselves as experts in agriculture. We do not think that we have brought down the tablets of wisdom from Mount Sinai on this subject," Yntema said before he and his associates stepped down from Mount Sinai with tablets, gospel and codification thereof.

And the CED plan became gospel and public policy, because *An Adaptive Program* expressed laws some 200 business leaders found acceptable and in compliance with the world market that their conjectural economics required.

The *Economic Report of the President* picked up added pages in 1962. For the first time an added line—"Together with the Annual Report of the Council of Economic Advisers"—was added to the cover, and inside, for the first time also, appeared the names of CEA members: Walter W. Heller, Kermit Gordon and James Tobin. Imperceptibly, the real public policy of the nation emerged in print.

"Many more children are born and raised on farms than will be needed to produce the nation's food and fiber. They must be educated, trained, and guided to non-agricultural employment," the *Report* said.

In the main, farm economic literature supported the CED plan because the bulk of tomes by schoolmen dealt with the sophisticated juggling of numbers, prices, demand, production and population—all quantitative matters. Isolated from the mainstream of farm life, the schoolmen undertook to handle farmers as a "gross economic quantity." The words are those of Johnson D. Hill and Walter E. Stuerman, who wrote *Roots in the Soil*: "The CED argues from finances to persons, rather than from persons to finances. And they argue about finances on the basis of the myth of a laissez faire economy. Their program boils down to a manipulation of persons in accord with a myth which they, as businessmen—men from the urban-industrial context—cherish and seek to propagate."

The great grain families from around the world [Europe—Fribourg (Continental Grain), Louis Dreyfus (Dreyfus Grain), George André (André Company); South America—Hirsch and Born families (Bunge); and America—Macmillan families (Cargil)] in the 1960s began rapidly increasing their control of the grain industry internationally.

Always, the signal word was SURPLUS! The surplus code word was a fiction, of course. In fact, there have been no surpluses in the aggregate—except seasonal—since 1910-1914, and there are none now.

At the end of the eleven year price support era that saw four national budgets balanced—six years of war, five of peace—total stocks approximated $2.5 billion. The inventories for three basic storable crops were 256 million bushels of wheat, 2.8 million bales of cotton, and 487 million bushels of corn. Such a corn supply was good for two months. The other *surpluses* constituted a bare inventory.

Data from Table 715, page 656, *Statistical Abstract of the United States*, 1944-1945, indicate that between 1933 and 1943—an eleven year period—U.S. exports of farm products totaled $8,723,787,000. Imports for the same period came to $12,786,725,000. The U.S. imported $4,062,938,000 more of farm production than was exported. In composite terms, the U.S. excess of imports of farm products over exports of the same products for the period amounted to about ten entire crops of wheat. Thus the surplus ploy was used to hold down farm prices before WWII. It was used to annihilate parity. Then it was used to shore up the intellectually indefensible premise on which the *CED Report* and the *Young Executives Report* was constructed. And this fiction is still being used by GATT to burn down the bridges so there can be no retreat to parity even if economic reality arrives.

Data covering the three decades between 1960 and 1990 suggest that, indeed, there have been no surpluses—except short term. And this stretches the general balance in farm production from 1910-1914 to the present, a period in which only short term surpluses have existed. And yet this fiction of *surpluses* has been used to literally kill off broad spectrum distribution of land and income for America, and thereby usher in fantastic changes in our political and institutional arrangements.

The table illustrates production of wheat and coarse grains, and the percentage of annual production consumed each year.

Data on the chart in this Afterword illustrate that ending grain stocks in 1985—at the height of the foreclosure mania—were less than stocks in the early 1960s, even though annual usage increased by 76%. Ending stocks, as a percentage of annual use, actually decreased from 71% in 1961 to 28% in 1985.

Ed Butcher, schoolman, lecturer, historian, College of Great Falls, Montana, with his analysis on a facing page, concluded that ending stock figures seemed to vanish by the end of the next harvest season. Although fluctuations in ending stock figures are always evident, there seems never to be a continuing increase in grain stocks, which must happen over time if a true surplus in fact exists.

Once lawmakers realize that there are no surplus grains—only marketing inventories—then they will realize that there is no mandate to bring night to the farms of the Great Plains by cutting lifeline loans.

The story has been told that, once upon a time, Socrates interrogated a young statesman to determine his qualifications. The budget of Athens, the strength of the army, the dwellings used to house the people—all passed in review. Finally Socrates asked, *And how much wheat will it require to feed the people of Athens for a year?* The young statesman fell silent. The interview was over. Nobody, said Socrates, *is qualified to become a statesman who is entirely ignorant of the problems of wheat.*

—*Charles Walters Jr.*
Publisher

USE GREATER THAN PRODUCTION
U.S. WHEAT AND COARSE GRAINS
(Million Metric Ton)

Year	Beginning	Production	Use	Imports	Ending	Percentage of Annual Production
60/61	105.6	178.8	166.7	0.6	118.3	93%
61/62	118.3	161.0	175.5	0.5	104.3	109%
62/63	104.3	159.3	170.8	0.3	93.2	107%
63/64	93.2	171.5	175.0	0.4	90.1	102%
64/65	90.1	157.5	172.9	0.4	76.5	109%
65/66	76.5	179.1	197.8	0.3	58.2	110%
66/67	58.2	180.7	189.7	0.3	49.5	104%
67/68	49.5	203.9	191.0	0.3	62.7	93%
68/69	62.7	197.6	188.9	0.3	71.8	95%
69/70	71.8	201.0	200.4	0.4	72.8	99%
70/71	72.8	182.9	201.6	0.4	54.6	110%
71/72	54.6	233.6	215.1	0.4	73.4	92%
72/73	73.4	224.1	250.0	0.5	48.0	111%
73/74	48.0	233.3	250.5	0.3	31.1	107%
74/75	31.1	199.4	203.7	0.6	27.3	102%
75/76	27.3	243.3	235.7	0.5	35.5	96%
76/77	35.5	252.8	228.4	0.4	60.3	90%
77/78	60.3	261.4	248.6	0.4	73.5	95%
78/79	73.5	270.5	272.7	0.3	71.6	100%
79/80	71.6	296.5	291.2	0.4	77.2	98%
80/81	77.2	263.1	279.1	0.3	61.6	106%
81/82	61.6	322.4	284.6	0.4	99.8	88%
82/83	99.8	326.0	287.7	0.6	138.7	88%
83/84	138.7	203.0	272.7	0.8	69.8	134%
84/85	69.8	307.6	294.8	0.9	83.5	95%
25 YEARS		5610.3	5645.1	11.0		100.6%

NOTE: Coarse grains include corn, sorghum, barley, oats, rye.

SOURCE: United States Department of Agriculture
                           Foreign Agriculture Circular
                           World Grain Situation and Outlook
                           February 12, 1985

AVERAGE ANNUAL PRODUCTION   234.4 Million Tons
AVERAGE ANNUAL TOTAL USE   225.8 Million Tons

INDEX

INDEX

Aberdeen, South Dakota, 87, 88
Accelerated Cost Recovery System
(ACRS), 55-57, 59, 61-65;
depreciation, 266
accident, deaths by, 126
Acres U.S.A., 26, 251, 252; publish-
er, 136
Act, Administration Procedures,
135; Agriculture Adjustment
(AAA), 12, 15-17, 19, 23, 29;
second, 20; Copper-Volstead, 9;
Federal Farm Loan, 10, 75;
Federal Reserve, 10; Gramm-Rud-
man, 24, 26; Homestead, 8, 9;
Maximum Hours, 21; McNary-
Haugen, 10; Minimum Wage, 21;
Morrill, 8; National Labor Rela-
tions, 21; Rural Electrification,
27; Sherman Anti-trust, 9; Smith-
Hughes, 10; Smith-Lever, 10;
Smoot-Hawley Tariff, 11; Social
Security, 20, 29; Soil Bank, 28,
29; Soil Conservation, 27; Tax
Credit, 60; War Stabilization, 23
*Adaptive Program for Agriculture,
An*, 272
Administration Procedures Act, 135
Afghanistan, 38
Agricultural Credit Act of 1987, 248
Agriculture Adjustment Act
(AAA), 12, 15-17, 19, 23, 29;
second, 20
Aiken bill, ix, 24, 25, 28, 110, 137
Albuquerque, New Mexico, 87
Alfalfa County, Oklahoma, 4, 47,
65, 92, 109, 151-204, 205-207, 228,
231, 260, 263
Allowance for Funds Used During
Construction (AFUDC), 57-59
Amarillo, Texas, 2
Amendment, Income Tax, 9
Amendment, Steagall, ix, 23-25
Amendment, Thirteenth, 118

American Agricultural Movement,
36, 37, 59
Ames, Iowa, 28
*An Adaptive Program for Agricul-
ture*, x
Anderson, Clinton P., 32
André, George 273
Argentina, 6
Arkansas, 1, 14, 19, 114; Dyess,
114; Fort Smith, 14; Tyronza, 19
Ashland, Kansas, 205, 206, 268
attorney fees, 195, 196
auction, style of, 93-98, 101, 104
Austin, Texas, 27, 74, 88, 226, 228
Australia, 6

bank failures, 27
bankers, and FmHA, 124
Bankhead Cotton Control program,
19
Banking Committee, House, 23
Bankruptcy Act of 1986, 248, 253
banks, number in U.S., 68
base period "100," vii
basket, market, vii
Belknap, William W., 51, 52
Bellmon, Henry L., 34, 35, 84, 110,
152, 204
Benson, Ezra Taft, x, 12, 25, 27, 29-
33, 77, 100
Bentsen, Lloyd, Senator, 141, 248
Bergland, Bob, 32, 36
Bill of Prohibitions, 168
Bill of Rights, 168
bill, Aiken, 24, 25, 28, 110
binder insurance, 172
Bismarck, North Dakota, 3, 88,
167, 221
Bison, Oklahoma, 33
Black Codes, 119
Black Hills, 1
blacks, 22